60

DYNAMICS OF SUSTAINABLE RURAL DEVELOPMENT

DYNAMICS OF SUSTAINABLE RURAL DEVELOPMENT

Edited by
G. Raghava Reddy
Director
Rural Development Academy
Tirupati

P. Subrahmanyam, *I.A.S*

SERIALS PUBLICATIONS
New Delhi

First Published–2003

ISBN: 81-86771-17-4

PUBLISHED BY

Head Office : **SERIALS PUBLICATIONS**
4, B.S.S. Hall, Khyber Pass Market,
Civil Lines, Delhi–110054 (India)
Phone: 0091-11-23811659
Fax: 91-11-23812678
E-mail: serials@satyam.net.in

Branch Office : *4830/24, Prahlad Street, Ansari Road,*
Darya Ganj, New Delhi-110002 (India)
Phone: 23245225

Printed at : Tarun Offset Printers, (Delhi)

Preface

The study of Rural Development is receiving greater attention in recent times for a variety of reasons. The stubborn persistence of poverty in general and rural poverty in particular poses a great challenge for the development agencies of all types at all levels. The very number of people i.e., 1.2 billion trapped in it is not politically acceptable and socially desirable. The strategies of rural development evolved and experimented in different countries have also undergone a big change due to the changing conditions at global, national and local levels. The agencies of civil society are gradually evincing greater interest in tackling the different dimensions of rural poverty. The State itself is deeply committed to the challenge of overcoming it. The World Bank and the UNDP are on the job of innovating, designing and experimenting with different strategies for attacking poverty. The emphasis in most of the contributions in this volume is on sustainability of the programmes and policies.

There are several books and reports dealing with different aspects of Rural Development. Yet another book needs some justification. This book draws a cross-section of writings on the subject covering the evolving strategies, policies and programmes at different levels as also a few micro-level studies on specific aspects. The experiences of some of the policies executed such as land reforms, credit reforms and the emerging role of institutions such as self-help groups are covered by scholars in the field. Hence, the present book will be useful for those who are engaged in the work of rural development as academicians, researchers, policy makers and executives of the programmes besides the community of students of Rural Development.

We are highly grateful to the contributors and publishers of some of the contributions for kindly permitting us to include them in the present volume. Our efforts will be amply rewarded if the book is found useful for those to whom it is intended. We welcome suggestions for its improvement from all quarters.

G. Raghava Reddy
P. Subrahmanyam

Contributors

G. Raghava Reddy, is Director, Rural Development Academy at 7-154, Santhi Nagar, M.R. Palli Road, Tirupati, India. He is closely connected with several professional bodies like the IEA, ISLE, ISAE, and served in different universities of Andhra Pradesh. Author and Editor of several books, he is a well-known figure in academic and research circles in social sciences.

Dr. P. Subrahmanyam, I.A.S. is presently programme co-ordinator United Nations Office for Programme Services (UNOPS) at Kathmandu. Earlier, he was Director, Pilot projects at CIRDAP, Dhaka. He is a Senior Civil Servant with proven track record in the design and implementation of poverty alleviation programmes. He is a resource person at workshops/seminars on Rural Poverty-Alleviation programmes at Regional and Global level organized by multi-lateral Funding Agencies.

Dr. P. Krishnaiah, IAS is the executive officer of the TTD, the richest and internationally renowned temple of Lord Balaji at Tirupati. Earlier he was collector of Chittoor and Mahaboob Nagar districts. He is a pioneer on research relating to Self-Help Groups as instruments of social mobilization and poverty alleviation and an able administrator of rural development programmes.

Keith Griffin, is a noted international authority on agrarian change and Rural Development. He has been the Director of several research projects on issues relating to rural poverty and unemployment. He has been a consultant to different national and International organizations. Presently he is engaged in research on Transitional Economice and associated with the university of California, Riverside, U.S.A.

Amyickowitz, is a graduate student and Research Associate of Keith Grifin.

Dr. H.P. Singh, is Director, Central Institute for Research on Dryland Agriculture, Hyderabad. He is a reputed Agricultural Scientist with Research, Extention Training interests in Agricultural Development with focus on semi-arid regions.

R. Radhakrishna, Currently is Director, Indira Gandhi Development Research Institute, Mumbai. Prior to that he was Vice Chancellor of Andhra University, Secretary ICSSR, and Director CESS, Hyderabad. A distinguished economist, he has been the recipient of several awards and rewards.

K. Venkata Reddy, Formerly Vice-Chancellor, S.K. University, Ananthapur, is a noted Gandhian. He has several books to his credit on Rural Development. His approach is basically empirical mostly based on personal and field experience. He is a liberal and a staunch advocate of Gandhian ideology to the issues of poverty and development.

Mahendra Dev, is the Director of CESS, Hyderabad. A renowned scholar and writer. He was formerly with GDRI, Mumbai.

V. Reddappa Reddy, is Professor in the Department of Rural Development, S.K.U. Ananthapur. Before joining S.K.U. he was in government service. A devoted teacher, able researcher and writer.

Dr. P. Purushotham, is Director, Rural Industries and Employment. NIRD, Hyderabad. He has undertaken several explorative studies on Micro-Credit and enterprises.

Azizur Rahman Khan, is presently professor of Development Economics, University of California, Riverside. A consultant on Rural Development to several international organizations and author of several books and reports on issues of rural development.

Dr. B. Ramachandra Reddy, is an Associate Professor, Department of Commerce S.V.U, Tirupati. An active researcher and prolific writer.

Dr. P. Kothandarami Reddy, is an Assistant Professor of Economics at SKIT, Srikalahasti. Earlier he was a post-doctoral fellow of the ICSSR.

Dr. I.S. Sundaram, is Research Director, P.G. Department of Economics, Hindu college Machilipatnam. A prolific writer and an active researcher.

Dr. V. Muniramaiah, is a Post-Graduate Teacher, in Novodaya Vidyalaya, 'Lepakshi', Ananthapur District. He is specialized in banking and finance and is widely travelled.

Dr. N. Sugayya, is Professor of Economics, S.V.U., Tirupati.

Dr. P. Jagadish, Gandhi is Honorary Director, Vellore Institute of Development Studies, Vellore, Tamil Nadu.

Dr. D. Nagayya, is Consultant on Small Enterprises at Guntur and was formely Director (Industrial

Development), National Institute of Small Industry Extension Training (NISIET), Hyderabad.

Anil K. Rajvanshi, is Director, Nimbalkar Agricultural Research Institute, Maharashtra.

J.M.J. Vinodhini, is RA, RDA, Tirupati. A.P.

S.P. Jain, is Consultant on Panchayati Raj and Rural Development at NIRD, Hyderabad.

Contents

PART—III
Role of Institutions

Part—I

APPROACHES TO RURAL DEVELOPMENT

1

The Distribution of Wealth and the Pace of Development*

Keith Griffin and Amy Ickowitz

Economists have long been interested in the relationship between the distribution of income and the rate of economic growth. Two propositions have tended to dominate the literature. The first, associated with the name of Simon Kuznets, asserts that the degree of inequality varies systematically with the level of income per head, initially increasing as incomes rise and then, beyond some point, decreasing with further increases in income per head (Kuznets 1955). The second proposition, often associated with Arthur Okun, asserts that there is a "great trade-off" between equality and efficiency and hence policy interventions intended to reduce inequality have a high cost in terms of a lower average income (Okum 1975). Taken together, the two propositions have been used to argue against public policies intended to create a less unequal society, since the Kuznets

* This paper was published in Terry Mckinley, ed., Macroeconomic policies, Growth and poverty reduction, London: Palgrave, 2001.

proposition indicates that in the long run policy interventions are unnecessary and the Okun proposition indicates that in the short run they are harmful.

In this paper we attempt to do three things. First, we reconsider the evidence behind the Kuznets and Okun propositions. Second, we explore the implications for development of shifting the focus of analysis from the distribution of income to the distribution of productive assets or wealth. Third, we consider where appropriate the implications for the analysis of substituting human development for an expansion of gross national product (GNP) as the objective of development policy. Our conclusion is that a more equal distribution of wealth is more likely to accelerate the pace of human development than retard it and hence the earlier view that emphasized a conflict between equality and development is seriously misleading.

The belief in a trade-off between equity and growth, in both developed and developing economies, is widely held. Recent evidence, however, indicates not only that the two are compatible but that they are mutually reinforcing. Traditional analyses of the relationship between inequality and growth have focused on the relationship between income inequality and the growth of GNP. In this essay, in contrast, we will examine inequality not only in terms of income but also in terms of the distribution of productive assets, i.e., natural, physical and human capital. Furthermore, while all of the empirical testing thus far defines growth as an increase in GNP, the results will have to be carefully reinterpreted if one assumes that growth of GNP is not the ultimate goal of development but simply a means to the end of increasing human development. Economic growth may help to advance human development, and per capita income enters into the human development index, but the two are not synonymous.

In Section I of this paper we examine the empirical evidence that has been gathered to date on the relationship between growth and inequality. We begin with a review of the evidence on income inequality and then discuss the evidence on inequality in the distribution of assets. In Section II we explore some of the current theories which try to explain why growth and inequality might be inversely related. In Section III we consider some of the evidence from individual countries. Finally, in Section IV we raise some of the policy implications that arise from this reexamination of the data, the theories and actual experience. Our ultimate objective is to show that a redistribution of productive assets could serve as a catalyst for growth, both in terms of an expansion of GNP and in terms of higher levels of human development.

I. Empirical Evidence

Discussion of the empirical evidence begins with the famous Kuznets hypothesis. We then consider more recent work on the distribution of income and its link to economic growth. Next, we consider the importance of natural capital, concentrating on the distribution of land ownership. Lastly, we consider human capital, taking as an example the distribution of education.

The Kuznets Hypothesis

For nearly four decades the Kuznets hypothesis was a stylized fact by most economists. The well known inverted U-shaped relationship between income inequality and the level of income affected the way economists approached theory as well as policy. In the early 1990s, however, economists increasingly began to question the idea that there was a close relationship between the level of income per head and the degree of inequality. The need for a reevaluation had been apparent for quite some time. The insights from human capital theory, the refinement of endogenous growth theory and apparent real world anomalies combined to encourage scholars to take a second look at the Kuznets hypothesis. Several papers were published in the early years of this decade which claimed that not only was there no inverse relationship between growth and income equality during the first stages of development but that on the contrary, initial inequality in the distribution of income was inimical to growth.

Simon Kuznets, writing in the 1950s and 1960s, developed his hypothesis that income inequality tends first to rise and then fall with increases in real income per capita after examining the historical experience of the developed countries and a very small sample of developing countries for which data were available. He believed that the historical record showed that such a relationship existed, but he was very careful to point out that this did not mean that there was an inherent trade-off between growth and equality, as he is sometimes interpreted to have argued:

> "All we can say is that the unequal distribution of income in the earlier decades in the presently developed countries did not prevent rapid economic growth. But our data do not reveal the specific social and economic circumstances, and we cannot say that a somewhat less (or more) unequal size distribution might not have contributed to even faster growth". (Kuznets 1963,69)

During the years after Kuznets first published his observations regarding the historical relationships between growth and income equality, several empirical studies were done using cross-sectional data to test whether this inverse relationship held, using the larger amount of data that had become available from the developing countries. In 1973, Felix Paukert, using cross-sectional data on 56 countries originally gathered by Adelman and Taft Morris (1971), concluded that "the data...support the hypothesis expressed but not fully tested by Kuznets that with economic development income inequality tends to increase, then becomes stable and then decrease" (Paukert 1973,120). Perhaps the most well known of the empirical studies is that done by Ahluwalia (1976) using cross-sectional data from 60 countries. He was convinced enough by the data of the existence of a U-shaped relationship between equality and growth to call it a "stylized fact'. Sherman Robinson went even further and claimed that the U hypothesis "has gathered the force of economic law" (Robinson 1976,437).

Not all economists agreed that the empirical tests were convincing enough to elevate the status of U hypothesis to "stylized fact", let alone "economic law". In 1983, Ashwanti Saith criticized Paukert and Ahluwalia's use of cross-sectional data to test what is really a secular relationship. By using cross-sectional data they implicitly assumed that every country travelled along "one well-trodden U-path". They thus ignored the fundamental inter-country differences pointed out by Kuznets in "size, historical heritage, and timing of their industralisation process" (Kuznets 1967, 153) among other things. Saith proceeded to question the robustness of Ahluwalia's results. He re-ran Ahluwalia's regression on his sample of developing countries, dropping those observations which he considered to be outliers and Spain since he believed that it could not really be called a developing country. He found that Ahluwalia's coefficients were no longer significant and concluded that "Ahluwalia's quadratic fit, and hence the U-curve, are the products of a few outliers, and if these are excluded from the sample, the U-curve fades into insignificance". (1983,378).

Ahluwalia and the authors of later studies performed in the 1970s and 1980s relied on a data set assembled by Shail Jain (1975). Much of this data is of poor quality and therefore calls the conclusions of these investigations into question. Deininger and Squire (1996a) have specified three basic criteria that data must meet in order for them to qualify as "quality" data:

1. the data must come from nationally representative household surveys;
2. all sources of income (or uses of expenditure) must be included (and not, for example only wage income);
3. the survey must be representative of the country's entire population and results must not be based on extrapolations from information gathered only from specific subgroups (e.g., it should not be a survey of only the urban population or only whites).

These appear to be reasonable criteria, but much of the data used in past empirical investigations of the relationship between inequality and growth have not met these basic standards. Only 61 of Jain's original 405 observations, for example, meet the minimum requirements set by Deininger and Squire.

The World Turned Upside Down

More recent empirical research not only questions the validity of the Kuznets hypothesis but seems to reverse the conclusions. Persson and Tabellini were perhaps the first to find econometric evidence that there might be a negative relationship between initial income inequality and the rate of growth. They used two sets of data, one based on historical data from nine developed countries and other cross-sectional data from 56 countries since the end of the Second World War. On their historical sample, they performed what has become a standard growth regression of GDP growth on various variables including the income share of the top twenty per cent of the population as a measure of inequality. In their sample for the postwar period, they focus on the median voter and therefore, rather unpersuasively, use the income share of the third quintile as their measure of inequality. They reported that "a strong negative relation between income inequality at the start of the period and growth in the subsequent period is present in both samples" (Persson and Tabellini 1994, 601). That is, high initial inequality is associated with slow growth of output and incomes.

Alesina and Rodrik perform similar regressions for two periods, namely, 1960-1985 and 1970-1985. In addition to using a Gini coefficient on income as a measure of inequality, however, they also include a Gini coefficient on land as one of their regressors. Their high quality data set uses Jain's data from OECD countries and data from Fields (1989) for 29 developing countries. "The results indicate that income inequality is negatively correlated with subsequent growth" (Alesina and Rodrik 1994, 481). When they use the Gini coefficients for land and for income separately, they find both to be significant at the 5 per cent level or higher, depending on the sample. When they use them both together, however, the Gini coefficient for land stays significant at the 1 per cent level, but the significance of the Gini coefficient for income declines to 10 per cent for the sample from the longer period and to 5 per cent for the shorter period. George Clark runs similar regressions using various income inequality measures and then performs sensitivity analysis to test the robustness of the negative relationship between income inequality and growth. His results "confirm a robust and negative relationship between inequality and growth" (Clark 1995, 422).

It seems that the most recent work using more and better data comes to a different conclusion regarding the relationship between inequality and income growth from those studies done in the past. However, even the data used in the most recent studies are still far from perfect. Deininger and Squire question the quality of Persson and

Tabellini's data on quintile shares of income. Only 18 out of Persson and Tabellini's 56 data points meet their criteria for quality data. "The negative relationship between income inequality and growth evaporates if, for example, we rerun the regressions by Persson and Tabellini using only the eighteen...high quality observations contained in their sample" (Deininger and Squire 1996b, 573).

Deininger and Squire are also critical of the data in Alesina and Rodrik as well as in unpublished work by Perotti. Both studies include observations for developed countries from Jain's data set. Some of the income figures for these countries are based on wage income, which can create the impression of high disparities in countries which may have low inequality of net household income. Also, a large number of observations from developed countries (36 out of the 69 in Alesina and Rodrik and 50 out of Perotti's 67) "gives rise to the suspicion that the statistical analysis captures structural differences between developed and developing countries more than regularities that are equally valid for both groups" (Deininger and Squire 1996a, 7). Deaton also argues that "Jain's figures are not a sound basis on which to make international comparisons, and results that rely on them should be viewed with great skepticism, although the lesson is widely ignored in the recent political economy literature, for example Persson and Tabellini (1990) and Alesina and Perotti, (1992)". (1995,1803).

Deininger and Squire use a new data set on income distribution to re-examine the relationship between growth and inequality. They collected as many observations of income distribution as they could from both primary and reliable secondary sources and obtained a total of 2,600. After applying their criteria for quality data outlined above, they were left with 682 high quality observations, which is substantially more than that are contained in the data sets used in previous studies. Not only do they have more cross-sectional observations, they also have a significantly greater number of time series observations for each country. This is crucial because the empirical testing of the Kuznets hypothesis in the past used cross-sectional observations, they also have a significantly greater number of time series data to try to draw conclusions about what is, in reality, a longitudinal relationship. According to Deininger and Squire, "Indeed, our data provide little support for an inverted-U relationship between levels of income and inequality when tested on a country-by-country basis, with no support for the existence of a Kuznets curve in about 90 per cent of the countries investigated" (1996b,573).

When they run the standard growth regression used in the past but with their high quality data, Deininger and Squire's results appear at first to corroborate those of Perrson and Tabellini, Alesina and Rodrik and Perotti, in showing that initial inequality has a negative effect on future growth. This effect, however, is no longer significant when regional dummies are introduced into the regression. This suggests to them "a wide range of region-specific characteristics which may, but need not, include inequality, could be at the root of the relationship that has been observed in much of the literature" (1996a, 13). While their results do not confirm that there is an inverse relationship between initial income inequality and growth, they do not confirm the initial income inequality is not positively correlated with growth. Thus the idea that income redistribution is incompatible with growth receives no support from the cross-section evidence and the view that inequality is a precondition for growth is increasingly untenable.

Even though Deininger and Squire do not find a significant correlation between aggregate growth and overall income inequality, they do find a significant and positive correlation between growth and increases in income of all but the top quintile. The relationship is strongest for the bottom quintile, implying that growth is associated with a reduction of poverty. They found that during decadal growth episodes, the incomes of the bottom quintile increased in more than 85 per cent of the cases they examined (1996a, 7).

What does this imply for human development? It is reasonable to suppose that an increase in income increases human capabilities but that it does so at a diminishing rate. That is, there are diminishing returns to income in terms of its ability to increase human development. This assumption, in fact, is incorporated into the construction of the human development index. It follows from this that, for any given increase in the average level of income, the more evenly distributed is the increase in income, the greater will be its contribution to raising human development. In other words, an egalitarian pattern of economic growth contributes more to human development than an inegalitarian pattern (Griffin 1997, 4)

The Distribution of Land

As we have seen, empirical testing of the relationship between inequality and growth has traditionally been done using data on the distribution of income. Like Alesina and Rodrik, however, Deininger and Squire have also used data on the distribution of land. They hoped to use these data as a proxy for the distribution of assets in general. Quite apart from the problem of using land as a proxy for productive assets as a whole, data on the distribution of land almost always understate the degree of inequality. There are several reasons for this.

First, measures of land concentration ignore those who own no land at all, e.g., landless agricultural wage labourers. That is, the data refer to the distribution of land among landowners and not among the entire rural population. Second, most of the data refer to the distribution of land holdings and not to units of ownership. Thus, for instance, an estate that is divided into ten tenant farms would be counted as ten holdings and not as one unit of ownership. This results in an underestimate of the degree of inequality since land holdings tend to be distributed more equally than land ownership. Many owners of large farms prefer to rent out their land to tenants rather than cultivate the entire area themselves. Third, measures of land concentration ignore those who own more than one farm by counting each farm as a separate unit of ownership. This too, results in an underestimate of the degree of inequality. Finally, land is treated as a homogeneous asset of uniform quality. That is, measures of land concentration are in practice of inequality in surface area and not measures of inequality in the value of land as a productive asset. If, as is often the case, most of the best land is owned by large landowners, the degree of inequality will be understated by most conventional measurements.

Despite these problems, Deininger and Squire are right to underline the importance of land inequality, particularly since the "possession of land could be a major determinant of an individual's productive capacity and their ability to invest, especially in agrarian societies where land is a major asset" (Deininger and Squire 1996a,8) Using regression analysis, Deininger and Squire find that the relationship between initial degree of inequality in the distribution of land and subsequent growth is negative, significant and robust. Greater land inequality leads to slower growth. When regional dummies are added to the regression, the significance of the coefficient on land distribution is reduced, but it remains statistically significant. Given the fact that the degree of inequality as measured by the Gini coefficient for land distribution is almost certainly understated, the true relationship would be even stronger than the estimated relationship.

The Distribution of Human Capital

While land is an important asset in most developing countries, human capital is perhaps an even more important determinant of a country's growth potential. Recent evidence suggests that the contribution of human capital to growth is higher than that of either natural or physical capital, and perhaps more than the two combined (Griffin 1997, 3; UNDP 1996; Asian Development Bank 1997). This is especially true if one reinterprets growth to mean an increase in human development, since improvements in health and education contribute directly to human development as well as indirectly through their effects on increasing the growth of output and incomes.

Using data on 98 countries from the period 1960-1985, Robert Barro finds that the growth rate of real GDP per capita is positively related to the initial stock of human capital as proxied by primary and secondary school enrollment rates (Barro 1991). Thus the more equitably distributed are educational opportunities, i.e., the higher is the percentage of the population enrolled in primary and secondary schools, the higher is the growth rate. The effects on raising human development would be stronger still, because of the direct contribution of education to human development.

The microeconomic evidence supports these findings. Rati Ram estimates that the returns to schooling are 13 per cent on average for all countries, with a higher return in developing countries compared to developed countries (Rati Ram 1996, 848). Evidence also indicates that the returns to primary and secondary education are higher than the returns to tertiary education. George Psacharopoulos explains that " for primary education, unit costs are small relative to the extra lifetime income or productivity associated with literacy. For university education, the opposite is true" (Psacharopoulos 1998, 101). Given that tertiary education usually favours the elite in developing countries—and even in developed countries the middle and upper classes are disproportionately represented—a more equal distribution of expenditures on education would increase efficiency and growth as well as equity. Indeed in another paper Psacharopoulos finds that in developing countries the rates of return on investments in primary education are more than 25 per cent, whereas they fall sharply at higher levels, namely, to 15-18 per cent in secondary education and to 13-16 per cent in tertiary education (Psacharopoulos 1994).

A recent study by the Asian Development Bank enables one to estimate the contribution of various factors to the difference in the rate of growth of per capita income in East and Southeast Asia during the period 1965-1990, on the one land, and three other regions during the same period, on the other hand. Consider, for example, sub-Saharan Africa. During the twenty-five years under examination, the rate of growth of output per head in sub-Saharan Africa was four percentage points a year slower than in East and Southeast Asia. This difference of four percentage points can be decomposed as follows: 2.3 percentage points are due to differences in human capital (namely, "schooling" and "demography"), one percentage point is due to differences in natural capital (namely, "resources and geography"), and 0.1 percentage points are due to differences in physical capital (specifically, "government savings rate"). The remaining 0.6 points are attributed to other factors (Asian Development Bank 1997,80). A broadly similar result was found in South Asia but not, curiously, in Latin America, where "initial conditions" and "openness" appear to have been much more important.

While such decomposition exercises must be treated with some scepticism, the Asian Development Bank study confirms the importance of human capital in accelerating economic growth and, in the cases of East and Southeast Asia and South Asia, suggests that human capital was more than twice as important as natural and physical capital combined in explaining differences in economic performance. These results are therefore consistent with other recent empirical findings.

II. Theoretical Explanations

Why might one expect that inequality in the distribution of income and wealth could harm development and that reduced inequality could accelerate it? Both political and economic explanations have been put forward. Let us begin with the insights of political theory and then turn our attention to possible economic reasons.

Political insights

There are three separate strands of argument to the analysis which connects inequality in the distribution of income and wealth to political instability. First, it has been argued that inequality can result in redistributive taxation which is harmful to growth of output. Second, it has been argued that inequality can result in a change in the composition of public expenditure which increases unproductive outlays and in the process reduces both the rate of growth of output and human development. Third, it has been argued that inequality can result in class conflict and uncooperative behaviour which reduces technical and institutional change and the growth of output.

Several papers published in the early 1990s examined the possible link between inequality and growth through the channel of voting behaviour. Each of these papers involves the construction of a theoretical model designed to capture both the economic and the political choices of the members of an economy and a polity. All of the papers make use of the median voter theorem which purports to demonstrate that when people vote on different possible tax rates, the tax rate preferred by the median voter will be the one chosen.

Persson and Tabellini were the first to set up such a model and used an overlapping generations framework in which different individuals are assumed to have different incomes. An individual acts as an economic agent as well as a voting citizen. It is assumed that the role of the government is to redistribute income from those who invest more than the average to those who invest less than the average. Agents work and invest in human capital. Individuals with more skills accumulate more capital. The government levies taxes at a rate proportional to income, while the revenues are redistributed in a lump sum manner to all agents so that poor agents benefit as much as rich ones but pay a relatively smaller amount in taxes.

The authors assume that the more of the returns on her investment an individual can retain, the higher will be the growth rate. This is because investment (and hence growth) is sensitive to the after-tax rate of return. On this basis the authors conclude that inequality is harmful to growth and offer the following explanation:

> "…if the median voter coincides with the average investor, he prefers a nonredistributive policy, whereas he prefers a tax (a subsidy) on investment if he is poorer (richer) than the average. More generally a median voter with higher individual skills… and therefore a higher k^m (median voter's capital accumulation)) prefers more private appropriability. A higher average skill level…gives higher average accumulation and hence increases the cost of redistribution, so that the voter prefers a less interventionist policy" (Persson and Tabellini 1994, 604)

The chain of causality is thus lower income inequality leads to less voter preference for redistributive tax intervention; less government intervention leads to more investment and hence to faster growth.

The idea behind Alesina and Rodrik's model is similar to that in Persson and Tabellini, but the technical details are slightly different. They use an endogenous growth model and instead of differentiating between individuals based on income, they focus on differences in the relative shares of labour and capital endowments. The government, in their model, uses proportional taxation of capital income to finance public investment. A large increase in taxation lowers the after-tax return on private capital investment and thus reduces the incentive for agents to invest and therefore reduces the growth rate of the economy. They too make use of the median voter theorem and argue that "the higher the proportion of capital income to total income of the median voter, the lower the tax rate chosen by the voting process and the higher the rate of investment and growth. In terms of income distribution, the poorer the median voter in relation to the voter with average income, the higher the equilibrium tax rate and the lower the growth rate" (Alesina and Perotti 1994, 361).

Like Alesina and Rodrik, Bertola (1993) uses an endogenous growth model and focuses on relative capital and labour shares .The government's role in his model, however, is not public expenditure, but redistribution from capital to labour through a proportional tax on capital. The intuition of the results is similar to that in Alesina and Rodrik. The higher the level of taxation, the lower the after-tax return on capital which results in a lower investment rate and a lower growth rate. The higher the ratio of profit income to wages for an individual, the less likely she is to vote for a high tax rate. Again using the median voter theorem, the tax rate that will emerge will be inversely related to the profit-wages ratio of the median voter. An implication of both papers is that the more even is the initial distribution of profits, and hence of productive wealth, the more rapid is likely to be the rate of growth. This follows from an assumption that government interventions are harmful to growth, e.g., that taxes reduce the return on private investment, that the return on public investment is lower than the return on private investment or that public investment is a very small share of total public expenditure on the margin.

A surprising implication of the idea that political behaviour is the crucial link between equality and growth is that this relationship is likely to be stronger in democracies than in authoritarian regimes since it is only in democracies that the median voter can vote on tax policies. Persson and Tabellini divided their sample into two groups—democratic and non-democratic—and found that indeed the positive relationship between equality and growth held only for their democratic sample. Alesina and Rodrik, however, in performing a similar test with their data found that the coefficient on the dummy variable for democracy in their regression "is not statistically significant, rejecting the hypothesis that the relationship between inequality and growth is different in democracies and nondemocracies." (Alesina and Rodrik 1994, 481) While Deininger and Squire take this as incontrovertible evidence that the political instability argument fails to explain the reason for the inverse relationship between inequality and growth, Alesina and Rodrik offer an alternative interpretation of their result. They argue that it is possible that "the pressure for redistribution coming from majority is felt not only in democracies but also in other regimes... some dictators are subject to political influences similar to those experienced by elected representatives" (Alesina and Rodrik 1994,483).

Alesina and Rodrik are correct to point out that even a highly authoritarian regime is unlikely to be totalitarian and hence often will have to respond to political pressures in one way or another. In some cases the response may be accommodating, e.g., through adjustments of tax rates or the level of transfer payments. In other cases, however, the response may be increased repression, e.g., through higher spending on police, prisons, the judiciary, secret police and perhaps the armed forces. That is, the adjustment may occur not on the revenue side but via changes in government expenditure which reduce resources available for redistribution and accelerating growth. In this second case, "inequality can be costly to maintain" (Griffin 1996,144). Bowles and Gintis argue in a similar vein that one explanation for "the sharply contrasting economic performances of the very unequal Latin American and less unequal East Asian economies over the 1980s and early 1990s is related to the high enforcement cost of economic inequality" (Bowles and Gintis 1995,411).

Moreover, countries with a highly unequal distribution of wealth are likely to be charcterised by sharp class conflict and periodic civil violence. Quite apart from the costs of repression, such conflicted and polarized societies will find cooperation between workers and asset owners to be difficult, be the asset owners large landlords or urban capitalists. "Each will be suspicious of the other; each will resist changes proposed by the other. The result will be greater risk, lower levels of investment, slower rates of technological and institutional change and a slower long term rate of growth" (Griffin 1996,144).

Thus there are several political channels which can link inequality and growth. Statistical regularities that can be captured in a regression equation probably do not exist and if they do exist, they are likely to be hard to detect.

Insights from Economic Theory

Economic theory offers a number of insights that help one to understand why reduced inequality of income and wealth could increase the pace of development, whether measured in terms of growth of GNP or expansion of human capabilities. We shall concentrate on investment in human capital, asset distribution and the rate of savings, and employment and the distribution of physical assets.

Stiglitz and Weiss (1981) have argued that because of imperfect information about the characteristics and future behaviour of borrowers, the loanable funds market does not produce a market clearing price in equilibrium but instead is characterized by credit rationing. One consequence of this is that agents (individuals and firms) are able to borrow only if they own an asset that can be used as collateral. This restricts the number of investors in general and in particular makes it difficult to finance human capital formation.

Investments in human capital are lumpy and usually require either accumulated savings or credit. If credit rationing limits access to funds, then those who have more initial wealth are better able to invest in human capital, partly because they have more of their own funds to use and partly because their wealth provides collateral which, in turn, gives them greater access to credit. The distribution of wealth will thus affect investments in human capital which, in turn, will affect output and growth (Loury 1981). "A more unequal initial distribution of assets would then imply that, for any given level of per capita income, a greater number of people are credit constrained. In an economy where individuals make indivisible investments—in schooling and education for example — that have to be financed through credit, this would imply lower aggregate growth"(Deininger and Squire 1996a, 10). This is even more true if by "growth" one means human development since education contributes directly to enhanced capabilities. Hence if the poor were to own more assets that could be used as collateral, e.g. land, they could borrow money to invest in the human capital of their families and thereby become more educated, healthier and more prosperous citizens.

Deininger and Squire believe that credit market imperfections provide a stronger link between inequality and growth than do the political channels discussed above. They cite two pieces of evidence in support of this view. First, in the advanced economies where one would not expect land to be an important source of collateral, the initial distribution of land does not in fact appear to be a significant determinant of growth. Second, in the developing countries the initial degree of land inequality is significantly and negatively associated with the average educational attainment of the population. This lends credence to the proposition that assets such as land may make it easier for people in developing countries to obtain access to credit which can be used to finance education.

While a greater supply of educated workers may be necessary for a faster pace of development, it is not sufficient. The human development approach sometime ignores the importance of demand for an educated labour force. From the human development perspective, the enhancement of human capital is of course a goal in itself, independent of its impact on accelerating the growth of output. However the impact of improvements in human capital on human development would be magnified if human capital formation were also to accelerate growth of GNP since economic growth contributes to an enhancement of human development. If investment in people is to have the desired impact on growth, there must be a demand for the skills created. Increasing the number of taxi drivers with advanced degrees is unlikely to have a strong effect on the growth rate. Hence it is important to take into account the social rate of return on different types of human capital when allocating resources. It is equally important that macroeconomic and trade policies, i.e., the development strategy in general, be supportive of an employment intensive pattern of growth.

In some developing countries enrollment ratios for women are still far below those of men. Enhancing the human capital of women through education bestows the same direct benefits on society as educating men in terms of having a more skilled and productive wok force. Birdsall, Ross and Sabot have shown that "substituting gender-specific primary school enrollment rates into the original Barro model (Produces) no significant difference between the coefficient values for males and females" (Birdsall, Ross and Sabot 1994, 10). There are however indirect effects or positive externalities of education associated with its effects on reducing fertility rates. It is widely known that rapid population growth rates have been an obstacle to development in many poor countries, even in those which have managed to achieve reasonable rates of growth of GNP. In all countries the education of women confers triple benefits: it raises human development directly, it contributes to a faster growth of output and, by reducing the fertility rate, it increases the rate of growth of per capita income.

Another possible link between asset inequality and growth arises from incentive compatibility problems which are common in highly unequal economies. Bowles and Gintis offer an example of how inefficient incentive structures can affect productivity and growth:

> "Consider an agrarian economy of a hundred households in which most of the land is owned by a single landowner who hires labour and/or leases land under share-cropping tenancy. Both of these forms of employment have adverse incentive effects. Wageworkers have little intrinsic work motivation, since they do not own the results of their work. As a result, the cost of supervising agricultural labour may be considerable. Share-croppers, too, have diluted incentives as they are only partial owners of their work. They will thus allocate less effort and care to their rented land than they would if they owned it themselves"(Bowles and Gintis 1995, 412).

A redistribution of land would clearly result in greater efficiency in the presence of these incentive and monitoring problems. One reason why this does not come about through the market mechanism is because of the credit market imperfections discussed above.

Let us turn now to the question of savings.

One theoretical justification for the Kuznets hypothesis was proposed by Nicholas Kaldor. (Kaldor 1978). He made two crucial assumptions: (i) that a high savings rate is essential for growth and (ii) that rich people have a higher marginal propensity to save than poor people. It follows from these assumptions that in order to ensure a high savings rate and hence rapid growth, income should be concentrated in the hands of the rich. We have already qualified the first of Kaldor's assumptions by arguing that the returns on human capital can be as high as the returns on saving and investing in physical capital. The second assumption also can be questioned, since it is not obvious that rich people always save proportionally more than poor.

Particularly in developing countries, the amount an individual or household saves is likely to be strongly influenced by available investment opportunities (Griffin 1974; Griffin and Khan 1972). The reason for this, as with investment in education, has much to do with the incomplete coverage and malfunctioning of capital markets. Because of the extreme credit market imperfections in most developing countries—in the rural sector and in the informal urban sector—most poor people have virtually no access to the formal credit market. They can neither save (deposit funds) through the banking system nor can they obtain loans (borrow funds) from formal sector commercial banks. In the developed countries, in contrast, the credit market intermediates between an investor and a saver, in principle (although not in practice) allowing all those with commercially viable projects to obtain finance capital.

In developing countries, for those who do not have access to the credit market, notably the poor, the investor and the saver must be the same individual, and the decision to save becomes identical to the decision to invest. In such cases an individual is likely to save only if she has a profitable investment opportunity within reach. A landless agricultural labourer, for example, has few investment opportunities and hence can be expected to save little whereas a small peasant landowner with a similar level of income can invest in the land and hence can be expected to save relatively more. The implications is that a more even distribution of assets could increase the overall savings rate by giving land or other productive assets to the currently assetless-poor and thereby provide them with profitable outlets for their savings.

Some of the earlier literature suggests that this may be true. A study of rural savings rates in India, for example, showed that farmers with access to land ("cultivating families") saved on average 13 per cent of their income (not including direct investment of labour in their land, which would have raised the estimate to 20 per cent); landless households (or "non cultivating families"), in contrast, saved less than four per cent of their income, presumably for precautionary motives (Panikar 1961). In other words, those who had an outlet for their savings actually saved three to five times more than those who did not. A study in then undivided Pakistan showed that rural inequality and average incomes were lower in East Pakistan than in West Pakistan, but personal savings rates were higher in rural East Pakistan (12 per cent) than in rural West Pakistan (9 per cent) (Bergan 1967). That is, according to the conventional view, rural savings should have been higher in West Pakistan than in East Pakistan since the former was both less poor and had a greater concentration of income, but the opposite was the case.

Finally, there is some evidence that among those who do have land, there is no systematic tendency for large farmers to save more than small. A study of 72 holdings in Ludhiana District in the Punjab, in 1969-70, showed that net savings were highest on medium sized farms (26.5 per cent of total income), followed by large farms (25.1 per cent) and then small (16.7 per cent). In the Hissar District of Haryana, a study of 108 holdings again showed that net savings were proportionately highest on medium sized farms (35.5 per cent of total income), but small farms were a close second (34.2 per cent) followed by large farms (31.3 per cent). These data suggest a redistribution of land among already existing landowners would not reduce the savings rate. These conjectures are supported by the redistributive land reforms in Taiwan and mainland China, where if anything, savings rates increased after assets were redistributed

It is reasonable to ask however whether arguments that apply to the distribution of land apply with equal force to the distribution of physical capital such as machinery and buildings. The empirical studies by Deininger and Squire as a proxy for all assets and find that there is a positive relationship between a more equal distribution of assets and growth. Furthermore, as argued above, the true relationship is likely to be even stronger than the estimated relationship since the measurements used for empirical testing understate the true degree of land inequality. One must be cautious however before making a leap from the distribution of land to the distribution of productive assets in general. It is conceivable that there are peculiar features of land that make its equitable distribution more favourable to growth than might be true of other productive assets. It is well established, for example, that "output per hectare tends to be higher on small farms than on large, because small farmers use their land more intensively and utilize more labour-intensive techniques of production" (Griffin and McKinley 1994,81). It does not follow from this small businesses tend to adopt more labour intensive techniques than large or obtain a higher output per unit of capital. That is something that needs to be established.

As far as we know, there has not been a systematic attempt to test empirically the relationship between the distribution of physical assets and growth. There are reasons to believe, however, that this relationship is positive as well. First, there is abundant case study evidence that indicates that small and medium enterprises create more employment per unit of capital than large enterprises. A smaller average size of enterprise is therefore likely to be associated with greater labour intensity, a higher productivity of capital and, of course, a more equal distribution of income. Second, in most developing countries –particularly those which followed an import substituting pattern of industralisation—the industrial sector is dominated by large, monopolistic enterprises which are highly inefficient. A more equitable distribution of physical capital could lead to a more competitive market, greater efficiency and higher average incomes. Since most developing countries have a comparative advantage in relatively labour intensive processes and products, greater emphasis on small and medium sized enterprises would enable them to exploit their resources more efficiently and, in addition, accentuate human development by increasing the demand for skilled labour, i.e., human capital.

Third, as argued above, if savings in developing countries are in part a function of investment opportunities, then policies which give the majority of people greater access to physical assets will simultaneously give them an important reason to save and invest. Even adequate shelter can provide an investment opportunity, since many poor families can use a room in their house to establish a business, e.g., restaurant, bar or teahouse, a repair shop or a microenterprise (Griffin and Brenner 1997). Home based enterprises can be a stepping-stone to larger activities and they certainly are an advance over ambulatory vendors and sales by squatters on the sidewalk.

There are thus several advantages of basing industrial development on small and medium enterprises. The practical problems that have impeded the development of small scale, labour intensive enterprises in the past have been credit market imperfections discussed above, onerous government regulations, controls and licenses, and policies that have favoured large enterprises, including protection from imports, subsidized bank credit and tax benefits. Taiwan is a counter-example. It avoided a heavy bias in favour of large, capital intensive enterprise and instead emphasised the expansion of small scale industry. The results, in terms of equity and growth, were remarkable (Fei, Ranis and Kuo 1979).

III. Evidence from Country Studies

While the theoretical insights and the econometric studies discussed above have been instrumental in encouraging a reevaluation of the relationship between growth and inequality, perhaps the greatest blow to the Kuznets hypothesis and the Okun proposition came from the blatant anomalies represented by the experiences of several East Asian economies such as Japan, China, South Korea and Taiwan. A Southeast Asian country, namely Vietnam, probably should also be added to this list. These countries experienced outstanding achievements as measured by almost all indicators of development while they managed for long periods to maintain and even at times to improve their performance with respect to equality. Speaking specifically of South Korea and Taiwan, Tisor Scitovsky claims, rightly we believe, that "by the double criterion of growth and equity, they have been the most successful of all developing nations" (Scitovsky 1985). During the 1980s in particular, their performance was in stark contrast to those countries in Latin America and sub-Saharan Africa that experienced both slow (and in some case negative) growth rates and worsening inequality. Do any of the theories discussed in the previous section shed any light as to why the East Asian and say, Latin American countries performed so differently with respect to growth and equality?

Those theories which focus on class conflict and political instability do not appear at first glance to be relevant in the East Asian context. While there were indeed redistributive measures in several countries of the region, they did not take the form of income redistribution as described in the models, nor were the redistributive measures the outcome of a voting process. If however one thinks of the models as metaphors that express the advantages of redistribution in a political economy context, then perhaps some insights can be gained. The East Asian governments did not redistribute income or use tax-financed transfer policies, they redistributed assets instead. Taiwan, South Korea, China and Japan all implemented major land reforms following Second World War. These redistributions of wealth, however, were not a result of the voting process but of historical circumstances. Indeed the threat of communism, and the example of the land reform in China, provided strong political incentives to introduce land reforms first in Japan, then in Taiwan and last in South Korea.

In Latin America, in contrast, the elites were not as threatened by a communist revolution and could afford to disregard the alienation of poor. Even so, the modest land redistribution in Mexico during the interwar period and the much more radical land reform in Bolivia in 1952 were warnings that social justice could not be ignored completely. Pressure for land reform increased after the Cuban revolution, but only in Chile (during the Frei and Allende administrations) was there a significant redistribution of land, and even there land reform was reversed during the Pinochet dictatorship. Indeed, the usual response to inequality in Latin America was repression, unlike East Asia where several governments attempted to "ensure that all groups in the population benefitted visibly from growth" (Birdsall, Ross and Sabot 1994,2).

More generally, East Asian governments were more vigorous in promoting agricultural and rural development, partly by encouraging technological change (the green revolution) and partly by creating a more appropriate policy environment. While the Latin America countries tended, for example, to overvalue their exchanges rates to the detriment of the agricultural and export sectors, in East Asia the exchange rate was kept close to its free market value or even in some cases undervalued. This benefitted a large proportion of the working population, and particularly the poor, a majority of whom were employed in agriculture and the export sector

Birdsall, Ross and Sabot emphasize human capital as providing the crucial link between development and equality when comparing the relative performances of East Asia and Latin America. After regressing primary and secondary school enrollment rates on income per capita for over 90 countries during the period 1965-1987, they found that "countries in East Asia, with the exception of Thailand, had significantly higher primary and secondary enrollment rates than predicted by cross-country comparisons. The performance of Latin American countries is not nearly as strong as that of East Asia and is mixed relative to the international norms"(Birdsall, Ross and Sabot 1994,7). Moreover, while enrollment rates in both regions increased over time, the quality of education in East Asia has continuously improved, while the quality of education in Latin America has declined, as evidenced by lower completion rates.

The difference in performance between the two regions does not seem to reflect differences in government commitment to education, at least as represented by differences in public expenditure on education as a percentage of GNP. In fact, the differences are not great. For example, in 1960 public expenditure on education as a percentage of GNP was 2.0 per cent in South Korea and 1.9 per cent in Brazil, while in 1992 the figures were 4.2 per cent in South Korea and even higher in Brazil, namely, 4.6 per cent (UNDP 1990 and 1996). The East Asian countries, however, enjoyed the benefits of both rapid growth and rapid declines in fertility rates. These two factors combined to ensure that absolute expenditure per child on education was much higher in East Asia than in Latin America.

Compared to East Asia, slow economic growth in Latin America and a much less rapid decline in fertility rates meant that resources for spending on education increased slowly while the size of the school age population expanded rapidly. Since fertility rates are inversely related to the level of education (particularly female education), there is a virtuous circle wherein increased education leads to lower fertility which in turn results in greater education expenditures per child, which lowers fertility further (Bridsall, Ross and Sabot 1994). East Asia was caught in this virtuous circle where Latin America was not.

Latin America's relative disadvantage was exacerbated by differences in the composition of educational expenditure. Consider South Korea and Brazil again. In 1992 about 7 per cent of expenditure on education in

South Korea was allocated to higher education whereas Brazil it was 26 per cent. Yet we know that expenditures on primary and secondary education have a stronger impact on economic growth, human development and equality than expenditure on tertiary education. Brazil, in other words, chose her priorities within education unwisely. This does not necessarily mean that the priorities were irrational. Large investments in tertiary education usually subsidized the education of the elites, who are able to capture the resources of the state and use them to their advantage. It should not be surprising that in Latin America, where inequality is very great, the proportion of education expenditures allocated to tertiary education tends to be much higher than in East Asia.

Low enrollment rates are both a result of and a cause of inequality. Once again, there is cumulative causality. Williamson finds that much of the difference in secondary school enrollment rates between South Korea and Brazil can be explained by differences in inequality (Williamson 1993). By educating only part of a population, the human capital of that group is enhanced and as a consequence that section of the population has an asset which gives them an advantage over those who remain uneducated, thus exacerbating inequality.

Bridsall, Ross and Sabot describe two virtuous circles in East Asia wherein "education contributed to economic growth, which, in turn, stimulated investment in education" and then "education contributed to low levels of income inequality which, in turn, stimulated investment in education" (1995,482). Latin America, alas, was caught in two vicious circles where poor educational performance and inappropriate development strategies combined to impede growth. Slow economic growth then contributed to relatively low investment in education. At the same time, poor educational performance contributed to high income inequality which in turn limited investments in education.

Not only did the East Asian countries do better than other developing countries in terms of improvements in the supply of education—both quantity and quality—they also stand out as examples of countries which created a strong demand for labour. By promoting their agricultural and export sectors through investment in infrastructure, by adopting favourable exchange rate policies and by reducing distortions in factor markets, the East Asian countries encouraged labour intensive methods of production. These policies not only helped to increase living standards in the agricultural sector, they also raised wages in non-agricultural sector by raising the reservation wage. This was especially true in countries which had a redistributive land reform. That is, redistributive measures in agriculture also reduced inequality in the urban, industrial sectors of economy.

The export sectors in most countries of East Asia initially relied on intensive use of low skilled labour, but over time exporting became more and more skill intensive. The combination of expanding employment opportunities and increasing real wage rates ensured that the returns to education at the level of the individual remained high. In Latin America, on the other hand, the demand for labour remained weak. Many of the Latin America countries adopted an import substituting industralisation strategy in the 1960s and 1970s which discriminated against agriculture. Industrial production was highly capital intensive and thus did not require large numbers of educated and skilled workers. As a result, the private returns to education were reduced and hence the incentives for individuals and families to invest in education were lower than they might have been had the development strategy been different. Bridsall, Ross and Sabot underscore the importance not only of enhancing human capital by increasing educational opportunities, but also of ensuring that there is a demand for the skills created. They argue that "weak demand for educated labour may help to explain why countries such as Peru and Argentina, which like East Asia, had greater than predicted human capital endowments, nevertheless have tended to underperform, with respect to growth" (1994,12).

Finally, the extensive land reforms that took place in South Korea and Taiwan provided the majority of households with a valuable asset in which to invest. In addition, in Taiwan, the process of industrialisation was not concentrated in urban areas is usually the case, but encomposed the rural areas as well. Indeed Taiwan (like China and the Punjab of India) industrialized the countryside. This pattern of development gave farmers and their families an additional source of employment and income. In 1975, for instance, 53.7 per cent of farm incomes in Taiwan came from jobs off the farm (Scitovsky 1985). The industralisation process in Taiwan also was unusual in that much of the growth in industry originated as a result of increases in the number of small firms. That is, industralisation in Taiwan was led by small and medium enterprises, not by large private oligopolies or state enterprises as in most developing countries. John Mellor notes that "an extraordinarily high proportion of total nonagricultural output takes place in small firms. Indeed, 60 per cent of all exports come from firms of less than 100 employees. Those firms are broadly distributed through the previously rural areas" (Mellor 1995, 322). Thus the combination of land reform and small enterprise development in the countryside meant that natural and physical capital and hence investment opportunities in Taiwan were widely distributed among households. In addition, the labour intensive pattern of growth ensured that human capital was a valuable asset and this, in turn ensured that investment in education would enjoy a high rate of return.

IV. Policy Implications

The focus of attention in this essay has been on the microeconomics of asset redistribution. A supportive general development strategy is however essential. Macroeconomic policy must ensure that the rate of inflation is not so high that the functioning of the price mechanism is impaired; and it must ensure that the pressure of demand is not so low that the investment incentives and overall level of employment are depressed. International trade policy must not be strongly biased either against exporting or import substitution. Most important, a high level of investment is desirable to give flexibility to the economy and to enable the structure of incentives to operate effectively in allocating resources. In such an environment the opportunities created by asset redistribution are most likely to be grasped.

Economic theory, econometric evidence and historical experience combine to produce an eloquent message; relative equality in the distribution of wealth contributes to faster economic growth and enhanced human development. It goes without saying that a redistribution of assets in favour of the poor would reduce poverty, both once-for-all and over time, because of its effect on the rate of economic growth. This would be true whether poverty is conceptualized as insufficient income or as a deficit in capabilities. The question of how best to achieve this more equitable distribution of productive assets still remains. The answer is bound to be affected by the characteristics of the three types of productive assets, viz., natural capital, human capital and physical capital. In the abstract it appears that there are two possible paths which governments can take to redistribute wealth. One is the more direct rule of an immediate, once-for-all redistribution of the stock of existing assets. The other involves a more circuitous path of redistributing the flow of investments so that on the margin, new additions to the stock of assets are equitably distributed.

Of the three types of productive assets, only existing stocks of natural capital can be redistributed quickly and relatively easily. The class of natural capital however is large – including farm land, forests and plantations, pastures, water rights, fishing rights—and the importance of natural capital in the total stock of capital tends to vary inversely with the level of income per head. That is, the poorer the country, the more significant is natural capital likely to be in determining the overall distribution of wealth. At the other extreme, existing stocks of human capital evidently cannot be immediately redistributed since most human capital is embodied in human beings. An improvement in the distribution of human capital will consequently depend on reallocating and increasing expenditure on such things as education, training, health, nutrition programmes and family planning services. This redirection of the flow of investment in human capital, however, need not take long to have an impact on the composition of the stock of human capital. It takes less than a decade, for example, to provide primary and some secondary education to a child, and the provision of basic health services takes even less time. One should not imagine therefore that a redistribution of human capital is necessarily, a long term objective; much can be achieved rather quickly.

A redistribution of the stock of physical capital is more complicated than a redistribution of natural capital. Direct investment by the state in the manufacturing sector once was common in developing countries. In addition, partial or complete nationalization of assets has been attempted in many countries and the consequences for distributive equity have depended on whether the value added of the nationalized enterprises rose or fell and on how the value added was distributed among the population. Many formerly socialist countries have pursued the opposite strategy, denationalizing or privatising state owned enterprises, but the experience so far is not particularly encouraging. Indeed in many formerly socialist countries privitisation has resulted in an extremely unequal distribution of productive wealth with no compensating pay-off in terms of a sharp acceleration on the pace of development (Honakkila 1997).

The most promising approach is to ensure that access to finance capital is widespread, that obstacles to the creation and growth of small and medium enterprises are removed, and that relative factor prices provide incentives to adopt employment intensive patterns of growth. Beyond this, it may be possible to help the poor accumulate assets, e.g., where appropriate, by turning the assets constructed on public works programmes over to a cooperative composed of those who laboured to build them (Griffin 1996, 140). Similarly, housing policy can be designed to promote widespread ownership of dwellings and a house plot, which can provide not only shelter but a place of business.

The argument that savings are a function of investment opportunities, and that a redistribution of productive assets would accelerate growth and human development and reduce poverty, rests on an assumption that there are slack resources in poor households which can be mobilized. There is surplus labour that can be used for investment. There is a margin of consumption above physical subsistence that can be squeezed if attractive investments are available. There is a potential for savings to rise if access to financial markets can be improved. In other words, the poor are quantity constrained rather than price constrained, and opportunities for employment, investment and borrowing are more influential in determining the pace of capital accumulation and savings by the poor than the wage rate, the profit rate and the real rate of interest. Asset redistribution in effect, eases the quantity constraint and permits savings and the employment of labour to increase, thereby raising the level of investment.

It sometimes argued that although a land reform would increase the rate of growth, a rise in aggregate investment would have an even greater effect, and if a land reform were to lead to social unrest and a decline in overall investment, a redistribution of assets might not be worthwhile (Deininger and Squire 1996a, 25). However a classic study of Latin America by William Cline comes to the opposite conclusion (Cline 1972). He argues that even if one makes pessimistic assumptions about the effect of redistribution on aggregate savings and investment, a redistribution of income in Argentina, Brazil and Mexico to roughly the then British level of equality would benefit the poor. Assuming there is a fall in the annual growth rate by 0.66 per cent in Argentina and by approximately one per cent in Brazil and Mexico, the incomes of the bottom 70 per cent of the population nevertheless would rise considerably. In fact, for the poorest 70 per cent to reach the post-redistribution level of income with the undiminished pre-redistribution rate of growth would require 34 years in Argentina, 56 years in Brazil and 49 years in Mexico. By then, most of the poor would have died.

Moreover, theory and empirical evidence since the time Cline wrote suggests that a redistribution of productive assets could in some circumstances increase investment and accelerate the rate of growth. If correct, this strengthens the case for redistribution. Similarly, while redistribution of land and other assets, or the threat of redistribution, could lead to social unrest and lower investment, as Deininger and Squire suggest, the perpetuation of inequality also can be costly in terms of resource use and this can lower the level of investment and the rate of growth. At the very least, the case against a redistribution of wealth is much weaker than once thought and the case in favour of redistribution is much stronger. Finally, asset redistribution is occurring willy-nilly in the ex-socialist countries and in many others (particularly in Africa and Central America) racked by civil conflict. The redistribution of wealth in these cases is disorderly and arbitrary rather than purposive and an opportunity is being missed to redistribute on a more systematic basis to encourage equity and long term material and human development. In economies entering a period of post-war reconstruction or a transition from central planning to a more market oriented economic system, the fluidity of politics may provide a brief opening for imaginative policies which link the distribution of wealth to the pace of development.

REFERENCES

1. Adelman, Irma and Cynthia Taft Morris. 1971. "An Anatomy of Patterns of Income Distribution in Developing Nations", Part II of *Final Report.* Grant AID/csd-2236: Northwestern University.
2. Ahluwalia, Montek S. 1976. "Inequality, Poverty and Development". *Journal of development Economics* 3: 307-342.
3. Alesina, Alberto and Roberto Perotti. 1994. "The Political Economy of Growth: A Critical Survey of the Literature". *The World Bank Economic Review* 8(3): 351-371.
4. Alesina, Alberto and Dani Rodrik. 1994. "Distributive Politics and Economic Growth". *Quarterly Journal of Economics* 108: 486-490.
5. Asian Development Bank. 1997. *Emerging Asia: Changes and Challenges.* Manila: Asian Development Bank.
6. Barro, Robert J.1991. "Economic Growth in a Cross Section of Countries". *Quarterly Journal of Economics 106* (May): 407-443.
7. Bergan, A. 1967. "Personal Income Distribution and Personal Savings in Pakistan, 1963/64". *Pakistan Development Review* VII (2).

8. Bertola, Giuseppe. 1993 "Factor Shares and Savings in Endogenous Growth". *American Economic Review* 83(5): 1184-1198.

9. Birdsall, Nancy, David Ross and Richard Sabot. 1995 . "Inequality and Growth Reconsidered: Lessons for East Asia". *The World Bank Economic Review* 9(3): 477-508.

10. Birdsall, Nancy, David Ross and Richard Sabot. 1994."Inequality as a Constraint on Growth in Latin America". Inter-American Development Bank. Processed.

11. Bowles, Samuel and Herbert Gintis. 1995. "Escaping the Efficiency-Equity Trade-off: Productivity-Enhancing Asset Redistributions". In Gerald A.Epstein and Herbert M.Gintis, eds., *Macroeconomic Policy After the Conservative Era.* New York: Cambridge University Press.

12. Clarke, G.R.G.1995. "More Evidence on Income Distribution and Growth. "*Journal of Development Economics* 47(2): 403-427.

13. Cline, William R. 1972. *Potential Effects of Income Redistribution on Economic growth: Latin American cases.* New York: Praeger.

14. Deaton, A.1995. "Data and Econometric Tools for Development Analysis", in Jere Behrman and T.N.Srinivasan, eds. *Handbook of Development Economics,* Vol. IIIA. New York: Elsevier Science B.V.

15. Deininger, Klaus and Lyn Squire. 1996a. "New Ways of Looking at Old Issues: Inequality and Growth". Mimeo.

16. Deininger, Klaus and Lyn Squire. 1996b. "A New Data Set Measuring Income Inequality". *World Bank Economic Review* 10(3): 565-591.

17. Fei, John C.H., Gustav Ranis and Shirley W.Y.Kuo. 1979. *Growth and Equity: The Taiwan Case.* New York: Oxford University Press.

18. Fields, Gary. 1989."Changes in Poverty and Inequality in Developing Countries". *World Bank Research Observer* 4:167-186.

19. Griffin, Keith. 1974. *The Political Economy of Agrarian Change.* London: Macmillan.

20. Griffin, Keith. 1996. *Studies in Globalisation and Economic Transitions.* London: Macmillan.

21. Griffin, Keith. 1997. "Culture, Human Development and Economic Growth". UNRISD/UNESCO, Occasional Paper Series on Culture and Development, No. 3.

22. Griffin, Keith and Mark Brenner. 1997. "Domestic Resource Mobilisation and Enterprise Development in Sub-Saharan Africa". Department of Economics, University of California, Riverside, Working paper 97-01.

23. Griffin, Keith and Azizur Rahman Khan. 1972. *Growth and Inequality in Pakistan.* London: Macmillan Press.

24. Griffin, Keith and Terry McKinley. 1994. *Implementing a Human Development Strategy.* London: Macmillan.

25. Honkkila,Juha.1997. *Privatisation, Asset Distribution and Equity in Transitional Economies.* United Nations University, World Institute for Development Economics Research, Working Papers No. 125.

26. Jain, Shail. 1975. *Size Distribution of Income: A Compilation of Data.* World Bank.

27. Kahlon, A.S, and Harbhajan Singh Bal. n.d. *Factors Associated with Farm and Farm Family Investment Pattern in Ludhiana (Punjab) and Hissar (Haryana) Districts (1966-67 through 1969-70).* Department of Economics and Sociology, Punjab Agricultural University, Ludhiana.

28. Kaldor, Nicholas. 1978. "Capital Accumulation and Economic growth". In Nicholas Kaldor, ed., *Further Essays on Economic Theory.* New York: Holmes and Meier.

29. Kuznets, Simon. 1955. "Economic Growth and Income Inequality". *American Economic Review* 45: 1-28.

30. Kuznets, Simon. 1963. Quantitative Aspects of the Economic Growth of Nations: VIII. Distribution of Income

by Size. "*Economic Development and Cultural Change* 11(2): 1-80.

31. Kuznets, Simon .1967. "Underdeveloped Countries and the Pre-Industrial Phase in the Advanced Countries". In A.N.Agarwala and P.S. Singh, eds., *The Economics of Underdevelopment*. New York: Oxford University Press.
32. Loury, G.C. 1981. "Intergenerational transfers and the Distribution of Earnings". *Econometrica* 49: 843-867.
33. Mellor, John.1995. *Agriculture on the Road to Industralisation*. Baltimore: The Johns Hopkins University Press.
34. Okun, Arthur. 1975. *Equality and Efficiency: The Big Tradeoff*. Washington D.C.: Brookings Institution.
35. Panikar, P.G.K.1961. "Rural Savings in India". *Economic Development and Cultural Change* 10(1).
36. Paukert, Felix. 1973. "Income Distribution at Different Levels of Development: A Survey of Evidence". *International Labour Review* 108: 97-125.
37. Perotti, Roberto. 1991. "Income Distribution, Politics and Growth: Theory and Evidence". Columbia University. Mimeo.
38. Persson, Trosten and Guido Tabellini. 1994. "Is Inequality Harmful for Growth". *American Economic Review* 84(3): 600-621.
39. Psacharopoulos, George.1988. "Education and Development. A. Review". *World Bank Research Observer* 3(1): 99-116.
40. Psacharopoulos, George. 1994. "Returns to Investment in Education: A Global Update". *World Development* 22: 1325-1343.
41. Ram, Rati. 1996. "Level of Development and Returns to Schooling: Some Estimates from Multicountry Data". *Economic Development and Cultural Change* 44(4): 839-857.

42. Robinson, Sherman. 1976. "A Note on the U-Hypothesis". *American Economic Review* 66(3): 437-440.

43. Saith, Ashwanti. 1983. "Development and Distribution: A Critique of the Cross-Country U-hypothesis." *Journal of Development Economics* 13: 367-380.

44. Scitovsky, Tibor. 1985. "Economic Development in Taiwan and South Korea". *Food Research Institute Studies* XIX(4): 215-264.

45. Stiglitz, Joseph and Andrew Weiss. 1981. "Credit Rationing in Markets with Imperfect Information". *American Economic Review* 71: 393-409.

46. United Nations Development Programme. 1990. *Human Development Report.* New York: Oxford University Press.

47. United Nations Development Programme. 1996. *Human Development Report.* New York: Oxford University Press.

48. Williamson, Jeffrey G. 1993. "Human Capital Deepening, Inequality and Demographic Events along the Asia-Pacific Rim". In Naohiro Agawa, Gavin W. Jones and Jeffrey G Williamson eds., *Human Resources in Development Along the Asia-Pacific Rim.* New York: Oxford University Press.

2

Rural Development Policies and Some Innovative Projects in Asia and The Pacific:

*An Overview**

Dr. P. Subrahmanyam

1. Introduction

In the 1940s, the newly independent nations, liberating and emerging as they were, from the yoke of imperialism, realised that potentials and constraints to (rural) development were largely rooted in the society itself. Barring some islands of affluence in their societies, the majority was reeling under the weight of poverty, darkness of illiteracy and filthiness of squalor (Myrdal, 1968). They pinned their hopes on achieving a higher economic growth rate for improving their people's standard of living.

The rural development pursued in the 1950s and 60s was largely centred around 'growth-first' models. Despite

* A modified version of the paper submitted to APO's workshop held at NIRD, Hyderabad, 1999.

robust growth in the 1960s, economic benefits did not 'trickle down' and majority of the population was languishing in abject poverty, rising unemployment and increased inequalities (ILO, 1977). The general disenchantment with the performance of the 1960s of 'economic growth without distributive justice', prompted the economists of the day to engineer such theories and models as 'redistribution with growth'[1], 'basic needs approach'[2], 'integrated rural development' and a demand for the establishment of 'new international economic order'[3]. Therefore, the 1970s could be described as a decade of equity and justice[4]. The 1980s were a mixed bag. It was a decade of structural adjustments 'without' a human face[5] to qualify itself to be labelled as a "lost decade"[6]. It was also a decade which laid foundations for the people's participation, integrated approach to development, and for socio-economic development of many Asian countries. The 1990s are a decade that belongs to democratic forces, participatory decentralised rural development, civil societies and human development.

This paper is divided into three Sections. Section-I reviews the rural development experience from the 1950s to 1990s and analyses the approaches to rural development paradigm. Section-II discusses some of the major issues in rural development. In Section-III, some selected innovative projects in Asian region along with the conclusions are presented.

2. Section—I: Experiences

Rural development is defined as a process of "improving living standards of the masses of the low income population residing in rural areas and making the process of their development self-sustaining" (Lele, 1975:20). It is also defined as a process which leads to a rise in the capacity of rural people to control their environment resulting from more extensive use of the benefits which ensue from such a control (Webster, 1975).

The World Bank defined it as '...a strategy designed to improve the economic and social life of a specific group of people-the rural poor' (quoted in Harriss, 1982).

Rural development has become a distinct approach and strategy implemented mainly by the Government, (or occasionally, by NGOs and private agencies) in developing countries. It encompasses multi-sectoral components and is broader in its approach than 'agriculture'. It, therefore, requires inter-disciplinary approach. Its focus on poverty, inequality and distributive justice makes it stand in a special category of interventions for bringing about socio-economic change (World Bank, 1997).

Many countries adopt IRD as an approach and a strategy. But there is no definite uniformity. (It is neither feasible nor desirable to have uniformity of approach for rural development for different countries with such huge diversities as in Asia and the Pacific region). This offers both a challenge and an opportunity to the policy makers: challenge because of the difficulties involved in the concept and implementation of rural development activities in a given socio-economic and political framework; opportunity because it offers enormous scope for introducing variety of programmes and projects.

Rural Areas and Rural People

As seen from the Table 1, these countries are, except South Korea, predominantly rural and agricultural. In Bangladesh, India, Nepal, Thailand, Vietnam and China about three-fourths of the population live in rural areas.

The following inferences can be made from Table 1.

- In countries such as South Korea, Malaysia and the Philippines though urbanisation is taking place at a rapid pace, agriculture still plays considerable role in providing employment to their

Table–1. Some Basic Characteristics of the Developing Countries of Asia

Countries	Population (millions)	Rural population (as % of total		%share of agriculture in				Population below income poverty line (%)	
				Labour force		GDP		$I a day (1985 ppp$)	National povertyline
	1997	1970	1996	1970	1990	1970	1997	1989-94	1989-94
Bangladesh	124	92	82	84	65	55	30	28.5	48.0
India	961	80	73	73	64	45	27	52.5	n.a
Pakistan	137	75	66	65	52	37	26	11.6	34.0
Nepal	23	96	90	94	94	67	43	n.a	n.a
Thailand	61	87	80	80	64	26	11	0.1	13.0
Malaysia	21	66	46	54	27	29	13	5.6	16.0
Philippines	73	77	46	58	46	30	20	n.a	41.0
Vietnam	77	82	81	77	71	n.a	27	n.a	51.0
South Korea	46	59	19	49	18	25	06	n.a	n.a
Indonesia	200	83	65	66	55	24	16	14.5	8.0
China	1227	83	70	78	72	34	20	29.4	11.0

Source: 1. UNDP (1998)
2. World Bank (1995,1998)

labour force. The development experience of these countries, as in the case of developed countries, reveal that there has been a definite shift in labour force from agriculture and allied activities to industry and services buttressing the hypothesis of Colin Clark.

- It is a well-known fact that the occupational structure of an economy undergoes a change in favour of non-agricultural sector. This is partly mirrored in the declining share of agriculture in GDP. But in countries such as India, Bangladesh, Nepal and Pakistan, despite the steep fall in the share of agriculture and allied activities in GDP (Table-1) the share of labour force in the primary sector remains more or less around 65 to 70 percent. The presence of disguised unemployment and underemployment in the agriculture makes things more difficult. The industrial sector in these countries is experiencing what UNDP (1993) called "jobless growth". This is one of the major structural factors explaining the stubborn persistence of rural poverty in these countries.
- In countries like Bangladesh, India, Pakistan, Nepal and Vietnam there is a mass poverty: one-third to two-fifths of population in these countries live below poverty line (Table 1).

3. Rural Development Strategies

In the 1950s, most of the national governments in Asia formulated 'community development' programmes with a view to achieving self-reliance and development through local institutions and participation of the rural communities for their development[7]. In the 1950s the United Nations identified community development as "synonymous with community participation" (Moser, 1989). The community development was seen as a "process designed to create conditions of economic and social progress for the whole community with its active participation" (UN definition quoted in Moser, 1989).

The core elements in community development were (a) participation of the people in local community development projects, (b) democratic decentralisation, (c) transfer of technology, (d) self-help efforts.

The Indian government, for instance, had initiated in 1952 the community development movement. Among others, this programme was to help agricultural community by providing technical guidance and leadership. The Village Level Worker (VLW) was backed by the specialists in agronomy, soil and water management, pest control etc., responsible for larger area. At the block level, the Block Development Officer (BDO) carried out the development work. The American agricultural specialists had shown a lot of interest in the programme and the Ford Foundation gave generous support (Galbraith, 1979).

Similarly, the community development programme in the Philippines was started in the 1950s under President Ramon Magsaysay. The objective was to integrate all rural development activities at the *barrio* or village level. United States gave a big support to this programme (Nietes, 1991). In Thailand, a National Community Development Programme was launched in the 1960s (CIRDAP, 1996). The Tribhuwan village development programme initiated in 1952 in Nepal was the first significant development effort. Nepal has, more or less, followed the Indian model (ESCAP, 1989).

The community development movement expanded rapidly during the decade of the 1950s. By 1960 over 60 nations in Asia, Africa and Latin America had launched national or regional community development programmes (Ruttan, 1984).

The community development programme had neither changed the status quo of the rural power structure, nor could ease the grip of rural poverty. By the mid-1960s, there was a food crisis in South Asia[8], which shifted the attention of policy makers from community development to green revolution. India had initiated the Intensive Agricultural Development Programme (IADP) and Intensive Area Programme (IAP).

In Bangladesh (formerly, of Pakistan) Akhtar Hameed Khan, the principal architect of the Comilla Approach, visualised an integrated approach to rural development. It aimed to raise agricultural production, income and employment by giving priority to small-scale irrigation and high yielding varieties. The Comilla Approach[9] had four major components:

1. A Thana Training and Development Centre (TTDC) in every Thana for training the local leaders and bureaucracy.

2. A Rural Works Programme (RWP) for the construction of roads, drainage and embankments etc.

3. A Thana-based small-scale irrigation programme (TIP); and

4. A two-tier co-operative system under the Thana Central Co-operative Association (TCCA) consisting of Krishi Samabaya Samiti (KSS), which were village level co-operatives, linked with the Co-operative at the Thana level.

Similarly, the BIMAS programme in Indonesia, the Masagana - 99 Programme in the Philippines and several programmes of Agricultural Bank in Malaysia have all tried to increase production in the economy (CIRDAP, 1996).

4. Conventional Approach to Poverty Alleviation and Rural Development: A Critique

The conventional approach suffers from the following constraints:

- The conventional approach considered development as an output, which can be 'delivered' through 'planning from the top' (SAARC, 1992). (Development cannot be packaged and distributed to the target groups like a dairy factory distributes milk bottles to its customers).
- The conventional strategies have seen development as 'transfer of technology' for boosting the production. These projects, in practice, tended to benefit the medium to large-scale producers, supporting them with technology, credit and extension advice (ILO, 1977).
- Expectation of rapid growth did not materialise, except in East Asia, due to inadequate capital accumulation and human resources (World Bank, 1993).
- Another fallacy of the conventional approach was that it considered different communities as harmonious entities. However, the relations are characterised by dominance-dependence relationships, whether at the village level in rural areas or in urban areas (ILO, 1987; SAARC, 1992).
- The conventional approach assumed that growth would take care of poverty and equity as benefits would "trickle down" to the poor. But this has rarely happened.
- The conventional approach failed to incorporate people's participation. Unless the rural poor are

given the means to participate fully in development, they will continue to be excluded from its benefits. The government may continue to implement programmes of what Chambers (1983) called 'rural development tourism'.

Growth with Justice Perspective

Disillusioned with 'growth-first' models, some economists gave a call to 'dethrone' the GNP and urged the planners and policy makers not to worship at the altar of GNP. They advocated that the economic logic of taking care of GNP should be reversed and asked them instead to take care of poverty as GNP could take care of itself (Haq, 1976).

(a) Redistribution with Growth

Redistribution with Growth was published in 1974. The authors recognised that the rural elite tends to capture the benefits of a government programme. To achieve equity, targeting is seen as a better alternative. Asset distribution such as land reform and provision of public goods emphasised. "A land reform breaks the power of large farmers and the rural elite will... provide a framework within which public goods and services can be directed to the target groups with minimum leakage" (Chenery et al., 1974:135). They have advocated need for a 'wholly new organisations endowed with ample resources and the best cadres' for executing these target-oriented programmes.

Communist countries such as China, Cuba, the Democratic People's Republic of Korea, the erstwhile USSR and Vietnam implemented various types of collective ownership of land. Other countries such as India, Japan, Pakistan, South Korea and Sri Lanka implemented land reforms. The implementation is, except in South Korea and Japan, far from satisfactory. However, the implementation of tenancy laws in West Bengal and Kerala in India stand out as an exception to this.

(b) The Basic Needs Approach

The basic needs approach is a radical departure from the conventional development approach. It was a shift from the growth approach to consumption approach. Consumption targets replace growth objectives. These are translated into specific targets or programme goals-'a life expectancy of 65 years or more; a literacy rate of at least 75%: an infant mortality rate of 50 or less per 1000 births; and a birth rate of 25 or less per 1000 population' (Streeten and Burki, 1978).

Since education is considered a key factor-in fact the key of all keys-for rising productivity and reducing poverty, the protagonists of the basic needs approach argued that expenditure on education should be viewed as investment. So is the expenditure on health and nutrition. The challenge of development, therefore, lies in the alleviation of poverty and in the provision of basic needs-food, shelter, safe water, education and health. China, Costa Rica and Sri Lanka provide good example of success. They made great strides in literacy, infant and under-5 mortality, safe drinking water, sanitation and other basic social services.

(c) Integrated Rural Development

The FAO had convened a big symposium on 'Agricultural Institutions for Integrated Rural Development' in 1971. This gave a new lease of life to the integrated rural development. By then, it was clear that the economic growth was no guarantee for reduction of poverty. In the wake of widespread poverty and rising unemployment, the integrated rural development strategy and approach was introduced with the explicit objectives of economic growth (rural development) and poverty alleviation. Under economic growth (rural development) it aims to have more agricultural and off-farm production, enhanced rural incomes, improved infrastructure and technology transfer to the rural areas etc. Under poverty alleviation, transfer/creation of assets, creation of jobs for the rural poor and provision of basic social services. Since growth will not necessarily decrease poverty, there is a need for frontal and direct attack on poverty. That is why the poverty alleviation is added to the list objectives of rural development.

In line with the dominant thinking of the 1970s for a bigger role for the State, many countries in South Asia took up several innovative programmes. In India, for instance, the notable ones are the Small Farmers Development Agency (1971), the National Rural Employment Programme (1980), the Rural Landless Employment Guarantee Programme[10] (1983), Minimum Needs Programme (MNP), Development of Women and Children in Rural Areas (DWCRA), Training for Rural Youth in Self-employment (TRYSEM), and Integrated Rural Development Programme (1978-79).

In Bangladesh, the Comilla approach was to be replicated through IRDP.IRDP also took up other programmes like Youth Programme (1977-82), and *Bittahin and Mohila Samabaya Samiti* (Assetless and Women Co-operatives)[11]. The IRDP, now known as Bangladesh Rural Development Board (BRDB) initiated a number of development programmes. Bangladesh and India, for instance, had also provided more space to civil society organisations and established mechanisms to support NGOs[12].NGOs like BRAC, Grameen Bank, Proshika in Bangladesh, Myrada, SEWA, the Working Women's Forum in India are doing yeomen service in poverty alleviation and rural development.

Structural adjustments and the 'lost decade': The 1980s saw the emergence of a new philosophy in the name of efficiency. It is linked to the neo-liberal school of thought, which is embedded to the theory of free markets and competition, getting prices right, slimming or even rolling back the State.

The typical package under structural adjustment is that the public spending should be trimmed to reduce fiscal deficit and balance the budget; the national currency should be devalued to promote exports. The panoply of controls should be dismantled and the economy should be liberalised. The national economy should be integrated with global economy. The government should withdraw from those activities which market could best perform.

The structural adjustment policies comprise of IMF 'stablisation' policies to reduce fiscal deficits and restore the balance of payments position to viable levels, and the World Bank's long-term 'structural reforms' to raise productivity and enhance efficiency. Usually these are complementary to each other. The principle of 'cross conditionality' implies that the World Bank rarely initiates a programme unless a government becomes a client of the IMF.

The IMF and the World Bank maintain that the structural adjustment policies contribute to poverty reduction. Firstly, failure to adjust will impose huge cost on the poor. Secondly, the 'social conditionality' that is now incorporated into the structural adjustment should take care of the provision of basic social services like education, health and nutrition etc. Thirdly, structural adjustment programmes would not only create conditions for good growth but also reduce poverty through pro-poor policies.

This is possible in theory. But in practice, the experience of the rural poor, particularly of the Sub-Saharan Africa, is contrary to the expectations of the IMF and the World Bank. Many poor people in Sub-Saharan

Africa suffered most. Zimbabweans have reinterpreted the acronym for their Enhanced Structural Adjustment Programme, ESAP, as 'Enhanced Suffering for African People' (Oxfam, 1992). The weight of poverty falls most heavily on certain disadvantaged groups like women and children; availability of less food due to fall in household income cast heavy burden on women and girls because of inequalities within households. In the context of poverty and structural adjustment in Bangladesh CIRDAP has documented that the poorer sections suffer most since the social investment is slashed considerably (CIRDAP, 1998).

5. Human Development Perspective

The central focus of human development perspective is human well being. The conventional economic thinking assumed that the purpose of development is to increase national income. But today, it is widely accepted that the purpose of development is to enlarge people's choice- economic, political, social and cultural. Increase in income is one of many choices people make; it is not the sum total of human life (UNDP, 1993). Increases in income are considered as one of the means to achieve human development (Haq, 1996). The aim of economic growth is to enrich people's lives. Development must, therefore, be woven around people; not people around development. The UNDP has been using Human Development Reports, since 1990, to advocate such policies and strategies that link economic growth with human development in the World.

The innovative analysis of HDR is to present the Human Development Index and rank all countries as per their performance. While preparing the HDI, the UNDP uses three key components: longevity, knowledge and income[13].

The Basic Needs Approach and the Human Development Perspective maintain that it is possible to attain good progress in basic social services even at low level of income. In Table 2, we present evidence of how different countries, with similar income, fare differently on human development indicators.

Though the per capita income of Sri Lanka and Cameroon is more or less, the same, in 1994, they have different achievement level. Sri Lanka's literacy rate of 90.1% is far ahead of Comeroon's 62.1%. Its infant mortality rate (IMR) and U-5MR are less than one-forth of Cameroon's. Life expectancy at birth in Sri lanka, in 1994, was 72.2 years, which is 21.1 years longer than Cameroon's 51.1 years. Sri Lanka has scored higher HDI value (0.711) positioning itself in medium human development country group than Cameroon with a HDI value of (0.468) remained as a low human development country (UNDP 1997).

Ecuador and Papua New Guinea produce different HDIs with similar per capita income. Ecuador has shown better performance, in terms of HDI rank, literacy rate, life expectancy, infant mortality and U-5 mortality rate than Papua New Guinea. Similar variation is found between Costa Rica and Turkey and Gabon and Trinidad and Tobago (Table 2).

Based on the evidence presented in Table 2, the following inferences can be made:

1. There is no automatic link between economic growth (and per capita income) and human development and poverty reduction.

2. It is possible to achieve poverty reduction and human development even at relatively low per capita income levels.

3. The quality of economic growth-of what kinds of goods and services are produced-and how the benefits of that growth are distributed is more important that the quantity of rate of growth.

Table–2. Similar Income, Different HDIs, 1994

Country	*Total Population (millions) 1994*	*GNP Percapita (US$) 1994*	*HDI Value 1994*	*HDI rank 1994*	*Adult Literacy rate (%) 1994*	*Life expectancy at birth (Years) 1994*	*IMR (per 1000 live births) 1994*	*Under-5 Mortality rate per 1000 live births 1995*
1	2	3	4	5	6	7	8	9
Sri Lanka	17.8	640	0.711	91	90.1	72.2	16	19
Cameroon	12.8	680	0.468	133	62.1	51.1	62	106
Ecuador	11.2	1280	0.775	72	89.6	69.3	47	40
Papua New Guinea	4.2	1240	0.525	128	71.2	56.4	68	95
Costa Rica	3.3	2400	0.889	33	94.7	76.6	13	16
Turkey	59.9	2500	0.772	74	81.6	68.2	44	50
Trinidad and Tobago	1.3	3740	0.880	40	97.9	72.9	15	18
Gabon	1.0	3880	0.562	120	62.6	54.1	91	148

Source: UNDP's Human Development Report, 1997.

4. The public policy with regard to the provision of basic social services in a such a manner as to distribute benefits of economic growth more equitably as shown by Costa Rica, Sri Lanka (and China) are very instructive for other countries to design pro-poor policies.

5. The challenge of development is to translate the benefits of economic growth into improvements in the people' lives.

6. Economic growth is, of course, essential in developing world for gradual reduction and eventual elimination of poverty. There is a need for intensifying the direct and frontal attack on poverty. In other words, growth with equity holds well, but not growth for the sake of growth.

Section—II: Major Issues in Rural Development

(a) IRDP: Participatory Approach vs. Welfare Approach

Before releasing a new product to the market, a private company undertakes a market survey to find out the market potential, clientele response, changes required to the design of the product etc. In contrast to this, take the case of Government sponsored programme such as IRDP, for instance, in India. This programme is conceived and finalised by the top bureaucracy (on the direction of a political executive[14]) and handed down to the field functionaries for implementation. The programme is meant to help the poor below poverty line and expects them to 'actively participate'. The contradiction between the expectation of 'people's participation' in theory and the top-down strategy in practice is too stark to be camouflaged. Unfortunately, the poverty alleviation, the key component of which is empowerment, is seen as a welfare measure. Whatever may be the precept in the policy documents, but in practice, the attitude of various administrators implementing poverty alleviation projects is to treat it like a welfare programme. This shows the 'paternalistic' attitude of the planners, designers and implementers of the programme. The welfare approach treats people as recipients, as silent and passive beneficiaries. This approach alienates the intended beneficiaries from the programme for whom it is meant.

The programme content of IRDP in India, at least in the initial years, illustrates this point. There was no such thing like participatory assessment of the needs of the poor to devise suitable schemes for income generation. With the result the milch cattle programme constituted as high as 93% under IRDP in India in 1980-81, although it had gradually declined to 53% by 1984-85 (Mukhopadyaya, 1989). It means that most of the beneficiaries must take the milch cattle, irrespective of their needs. More often than not, the project administrators, caught up as they are in a 'jungle' of targets, would bother more about the "quantities" and less about the 'quality' and the 'process' which itself can be an educative, empowering one (Chambers, 1983). The outcome of the top-down target-oriented approach in IRDP in India, for instance, can be described as 'salt-sugar syndrome'. When our beneficiaries need salt, we offer them sugar. We do not know where and how to acquire salt from; and they do not know what to do with sugar. They ask us what they 'need'; but we give them what we 'have'. We think we have helped them; it is our state of mind; a sort of mental block. For them, it means nothing at best; for all you know, it may be a debt burden for them. This is not to denigrate the programmes. This is only to highlight the limitations of welfare approach and to stress the case for the participatory approach in poverty alleviation programmes.

The "participatory approach" on the other hand, lends itself to a situation where poor are seen as key actors in the development process, building on the experience of their own coping strategies. Programmes and projects should be left to the initiatives of the local people. The fundamental aspect in the participatory approach is to enable people to participate in planning, implementation and decision-making process. This process facilitates the community involvement and instils a sense of ownership, which are vital for its sustainability.

To implement government programmes through participatory mode may not be that easy, though not impossible. As observed by Oakley and Marsden (1984), there are number of obstacles. In most of the developing countries the political, social and legal systems do not favour citizens taking control over their lives. The dominant coalition, which constitutes the political, social and financial power base of the State still maintains its hold in decision making. They perceive the bottom-up participatory initiatives as direct threats to their pre-eminence and sway over society.

But it must be noted that most of the NGOs' main strategy is participatory approach. It is through this approach that they are able to reach the disadvantaged, organise, empower the poor and awaken their spirit of self-esteem. Government must learn this from the civil society organisations.

(b) Culture of accommodation and equilibrium of poverty[15]

One of the major objectives of IRD is to combat poverty that has a tremendous grip over the rural poor. Rural poverty, especially in South Asia, is not an incidence of isolation; it is a mass affliction. It denies them the means for improvement. If at all become available, the social and biological forces devour the improvement; the success eluded and poverty perpetuated. When the poor people's attempt to escape from poverty is, time and again, frustrated, they reconcile to the realities of life and prefer acquiescence to frustration. People say that poor do not have motivation and aspiration to escape from poverty. This is not correct. There are thousands of success stories. Moreover, motivation and aspiration, after all, are subject to conditioning by its culture. The conditioning is reinforced, at least partly, by the instruction of religious preaching. Though the pain of poverty is not denied, all religions talk of spiritual rewards that the poor would get. Christianity talks of the prospect of poor reaching the Paradise while the rich may not. It is easier for a camel to go through the eye of a needle than for a rich person to enter the Kingdom of God. Hinduism talks of acquiescence and good behaviour in the present life to improve the spiritual rewards and betterment in the next life. The poor people who are also illiterate, inarticulate, vulnerable may remain passive as self-blame and low esteem, or fear of the unknown, or fatalistic attitudes inhibit any tendency to exercise any control over their situation (ESCAP, 1996).

Be it as it may, given the iron grip of equilibrium of poverty the attack against poverty under IRDP should be launched on the socio-psychological front. Firstly, the programme should combat the sense of accommodation residing in the mind-set of the poor. They should be motivated and inspired to escape from the equilibrium of poverty. There should be conscientisation or awareness raising on the sociological realities of their life situations. This is very important because the perception about suffering is more important than the suffering itself. The poor should undertake the social inquiry into their life situations and analyse the social forces and processes, which create, reproduce and perpetuate their poverty and dependence (ILO, 1987). They should perceive possibilities of change through their individual and collective action. Secondly, there should be organised efforts to facilitate that escape (Galbraith, 1979).

There are a number of possible strategies for rejecting the accommodation and facilitating the escape from the equilibrium of poverty. Under the first category the following are the suggested activities.

(a) Provision of social animators or facilitators or catalysts to motivate and sensitise the poor.

(b) Use of participatory methodology for social inquiry and information gathering systems.

(c) Organisation of (homogenous) small groups.

(d) Organising the poor through social mobilisation.

(e) Arranging exchange visits/interaction with other more advanced communities.

(f) Awareness through education.

(g) Use of traditional art forms and folklore.

(h) Use of media.

Under the second category, among others, the programmes such as land reforms, asset creation and income generating programmes, employment-generation programmes, extension of micro credit, training and capacity building, provision of basic social services like education, health, sanitation, drinking water, family planning etc., should be implemented. Poor people's access to social services must be enhanced and ensured. This is very important because improvement in the provision of social services not only alleviate the immediate consequences of poverty but also attack one of the major causes of poverty (World Bank, 1990).

(c) Building Organisations of the Poor:[16]

Administration of rural development programmes poses peculiar problems. Inflexible, hierarchy based bureaucratic systems are antithesis of the participatory approach to development. A centralised, top-down administrative structure is hardly able to reflect the needs of the poor in the programme design. Added to this is the question of field functionaries' level of motivation. The development bureaucracy is ill equipped to deliver the job. Their class character and social composition is a major barrier in understanding the problems of the rural people, much less the rural poor. There is a Great Wall of China between the developmental administrators and the target group of beneficiaries separated by different socio-economic and cultural settings. Local self-governments are supposed to look after development work. They are considered vehicles of local development efforts. But most of them have become power-oriented than welfare or development oriented. Unless the class character changes, the local bodies may not be able deliver the goods. (But the point is whether this can be improved through training, sensitisation and awareness building etc). Given this situation, it is difficult to imagine that government organisation would be able to deliver the goods. This calls for an alternative organisation with different ethos, ideology and commitment.

(i) **Building Small homogenous groups of the Poor:** Poverty cannot be eradicated by an outside agency. Organisations of poor are an essential prerequisite if poverty is to be eradicated. This requires awareness building and sensitising the poor on the causes and consequences of poverty so that they gain deeper understanding of poverty and perceive possibilities of change. In order to initiate action, they need to build organisations in a manner that best suits their purpose. It may be self-help organisation or village organisation or in some other form as decided by them. The small groups can be networked into somewhat bigger organisations.

(ii) **Community Development Initiatives.** Initially, the poor people tend to take up simple activities for the benefit of the community. The resources required for such activities are mobilised locally through collective action. The initial success will give them confidence and they will embark on bigger projects as days pass by. This should be sustained by forward and backward linkages including market tie-up, raw material supply and buy back arrangements.

(iii) **Capacity Building of the Poor:** As the path to development unfolds, the poor would soon realise and develop their capacities using their latent for their betterment. The internal animators, managers and leaders from the poor people's organisations would emerge and take control and steer the development process for further development.

(iv) **Support service mechanisms:** It is necessary, at least initially, till the poor people's organisation becomes self-sufficient. It can be government, non-governmental organisation, co-operatives, or rural banks for the poor. The support service mechanism can help the poor to acquire management and technical skills, to develop liaison with other service agencies, improve saving, financial and accountancy capabilities and to help transform their ideas into implementable workplans etc.

(d) Self-reliance:17

Self-reliance should not be equated with self-sufficiency or autarky. It should be understood as one's own faith in one's own abilities for achieving one's own objectives. In the context of poverty alleviation, self-reliance should be understood as a process of de-alienation, regeneration and development of powers that people might have lost through dependence, exploitation and subordination (ILO, 1987). The question is how do the poor people pursue autonomous course of action? This requires a combination of material, intellectual, organisational and managerial self-reliance.

(i) **Material self-reliance:** It means that poor people would determine their own path, drawing as far as possible on local knowledge and resources to achieve that end. They should become fully aware of the range of local resources available to them. They should also eschew the thought that changing their life situation is beyond their means. In other words, self-reliance should be seen as a process in which the poor people should explore local solutions to their problems. Resources required for the development of the material base are acquired partly through own efforts (through either savings or eliminating the unnecessary expenditure) and partly through assertion of rights and entitlements. In a welfare state or in a situation where NGOs are actively providing micro credit and such other resources, it is possible to acquire/create assets and also gain access to government to common public resources.

(ii) **Intellectual self-reliance:** From the intellectual perspective, the rural poor can be broadly grouped under four categories[18]

- Literate and skilled
- Literate but unskilled
- Illiterate but skilled
- Illiterate and unskilled.

This broad classification is helpful for identifying suitable training programmes for either skill upgradation or functional literacy. Whenever the project officials, who are normally urban-oriented, well educated, meet with illiterate poor villagers, the transaction is quite strange. The educated feels shy of mingling well with the illiterate poor. If the illiterate person is explaining some thing on which s/he has enormous wisdom, the educated feels offended. Being an educated, s/he feels it is below dignity to listen to her/his lecture. Because the educated thinks s/he does not need to learn any thing from an illiterate. This is called 'intellectual arrogance'. To a lesser degree, this gap exists between rural literates and illiterates also.

The intellectual self-reliance should mean that rural masses must develop their indigenous knowledge base and acquire reading, writing and numeracy skills and build upon their practical experience in order to overcome the subtle forms of domination or exploitation arising out of control over knowledge. The poor people should think about their life situation and understand the forces that perpetuate their poverty and dependence. This should prompt them to search for and perceive possibilities of change. As earlier noted, perception about suffering is more important than suffering itself. They should also become aware of their rights and entitlements conferred by government legislation or court pronouncements or customary rights. They should acquire knowledge about outside world through reading, media such as press, radio, TV or exposure visits and relate macro-level policies to micro-level initiatives or impact. Cultural education, awareness building, conscientisation and social mobilisation through 'mission mode' would greatly help achieve intellectual self-reliance. The total literacy campaign (TLC) launched in Nellore district of Andhra Pradesh (India) is a case in point. The women got motivated and galvanised themselves into a formidable force and brought pressure on the state government to impose a total prohibition on arrack.

(iii) **Organisational and managerial self-reliance:** It means that poor people should possess ability to organise themselves around some productive activity and manage such programme which would bring about a change in their life situation. If they start an organisation, they should be able to manage, control and develop on their own. This requires that they learn some managerial functions like maintenance of records, market tie-ups, bookkeeping, cashbook maintenance, purchases etc. This is important because many self-help groups are taking up micro credit programmes and other income generating activities. They must build up their capacities, acquire skills through training and education.

(e) *Role of the State in Poverty Alleviation and Rural Development*

Development does not take place in a vacuum. It occurs in a system-be it capitalist, socialist or mixed. In the 1950s, the dominant thinking was that the State could do nothing wrong. The Pendulum has swung too far. By the mid-1990s, the thinking is that State could do nothing right. However, with the Asian crisis of 1997, a new consensus, reflecting a better appreciation of the limitations of market forces, is emerging (UNCTAD, 1998). The current wave is in favour of liberalisation, privatisation and globalisation. There is a greater reliance on the market mechanism. The argument is simple: 'Markets fail, but so do governments' (World Bank, 1991:131). But as rightly argued by Dreze and Sen (1995) it is futile to espouse a general 'pro-state' or 'pro-market' stand. In fact what a government can and will do depends on the nature and (class) character of those that constitute government. As the East Asian experience showed that it is not the mere state intervention but the quality, nature and form of intervention that matters (World Bank, 1993).

It is instructive to compare the South Asia's progress with the East Asia's in the field of education and heath, as given in Table-3. The South Asia's adult literacy rate of 48 per cent in 1993 is way below the East Asia's 98 per cent. In education and health, the per capita per annum investment in Malaysia is $150 and in the Republic of Korea it is $160, compared to $5 in Bangladesh, $10 in Pakistan, and $14 in India (HDC, 1997). It is this human capital that enables the East Asian countries to compete effectively in the global economy, while South Asia languishes like a sick person.

The lesson for South Asian countries is that they must increase investment in education (of what type, is very important) and health, which would enable people to participate in growth process and derive benefits from a dynamic and growing economy mainly through gainful employment. Because investment in human capital will lead to the creation and distribution of new wealth (World Bank 1995). Lack of human capital will be a major obstacle, especially for South Asia since several countries have embraced the regime of liberalisation. Its poor literacy rate of around 50 per cent coupled with ill-trained and unskilled labour force will be a major handicap in the global economy where market forces determine rewards based on competition. The South Asia and the Sub-Saharan countries are not able to harvest the benefits of the so-called forces of the 'liberalisation, privatisation and globalisation' due to illiteracy, poverty and structural rigidities (UNCTAD, 1998).

The international concern continued to echo for social development-be it in the World Conference on Education for All (1990), the World Summit for Children (1990), or the World Summit for Social Development (1995). Of particular interest is the idea of '20:20 compact' endorsed by the World Summit for Social Development. According to this proposal, governments should allocate 20% of their

Table–3. South Asia compared with East Asia on education and health

	1960		1993	
Items	*South Asia*	*East Asia (excl China)*	*South Asia*	*East Asia (excl China)*
Adult literacy (%)	32 (1970)	88 (1970)	48	98
Public expenditure on health (as% of GDP)	0.5	0.2	1.4 (1990)	2.3 (1990)
Public expenditure on education (as % of GNP)	2.0	3.7 (1980)	3.4 (1992)	4.3 (1992)
Military spending (as % of combined expenditure on education and health)	113	273	72 (90-91)	49 (90-91)

Source: HDC (1997)

budgets and donors should allocate 20% of their aid budgets to basic social services[19]. The UN Target of 0.7 per cent of donors GNP as official development assistance (ODA) is far from being met. It stands at 0.22 per cent in 1997 down from 0.35 per cent in 1985 reflecting the diminishing generosity of the rich.[20] In 1996, donors reported that 2.4% of their ODA was spent on basic health and 1.4% on basic education. Governments of developing countries, especially the South Asian countries, must invest more and improve the quality of programme delivery in education, health, shelter, poverty alleviation, and environment protection.

To quote Human Development Report, (1997:101) "A poverty eradication strategy requires not a retreating, weak state but an active, strong one, and that strength should be used to enable the poor rather than disable them".

The State should play an enabling role involving civil society organisations (CSOs) as institutions to correct the market failures and/or state failures. They can play crucial role (as alternative to privatisation) in demanding and demonstrating pro-poor policies. Their initiatives are justified in terms of the increased participation and empowerment of poor people. With the people's participation, a system of social surveillance can be put in place. This calls for a tripartite alliance-of government, non-governmental organisations and the community.

(f) **Tripartite alliance-Go, NGO and the Community:** The synergy between government and civil society organisations must be tapped for the benefit of poorer sections. Governments have men and material but lack participatory approaches. The NGOs and self-help groups, on the other hand, are known for flexibility to reach the poorest and empower the marginal group,

challenging the gender-stereotypes, advocating and implementing participatory development. Many of them are in micro credit, income generation activities, education, health and women's development. There are other NGOs, which are known for advocacy, and mobilising poor people to exert pressure on the government to act in time on issues of importance. Many NGOs work through people's organisations and self-help groups. In fact these have become alternative power centres to the feudal and entrenched powers in those villages where they exist. The lobbying and advocacy of NGOs have prompted many agents including government to reassess their policies and introduce necessary amendments (HDC, 1997). A covergence between these two can produce significant results. This collaboration is more urgent than ever before in view of the structural adjustment policies that are in place in most of the Asian countries.

Section-III: Selected Innovative Projects in Asia and the Pacific Region

1. **Micro Credit: The Grameen Bank of Bangladesh:** The brainchild of Prof. Muhammand Yunus, it was started as Action Research Project in 1976 in a small village called Jobra (Yunus, 1997). Then it became a Pilot Project and in 1983 became a full-fledged bank. It aimed to provide micro credit to the poorest of the poor and move them towards capital accumulation and asset creation (Grameen Bank, 1996).

Process: Its innovation lies in organising people into homogenous groups of five members. It offers loans without collateral but takes the group guarantee and use the peer group pressure to ensure its proper use and repayment. The group members hold weekly meetings, maintain close supervision and apply peer group pressure in case of non-repayment, if necessary. Besides credit, it encourages people to go in for better housing, education, environmental sanitation, health and nutrition as part of its commitment for overall social development.

Impact

- ❑ By 1996, it has 1050 branches spread over 35,780 villages with coverage of 2 million loanees of which 94% are women.
- ❑ Bank borrowers, the rural poor of Bangladesh, have become the owners of the Grameen Bank.
- ❑ Their accumulated savings exceed $125 million with a cumulative lending of about $2.1 billion. The repayment rate is 95-98%.
- ❑ Grameen Bank model is being replicated in forty developing countries.

Lessons

- ◆ The poor are credit worthy and are bankable.
- ◆ Emphasis on social development including better education improved nutrition, health and better housing for human development;
- ◆ Changed the pattern of ownership of means of production through micro credit.
- ◆ Micro credit programme is sustainable.

Social Development Projects: In addition to micro credit, there are some NGOs working in education, health and socio-political awareness building and empowering the marginal groups through a holistic strategy. The BRAC of Bangladesh and AKRSP of Pakistan are notable in this regard.

2. **Bangladesh Rural Advancement Committee (BRAC):** Established in 1972, it was engaged in rehabilitating

thousands of refugees returning from India. Later on, it moved on to community development. With its rich experience in poverty alleviation and rural development, from 1976 onwards it focuses on the bottom 40% of the population, with a special attention to the needs of poor women, landless, and other vulnerable communities. Its delivery package includes micro credit, non-formal education, health, rural marketing, and training. It has achieved big success in education and health sectors (BRAC, 1997).

Process: Each village has two village organisations (VOs)-one for women and one for men. Each VO consists of 50 members divided into groups of five. Each member participates in weekly meetings and undergoes a 40-lesson non-formal education. This capsule course is run to increase the awareness and conscientisation, which form a critical part in social mobilisation of the poor. Human development and income generation are complementary in BRAC framework.

Impact

- BRAC runs 34,334 non-formal schools where 72% of the students are girls and 95% of the teachers are women.
- It covers 2.3 million members (96% female) in 66,000 villages with 20,433 full time employees and 31,009 part-time staff.
- By directing education, jobs and credit at women, the NGOs such as BRAC, Grameen, Proshika and ASA etc. have created a social revolution in a conservative Muslim society (The Economist, 1998).
- Its rural health programmes, particularly its network for distribution of ORT, is so effective that the entire rural society looks to it for assistance.

Lessons

- ◆ Holistic approach towards poverty alleviation and rural development.
- ◆ Empowerment of rural poor is an integral part of poverty alleviation.

3. **Aga Khan Rural Support Project (AKRSP) of Pakistan:** Initiated by the Aga Khan Foundation, this was started in Gilgit in 1982 to improve the poor socio-economic conditions of about one million people in northern areas of Pakistan. AKRSP follows a 'package' approach. It provides basic education, health services, imparts technical training and skills, provides micro credit and undertakes infrastructure projects (World Bank, 1996).

Process: Forms a multi-purpose Village Organisation and villagers are empowered to select the projects. They contribute their labour and manage the project themselves. At each stage of the project cycle the people are involved. Participation has been the key for its success.

Impact

- ❑ About 1964 Village Organisations formed.
- ❑ Total savings of the VOs are Rs. 220 million
- ❑ Loans disbursed amounts to Rs. 518 million.

Lessons

- ◆ Comprehensive package to alleviate poverty and people's participation.
- ◆ Empower local communities to enable them to overcome difficulties.

4. **Sustainable Development through Integrated Watershed Development:** Anna Hazare has transformed the drought-prone and poverty-striken village of Ralegaon Siddhi through soil and water conservation

works and ecological regeneration. This has been well documented in the history of integrated watershed development management. Inspired by the work of Anna Hazare, the Chief Minister of Madhya Pradesh has taken up a statewide scheme called Rajiv Gandhi Watershed Development Mission. Anil Agarwal (1998) has documented on the outstanding work of watershed development in the district of Jhabua in Madhya Pradesh.

Process: There are institutional arrangements at three levels. An empowered committee headed by the Chief Secretary ensures interdepartmental co-ordination. At the District level, the district collector is the mission leader. The Chief Executive Officer (CEO) of the Zilla Panchayat is responsible for the project and reports to the District Collector. There are two other multi-disciplinary committees at the district level. At the village level, there is a watershed committee. The work begins with the participatory rural appraisal, in which the community decides details of planning including the structures to be built. The technical committee assists the watershed committee and the funds directly flow to the watershed committee. In order to involve the landless persons, the self-help groups and women groups are created.

Impact

- In Jhabua district, some 249 micro watersheds are in operation benefiting 374 villages.
- Some 143 new tanks have been built which has helped the groundwater table to come up by 0.64 metres in 19 watersheds.
- Increased irrigation raised the productivity by 7%. Area under Rabi (dry season crop) increased by 340 hectares in 7 micro watersheds.
- Food availability increased and 313 village level grain banks are established to help needy ones.

Lessons

- There is a need to learn from the tribals of Jhabua, from the poor people from Ralegaon Siddhi and from people like Anna Hazare.

5. **Economic Impact of Peripheral Infrastructure on the Rural Poor:** CIRDAP had evolved a participatory methodology for community participation in Integrated Rural Development through Community Information and Planning System (CIPS). This methodology has been tested in 13 countries and found that success and sustainability of a project hinges on the active participation of people in all phases of a project—planning, beginning from data collection and analysis, plan formulation, implementation, monitoring and evaluation (CIRDAP, 1991). Recently this was modified to incorporate some elements of 'project cycle management' to enable the intended beneficiaries to take control over the project activities. It is named as "CIRDAP Approach to Rural Development" (CIRDAP, 1997). This methodology is applied to a Pilot Project, which is under implementation in India and Lao PDR. The results available from India are given below in Table 4.

As seen from the Table 4, the CIRDAP's contribution is only 37% and 36% in Rukumpally and Chiguralapally respectively. The remaining money has come from other sources such as government, NGOs and the community. It shows the coalition building that was achieved in the pilot villages.

Process

The Pilot Project in India and Lao PDR uses Card methodology. It has three stages and seven steps. The three stages are planning, implementation and evaluation (CIRDAP, 1997b). The salient features of the CARD methodology are listed below:

Table–4. Mobilisation of Funds for Peripheral Infrastructure in Pilot Villages in India

US$

Name of Villages	*CIRDAP*	*PR/Govt.*	*Villagers*	*Others*	*Total*
Rukumpally	10,250	14,265	1,353	3,904	29,772
Chiguralapally	7,485	7,058	3,058	3,610	21,228

Fund Mobilisation for Income Generating Activities in Pilot Villages in India

Name of Villages	*Number of SHGs organised*	*Groups Savings*	*CIRDAP Seed Money*	*DRDA Subsidy*	*SBH Loan*	*Total*
Rukumpally	6(110)	2,200	7,118	3,794	4,095	17,171
Chiguralapally	11(219)	4,177	13,970	11,460	9,059	38,667

Source: Field Reports from ARF, India
Note: Exchange rate US$ = 34 (Indian Rupees)
SHGs: Selp Help Groups, Numbers in parenthesis indicate the total members in the SHGs).

6. Project initiation by participatory planning

(a) Modified Project Cycle Management (PCM) workshop

→ Bottom-up process

(b) Preparation of Project Design Matrix (PDM) and Plan of Operation (PO)

→ Clarity of project.

(c) Participatory Appraisal

→ Villager's consensus and accountability

1. Use of CIPS methodology for projects with IGA

→ Sustainability

2. Project management with PDM and PO

→ Logicality, Consistency

3. Maximum use of local resources such as manpower, wisdom of villagers and local materials

→ Efficiency/Ownership

4. Priority is given to the development of people's self reliance

→ Sustainability

Impact

- Construction and maintenance of peripheral infrastructure with the people's participation.
- All-weather road brought electricity and drilling machines to the village, converted dry land into wet helping the villages to raise two to three crops a year.
- Provided more employment and a sense of food security.

- ❑ Enhanced the capacity building of self-help groups in the project areas.
- ❑ Created more space for the NGO and developed a framework for tripartite alliance—of government, non-governmental organisations and the community.

Lessons

- ◆ Framework of tripartite alliance offers enormous potential for future replication.
- ◆ Integration of delivery of project benefits and dovetailing of resources with other agencies is worth looking at.
- ◆ Participatory approach holds the key for ending poverty and achieving development.

7. **Saemaul Undong of South Korea:** The Korean War left South Korea a battered country. 60% of its cultivable land was left fallow, its limited industrial capacity was destroyed. In 1961, their literacy was 30% and the per capita income was US$ 80 and the manufacturing accounted for less than 10% of GNP (Meier, 1984). But the First and Second Five Year Economic Development Plans (1962-66 and 1967-71) saw South Korea register 10% growth rate per annum and building modern industries with surging exports. In other words, with a set of appropriate government policies and indigenous efforts, South Korea transformed the situation and became a modern industrial economy within a single generation. But the rural-urban gap was widening. It is in this context that the Saemaul Undong was commenced in 1971 as a programme of rural development.

Process: Saemaul Undong means a 'movement to make a new village'. Since it has spread to urban areas, it is described as 'new community movement'. It is based on the spirit of diligence, self-help and co-operation.

- Diligence: It is a campaign for people to work hard diligently. Diligence here means voluntary efforts.
- Self-help: It means 'helping oneself'. Saemaul Undong movement is a drive to cultivate and practice the spirit of self-help.
- Co-operation: Saemaul Undong movement endeavoured to revive several informal co-operative groups in Korean villages. For instance, "hyangyak", a system of co-operation in which community members help each other, "kye" was a mutual saving association; "tonghoe" means community assemblies. Co-operation leads to solidarity. United efforts lead to success. Success will strengthen their co-operative spirit.

In addition to espousing the Saemaul spirit/philosophy, which is designed to improve people's (farmers) work ethics, the movement implemented projects based on village priorities (mostly physical development of rural life), trained village leaders, organised farmers in agricultural co-operatives and set-up village development committee. Thus the Saemaul Undong has taken up various rural development projects in a step-by-step basis. All these projects received strong government support. The movement was considered unique in two fronts: (a) it started not from institutional building but resources supplemented from the government and (b) it was implemented nation-wide with specific focus not on individuals but on the village as a whole.

Impact

- ❑ Rapid rural modernisation of the traditional villages in Korea was achieved through combination of individual action, the co-operative action of the villages and government action.

- Strong leadership and political will of the government contributed significantly to its success.
- Development of local administration and people's participation contributed to the development of democratic decision-making in rural areas.
- The long tradition of mutual co-operation in the village was recognised and used in implementing projects.
- Improvement of people's (farmer's) work ethics by promoting the Saemaul spirit contributed to enhanced human capital.

Lessons

- Inspired by the Saemaul Undong Philosophy, the Chief Minister of Andhra Pradesh, (India) has introduced a programme called "Janmabhoomi". This programme is designed to involve the villagers to participate in the construction of local level infrastructure. It has earmarked some budget for these works.

8. **Employment Generation: Jawahar Rozgar Yojna (JRY) Programme (India):** Launched in 1989 by merging earlier two programmes of National Rural Employment Programme (NREP) and Rural Landless Employment Guarantee Programme (RLEGP). It aims to provide employment opportunities to the rural poor while creating durable community assets in the rural areas.

Process: Works are executed through the Panchayat Raj institutions. Community involvement and participation are essential elements in the programme. The central government and the state governments share the cost of the project in the ratio of 80:20. The central funds to the states are allocated based on the proportion of rural poor in the state. It has two sub components:

Million Wells Scheme (minor irrigation) and Indira Awaz Yojana (housing) for the benefit of Scheduled Castes and Scheduled Tribe and other weaker sections (Government of India, 1996).

Impact

- 750 to 850 million mandays of employment are generated every year.
- One million houses have been constructed for the homeless persons in the rural areas.
- 320,000 irrigation wells have been constructed for the welfare and development of the Scheduled Castes and Scheduled Tribes.

Lessons

- The decision making had been decentralised down to the grassroots level.
- This is in line with the 'power to the people' philosophy. Though there are some problems at operational level, with the involvement of village panchayats and Gram Sabhas more accountability and transparency can be expected.
- Other countries, at least in South Asia, can examine it for replication.

9. **Conclusion:** The growth-first models of the 1950s and 1960s have failed to make any dent on poverty eradication, unemployment and inequalities. The 1970s saw a bigger role for governments in the name of equity, justice and poverty eradication. By the 1980s, it was felt that time has come to control the profligacy of the government and dismantle panoply of controls through structural adjustment policies. But the launching of the Human Development Reports since 1990, the UNDP has been drawing the attention of the world for initiating pro-poor policies for sustainable human development.

From the analysis of major issues in rural development and the selected innovative projects, it may noted that the answer to poverty alleviation does not lie in the unsustainable and declining public (donor) charity; nor does it lie in one time injection of slender assistance. The solution to end human misery and poverty should be found in organising the poor, harnessing the latent talent of the local community and implementation of proactive participatory rural development. Conscientisation should make the poor feel and perceive the suffering they are undergoing. They should dream and realise the possibilities of change. In fact, some of the case studies showed that the poor do not require charity. They need access to resources and equal opportunities and a level playing field. The mechanism of tripartite alliance should result in building human capabilities, in strengthening the institutions of civil society, in empowering poor people, and enabling them to stand on their own feet to shape their lives and destinies. Empowerment of the poor is an essential element in the poverty eradication. Participatory approach and people's participation holds the key for pro-poor policies, rural development and poverty eradication.

REFERENCES

1. Anil Agarwal, (1998): "The house that Digvijay built". Down *to Earth,* Scientific and Environment Fortnightly, Vol. 7, No. 15., December 31, 1998.

2. BRAC, (1997): *Annual Report,* Dhaka, Bangladesh,

3. Chambers, Robert, (1983): *Rural Development: Putting the Last First,* Longman Group UK Ltd, Harlow, England.

4. Chambers, Robert, (Nov. 1989): The State and Rural Development: Ideologies and an Agenda for the 1990s, Discussion Paper 269, IDS Publications, Institute of Development Studies, University of Sussex, Brighton, England.

5. Chenery, Hollis, Montek S. Ahluwalia, C.L.G. Bell, John H. Duloy and Richard Jolly, (1974), *Redistribution with Growth,* Oxford University Press, New York.

6. CIRDAP, (1987): *State of the Art, Integrated Rural Development in Asia-Pacific,* Dhaka, Bangladesh.

7. CIRDAP, (1991): *Community Participation through CIPS Model,* Dhaka, Bangladesh.

8. CIRDAP, (1996): *Report on Rural Development in CIRDAP Member Counties 1994-95,* Dhaka, Bangladesh.

9. CIRDAP, (1997): *CIRDAP Approach to Rural Development,* Dhaka, Bangladesh.

10. CIRDAP, (1998): Public Expenditure and Social Development in Bangladesh, Dhaka, Bangladesh.

11. Clark, Colin. *The Conditions of Economic Progress,* Macmillan, London.

12. Dreze, J. and Sen, A. (1995): *India: Economic Development and Social Opportunity.* Oxford University Press, New Delhi.

13. ESCAP, (1989): *Regional Experts Meeting on Integrated Rural Development in Asia and the Pacific* held in Suweon, Republic of Korea.

14. ESCAP, (1996): *Showing the Way; Methodologies for Successful Rural Poverty Alleviation Projects,* UN, ESCAP, New York.

15. Eurostep, ICVA, Action Aid and Norwegian People's Aid, (1998): *The Reality of Aid, 1998/99,* An Independent Review of Poverty Reduction and Development Assistance, Earthscan Publications Ltd, London.

16. Freiri, Paulo, (1968): *Pedagogy of the Oppressed,* The Seabury Press, New York.

17. Galbraith, J.K. (1979): *The Nature of Mass Poverty,* Penguin Books Ltd, Harmondsworth, England.

18. Government of India, (1997): *Annual Report,* Ministry of Rural Areas and Employment, New Delhi.

19. Government of Republic of Korea, (1983): *Saemaul Undong in Korea,* Ministry of Home Affairs, Seoul, Korea.

20. Grameen Bank, (1996): *Annual Report,* Dhaka, Bangladesh.

21. Haq, Mahbub ul. (1976): *The Poverty Curtain: Choices for the Third World.* Oxford University Press, New Delhi.

22. Haq. Mahbub ul, (1996): *Reflection on Human Development,* Oxford University Press, New York.

23. Harriss, John (1982): *Rural Development: Theories of Peasant Economy and Agrarian Change,* Hutchinson University Library for Africa, London.

24. Human Development Centre, (1997): *Human Development in South Asia 1997,* Oxford University Press, New York.

25. International Labour Organsiation, (1977): *Poverty and Landlessness in Rural Asia,* A WEP study, Geneva.

26. International Labour Organisation, (1987): *The Animator in Participatory Rural Development (Concept and Practice)* by S. Tilakaratna, Geneva.

27. Korten, David C., (1980): "Community Organsiation and Rural Development: a learning process approach", *The Public Administration Review,* Vol. 40, No. 5.

28. Lele, Uma (1975): *The Design of Rural Development: Lessons from Africa,* Johns Hopkins, Baltimore and London.

29. Meier, Gerald, (1984): *Emerging From Poverty—The Economics That Really Matters* Oxford University Press, Inc. New York, Oxford.

30. Moser, C.O.N. (1989): "Community Participation in Urban Projects in the Third World", *Progress in Planning,* Vol. 32 Part 2.

31. Mukhopadhyay, (1989): "Integrated Rural Development Programmes in Selected South Asian Countries", Resource Paper presented in the *Regional Experts Meeting on Integrated Rural Development in Asia and the Pacific* held in Suweon, Republic of Korea.

32. Myrdal, Gunnar. (1968): *Asian Drama: An Inquiry into the Poverty of Nations,* Vol. I, Kalyani Press, 1985 Edition, New Delhi.

33. Nietes, Pulcra M. (1991): "Integrated Rural Development: The Philippines Experience" in Integrated Rural Development in Asia, edited by H. Ramachandran and J.P. De Campos Guimaraes, Concept Publishing Company, New Delhi.

34. Oakley and Marsden, (1984): Approaches to Participation in Rural Development, International Labour office, Geneva.

35. Oxfam (1995): *The Oxfam Poverty Report,* by Kevin Watkins, An Oxfam Publication, U. K.

36. Ruttan, Vernow. W. (1984): "Integrated Rural Development Programme: A Historical Perspective" *World Development* V. 12, No. 4, p. 393-402.

37. SAARC, (1992) *Meeting the Challenge, Report of the Independent South Asian Commission on Poverty Alleviation,* Kathmandu.

38. Streeten, Paul P. (1979): "Basic needs: premises and promises", *Journal of Policy Modelling.*

39. Streeten, Paul P. and S.J. Burki, "Basic Needs: Some Issues", *World Development,* Vol. 6 March 1978), pp. 136-146.

40. *The Economist,* (1998): "The other government of Bangladesh". The Economist July 25th 1998.

41. UNDP, (1993): *Human Development Report,* Oxford University Press, New York.

42. UNDP, (1997): *Human Devolvement Report,* Oxford University Press, New York.

43. UNDP, (1998): *Human Development Report,* Oxford University Press, New York.

44. United Nations Conference of Trade and Development (UNCTAD), (1998): *The Least Developed Countries Report, 1998,* United Nations, New York and Geneva.

45. Webster, R. (1975): *Integrated Communication* East-West Communication Institute, East West Centre, University of Hawaii, Honolulu.

46. World Bank, (1980): *Meeting Basic Needs: An Overview,* Washington.

47. World Bank, (1990): *World Development Report,* Oxford University Press, New York.

48. World Bank, (1991): *World Development Report,* Oxford University Press, New York.

49. World Bank, (1993): *The Asian Miracle,* Oxford University Press, New York.

50. World Bank, (1995a): *World Development Report,* Oxford University Press, New York.

51. World Bank, (1995b), *Priorities and Strategies for Education,*—A World Bank Review, The World Bank, Washington D.C.

52. World Bank, (1996): *The Aga Khan Rural Support Programme,* A Third Evaluation, A World Bank Operations Evaluation Study, Washington, USA.

53. World Bank, (1998): *World Development Report,* Oxford University Press, New York.

54. World Bank, (1997): *Rural Development—From Vision to Action,* Environmentally and socially Sustainable Development Studies and Monographs Series 12, Washington, D.C., USA.

55. Yunus, Mohammad, (1997): "Towards Creating a Poverty-Free World", *D.T. Lakdawala Memorial Lecture,* delivered at the Institute of Social Sciences, New Delhi, India on August 8, 1997.

3

Sustainable Development:

The Gandhian Approach

K. Venkata Reddy

1. Introduction

In the course of multifarious ventures towards development, there has been over exploitation of Earth, without serious effort at recouping the loss to natural endowment. As such the greatest single challenge that India faces now is whether the country can continue to step up productivity and meet the needs of the fast changing society without damaging the carrying capacity of the basic inputs like land, water, etc., keeping in view of interests of future generations. It is in this context the concept of sustainable development assumes critical importance. The concept is viewed from different angles in a dynamic framework such as economic viability, environmental soundness and social equity. With the publication of THE REPORT OF THE WORLD COMMISSION ENIVRONMENT AND DEVELOPMENT (The Bruntland Commission, 1987) the need for sustainable development gained global importance. Calling for development that "meets the needs of the present, without compromising the ability of the future generations to meet their needs", the Brutland Commission Report highlights the need to simultaneously address development and environmental imperatives. FAO (1987) has formulated a more comprehensive definition: "sustainable development is the management and conservation of the material resource base and the orientation of technological and institutional change in such a manner as to ensure the attainment and continued satisfaction of human needs for present and future generations. Such sustainable development (in agriculture, forestry and fisheries sector) which conserves land, water, plant and animal genetic resources, is environmentally non-degrading, technically appropriate, economically viable and socially acceptable". From the definition it is evident that sustainable development aims at marshalling resources in such a way as to meet the requirements of the present as well as that of the future generations with due care of environment, technical soundness, economic viability and social equity. The implication is that we can conceive of strategies for managing resources which enhance the capacity of the present and future generations to meet their needs. Evidently sustainable development is a holistic concept and it calls for different measures on several fronts for achieving its objectives.

In the course of development, forest resources are more exploited, trees all around are fell, grazing lands and irrigation tanks are encroached upon, land is damaged and water and air are polluted with greenhouse gases and global warming. The loss to the natural endowment is not recouped and hence the eco-system is damaged and the carrying capacity of the supporting elements like land, water, etc is adversely affected. In the process, we suffer and make the life of our descendents miserable. Mollison (1991) in the work Permaculture rightly pointed out "There is too much of contemporary evidence of ecological disaster. Our life style has led us to the very brink of annihilation. We have expanded our right to live on the earth to an entitlement to conquer the earth, yet conquerors of nature always lose. To accumulate wealth, power or land beyond one's need in a limited world is to be truly immoral, be it as an individual, an institution or a nation-state...Like war, growth at any cost is an outmoded and discredited concept". That the earth is over exploited resulting in ecological disequilibrium is evident from calamities like earthquakes, droughts, floods, etc. which we experience. The need of the hour is a development strategy guided by the principles of ecology, economics, social and gender equity and ethics. Gandhiji long back warned that accumulation of wealth beyond one's need, exploiting, unmindful of the need of the poor and care of earth is unethical. His views on different aspects of development are still relevant in a large measure.

2. Agricultural Growth Trends and Gaps

The agricultural growth trends during the planning era clearly present the manner in which land resources are adversely affected. In the first phase of the land development upto 1960, the agricultural growth was achieved through the expansion of area under cultivation by way of bringing the fallow lands under the plough and through deforestation (C.H. Rao 1994). During the green revolution period commencing from 1965-66, water and fertilizer became crucial land-saving inputs. These resulted in depletion of ground water, excessive use of chemical fertilizers and pesticides leading to degradation of the soil and consequent adverse effects. Green revolution also adversely affected the land tenure system, causing eviction of tenant cultivators from the land by the landowners. In the absence of effective enforcement of land reform measures, and non-farm occupations, landless poor suffered a lot (G.P 1973). During the post green revolution period, rich-poor divide is found to be widening leading to extensive co-existence of un-sustainable living standards on one hand and unacceptable poverty on the other. The rural women and assetless poor are found to be much exploited segments in the rural areas. In 1972 at the UN conference on HUMAN DEVELOPMENT at Stockholm, Indira Gandhi, the then prime minister of India opined "development will not be socially sustainable unless considerations of economic and gender equity were integrated with those of ecology".

Agriculture continues to be a major source of employment and income to vast majority of about 65 per cent of total population in India, thereby making a case for sustainable agricultural development but the share of agriculture in the GDP and public investment on agriculture dwindled. The share of the agriculture in GDP declined from 50 per cent in 1950-51 to 27 per cent in 2000-2001, with almost same proportion of population depending on agriculture. In the First Five Year Plan agriculture claimed 32 per cent of the total outlay and this percentage declined to 11 per cent in 9th plan (1997-2002).

In very recent years even under the assured irrigation yield levels are stagnated. This situation is attributed to poor drainage, soil degradation and indiscriminate use of chemical fertilisers and pesticides. M.S. Swaminathan (1999) warns that excessive use of chemical fertilisers and pesticides would increase the incidence of dreadful diseases like cancer through toxic residues present in the grains and other edible parts.

3. Neglect of Rainfall Harvesting, At What Cost?

We in India, have a great tradition of preserving and managing well the rain water. Tanks impounding the rain water were constructed by various rulers in the past. In southern region of India minor irrigation tanks were mostly constructed during the Vijayanagara Rule on an average, six irrigation tanks for each revenue village. In recent years, pathetically enough most of these were converted into cropped area, housing colonies or bus depots. In the past "Neerukattu" arrangement as a part of "Jajman" system worked well in regulating water to the fields. Since most of the irrigation tanks/perculation tanks/ponds now remain defunct, rain water is not fully conserved with all the adverse effects on the ground and surface water and soil moisture.

In recent years, the thinking of the individuals and communities seems to be that water harvesting and management is the responsibility of the State. Further, the simple technology of storing water in the irrigation tanks has been neglected and now focus is on exploitation of rivers and groundwater through dams and tubewells. Dependency on the State for irrigation also meant higher cost of water supply. But cost recovery being poor, "the financial sustainability of water schemes has run aground" (Anil Agarwal). Excessive exploitation of groundwater through tubewells, deepening of the existing openwells with corresponding steps to recharge, results in fall in the groundwater with all the adverse effects.

Failure of harvesting rainfall on a wider scale has it's own adverse effects on vegetation, forest cover, bio-diversity and ecological balance. Further, increasing population and decreasing man-land ratio results in the over exploitation of the earth in terms of intensity of cropping and soil exhaustion, excessive dose of chemical fertilisers and encroachment of irrigation tanks

4. Poverty as Enemy of Environment

In recent years there has been a large scale deforestation. Poverty has become the worst enemy of the environment. Though the proportion of the population living below poverty line is estimated to be declining, the number of absolute poor increased from 290 million to 350 million during 1990-2001(9th Five Year Plan Reports). In many areas to eat and survive, the poor cut down trees and hunt almost everyday in the forests causing destruction to the forest wealth. Metallic ores and coal which are non-renewable are being mined or drilled and they leave the earth depleted. Surface mining without subsequent restoration leaves the land degraded. Destruction of forests causes not only extinction of flora but fauna too. Deforestation has very serious adverse effects on the sustainable development. FAO (1989) report rightly points out "in absence of effective national and international support and alternative employment opportunities, the rural poor are forced for mining of soil nutrients, the cultivation of steep slopes, the overgrazing of rangeland and the excessive collection of fuel materials in order to feed and warm themselves. It is they, therefore who govern the success or failure of policies to achieve sustainable production systems".

It simply means over exploitation of the earth results in the damage to forest wealth and ecological balance. For ecological security, nearly one third of the geographical area must be under the forest cover. But today in India the forest cover as per the State of Forest Report 1997, is only 19.27 per cent of the geographical area. In places where the forest cover is low the rainfall is low.

There is a vicious circle of drought, deforestation, ecological imbalance and failure of rainfall as each of these four elements is both the cause and consequence of the other. Of these four interlinked elements, rainfall is crucial facilitating vegetation and forest cover and ecological equilibrium needed for sustainable development. Drought works against sustainable development. Effective drought management demands drought proofing of the affected areas through harvesting rainwater on a wider scale with adequate number of mini water storing structures. Management of the livestock becomes an important component of the sustainable agricultural development. There is an urgent need for relating livestock population to the bearing capacity of available land and water. This calls for improving the quality of livestock.

As per the study of Anil Agarwal, India receives most of its rainfall in just 100 hours out of 8,760 hours in a year. If the rainfall in 100 hours duration is not captured there will be no water for the rest of year with all the adverse effects.

5. Population And Sustainable Development

Sustainable development is very much associated with the size of population. Now two issues crop up (1) the capacity of a given set of resources to support given population and (2) the capacity of the given population to sustain itself on the given resources (V.G 1992). In the development process land and water are two basic inputs. With a demographic pressure, the per capita arable land is getting reduced and it is now below one acre. Again, the availability of water per capita has come down from 5235 cubic meters at the time of independence to about 2227 cubic meters in 1992.The population of the country increased from 360 million in 1951 to 1000 million in 2001 or increased by two and a half times in a period of five decades. Food production requirement for the population in 2001 was estimated at 240 million tonnes as against the present production of about 200 million tonnes.

The sustainability of land calls for expansion of irrigation. Eco-friendly minor irrigation covers some 65 per cent of total irrigated area, but this sector is not receiving adequate attention. The Ninth Five Year Plan admits that "the upkeep of the tanks has not been attended to properly" In the absence of the effective administrative machinery at the village level, there has been encroachment of irrigation tanks. Sustainability of land and water calls for rational mix of chemical fertilisers and bio-fertilisers. The sustainability of the population on natural resources is also dependent on consumption habits. Wasteful consumption of water must be curbed. The consumption habits must be within the reach of one's resources.

6. Gandhiji's Concern for Sustainable Development

Mahatma Gandhi had a concern for ecological balance. "Sarvodaya" idealogy highlights welfare for all- not only all humans but also the entire creation. The latest science of ecology and bio-diversity has also come closer to the philosophical approach of the Gandhiji, highlighting that everything in the universe is so interdependent that if a part or section is destroyed, it will affect the whole system. This also gives a strong philosophical as well as scientific basis to the ideology of non-violence .If you harm others you are harming in the process yourself (Nirmala Deshpande 1994). Gandhiji desired extensive plantation of shade-giving and fruit-bearing trees all around the village. His advice to the rural people was to preserve land for grazing purpose and protect the forest cover as a community responsibility. He wanted the people to live in harmony with nature and cautioned the impending danger if forests are destroyed. He stressed on community-based eco-friendly minor irrigation schemes. Also, he emphasized eco-friendly small industrial units and cattle based economy in terms of dairying, bio-fertilisers, etc. Gandhiji's stress on "production by masses and not mass production" is compatible with laws of ecology as rightly pointed out by Schumchar in "Small is beautiful". To ensure better social environment he insisted on revival of traditional cultural activities and regular interaction among rural people at community centers built by the rural people collectively. He desired that each village to be evolved as a self-sufficient unit and through self-help the villagers should collectively strive for all round development. To strengthen the economy at grass root level with village as focal point, he pleaded for decentralization of administrative machinery and planning process.

Unfortunately the trend now is towards centralisation and neglect of villages. Malcom Adiseshaiah 1994 very rightly pointed out "The anti Gandhian aspect that characterises our life today is that in every aspect of it – political, economic and social – the trends are towards centralization and central direction even in areas which are clearly ear-marked in the constitution for action by the lower levels like the State and Panchayats". Towards the goal of sustainable development, in a country of India's size with varying Physo-geographical features and climatic conditions, regional variations in development, village panchayats have a crucial role to play. Hence there is a strong case for development of villages as an element of sustainable development with adequate resources and clear-cut functions.

7. The Need of The Hour

The need of the hour is sustainable agricultural development and this calls for measures on several fronts. There is a need for adopting a code of environmental ethics with a sense of personal responsibility for earth care. Mollison speaks about the Law of Return which underlines "whatever we take from nature we must return as nature demands a return for every gift received". He warns that nature has extreme penalties for those who break such law and for their descendants. He wanted that natural resources be used only in a situation of pressing necessity and wastage should be avoided in the use of natural resources. He wanted that the renewable resources be used at a rate less than their rate of regeneration. The rate of use of exhaustible resources should depend on the rate at which they can be substituted or recouped but the substitutability has its own limitations and hence a code of environmental ethics to be honored by individuals, institutions and Government. Under the policy of liberalisation and globalisation there must be effective check on the investment pattern of the Multi-Nationals in India so as to ensure sustainability of life-supporting resources, sustainability of small producers and sustainability of landless poor. Also, care must be taken that the policy of corporatisation of the agriculture will not (1) deprive the entrepreneurial opportunities to the individual farmers, (2) curtail employment opportunities on the farm front; (3) reduce the small and marginal farmers to the ranks of agricultural labourers; (4) Increase market dependency for food articles leading to reduction in food security and (5) render the policy of land reforms ineffective .In short, in the corporatisation arrangement, the equity issues should not become secondary (K.V. Reddy 2001)

8. Priority to Minor Irrigation

Water being a basic input for sustainable development, priority must be given to the community based rainwater harvesting and utilization. Eco-friendly minor irrigation schemes, as stressed by Gandhi must receive priority. All the residents of all villages in the country must be well organised in harvesting every drop of rain water, particularly the run off rainwater through mini structures. Harvesting of rainwater must become a people's movement. Government-oriented schemes of water preservation should be supplemented by community-oriented and decentralized programme. Voluntary organizations have a crucial role to play in organizing the rural people in the task of rainwater harvesting.

There must be proper cooperation between Gram Panchayats and voluntary organizations in the task of organising the villagers in harvesting the rainwater by the way of checkdams, perculation tanks or ponds. Water harvesting may be linked with some incentives to village Panchayats by way of assistance to common amenities like community hall, primary health centre, etc. Whereever needed, for every 50 to 100 acres, one rain water preserving structure may be designed. By effective harvesting of rainwater as social movement we will be able to store the moisture in the soils, preserve the water in tanks, feed the nearby wells and help recharge of groundwater. Besides new structures to preserve the rain water steps must be taken to restore the existing irrigation tanks/ponds by evicting encroachers and desilting the tanks. This is possible only when all the villagers are united for restoring "social capital", in which the interests of all are involved. The Ninth Plan did make mention of the strategy of sustainable development composed of nine elements. Surprisingly the element of droughtproofing of rainfed areas is conspicuous by its absence in the policy elements listed by planning commission.

9. Case for Mini Watershed Programmes

Mini watershed development programmes may be popularised aiming at rainwater harvesting along with the schemes of contour bunding and checkdams, social forestry. Dryland farming, horticulture, mixed cropping and inter-cropping. To economise the water use the drip irrigation and sprinkler irrigation systems may be popularised with necessary technical guidance and institutional support. As a water saving measure, farmers must be encouraged to take up cultivation of millets, pulses and groundnut rather than rice and sugarcane which need more water.

C.H. Hanumantha Rao opines that the country has the potential for achieving the higher agricultural growth of

4 to 5 per cent in a sustainable manner without causing pressure on its natural resources. In this context, it is stated that out of the total potential from the major and minor irrigation projects, about half the area remains to be exploited. Further nearly 25 million hectares can be added under minor irrigation sources including groundwater sources. As per the ICAR study reported in the Ninth Five Year Plan "about 25 to 50 per cent of irrigation presently in use can be saved through improved management practices without reducing yields and such savings in water would infact rise the yields substantially in respect of several crops". This calls for massive public as well as private investment in different irrigation schemes.

Towards the goal of sustainable development effective steps are needed in terms of stepping up of public and private investment in infrastructure covering irrigation, rural electrification, rural roads, agro-processing and warehousing. It is encouraging to note that in the union budget for 2002-2003 there are proposals (1) to increase the allocation for "The accelerated irrigation benefit programme" from Rs.2000 crores to 2800 crores, (2) to enhance the allocation for agricultural research from Rs 684 crores to Rs.775 crores and (3) a further allocation of Rs.2500 crores for 2002-2003 over and above Rs.5000 crores provided so far for the Pradhan Mantri Sadak Yojana.

10. Focus Attention on Dry Farming Technology and Extension Services

Dry farming technology must be strengthened as an integral part of sustainable agricultural development, focusing attention on evolving drought resistance strains and cultivation of such crops with less of water consumption. The problem of pesticide-resistance pests calls for a rational mix of chemical fertilisers and bio fertilisers. Now, the integrated pest management techniques must be popularised. Some of the recent studies reveal that with the progress of yield increasing technology pressure on marginal lands can be reduced. Extension services must address the problems of prudent use of fertilisers and pesticides which would go a long way in improving the crop yields and sustaining soil fertility as well. Also further research on the sustainability of agro-pastoralism i.e., the combination of livestock and crop reduction is very much needed.

Crop and cattle scheme should receive adequate attention. Every agricultural household must be encouraged to plan for supplementing income through dairying, poultry, etc. so as to ensure sustainability .Educated youth may be encouraged with necessary incentives to set up eco-friendly small scale industrial units based on local raw material, facilitating sustainable development

The self help groups (SHGs) such as Vanasamraksna Samithis and water users associations should be well structed representing a cross section, free from political polarization and they have to function under the supervision of village Pnachayats. The programmme of the Joint Forest Management can be strengthened by giving usufructuary rights over fuel wood species grown on fallow lands. Also, eucalyptus-based farm forestry in the relatively well endowed agricultural plains, degraded private and public lands involving landless poor would go a long way in easing the fuel wood crisis without causing de-forestation and environmental degradation.

Decentralised planning taking block or samiti as a unit for formulation of a plan with the active participation of the local people is the right approach towards sustainable development. The recent strategy of central assistance for rural development schemes through Village Panchayats is a right step towards participatory approach, highlighting the principle of self-help and development from below.

11. Tackle the Problem of Poverty

The most burning problem of poverty must be effectively addressed in terms of regular well paid employment to the poor and institutional support for them in asset building ensuring regular income and purchasing capacity. It is to be noted that strategies to achieve sustainable crop, livestock, forestry, fishery production systems will succeed only when they are complemented by policies to slow down population growth and enhance the alternative employment opportunities. Policy measures, therefore, should focus attention on crucial issues such as organizing people at the village level for community action in preserving natural resources in terms of rainwater conservation, protection of forest wealth, social forestry, use of bio-fertilisers, awareness building in preservation of natural resources, rural infrastructure, rural marketing and setting limits to population and consumption. In keeping with the Gandhian ideology, designing a decentralised plan of action making village a focal point of development, addressing simultaneously growth of agriculture and micro-enterprises, livelihood security and community based programmes for preservation of natural resources and adopting a code of environmental ethics is the right approach to attain sustainable development.

REFERENCES

1. FAO,1987. The State of Food and Agriculture, Rome, P.67
2. Molision, 1991. Permaculture, the Deccan Development Society and Permaculture, India, P.1
3. Nirmala DeshPande, 1994. All India Gandhian Constructive Workers Conference Publication, September.

4. C.H. Hanumantha Rao, 1994. Agricultural growth, rural poverty and environmental degradation in India, Oxford University Press, New Delhi,.

5. C.H. Hanumantha Rao, 2000. Inaugural Presentation at National seminar on Sustainable Development, Issues, Policies and Strategies, Department of Economics, S.V.University, Tirupati on March 31st and April 1st

6. G. Parhtasarthi, 1973. Changes in Rice Farming and their Social and Economic Impact:Study of a Delta Village, Andhra Pradesh, Department of Cooperation and Applied Economics, Andhra University pp. 33-52.

7. Indira Gandhi, 1972. UN Conference on Human Development, Stockholm.

8. M.S. Swaminathan, 1999. A Century of hope, East-West books Pvt. Ltd Madras.

9. Anil Agarwal Drought? Try capturing the rain, Centre for Science and Environment, Institutional Area, New Delhi p. 2. Government of India Planning Commission Ninth Five Year Plan 1997-2002 Vol. I and Vol. II.

10. Vasant Gowrikee, 1992 (Ed) Science, population and development, Unmesh Communications pp. 401-467.

11. FAO 1989, The State of Food and Agriculture, Rome P.85

12. Dr. Malcom. S. Adisheshiah 1994. "Some imperatives on Democratic decentralization in All India Gandhian Constructive Workers Conference 2-3 september.

13. M.K. Gandhi, 1927. An Autobiography, The stories My Experiments With Truth, Navajeevan Publishing House, Ahmedabad.

14. K. Venkat Reddy, 2001. Agriculture and Rural Development (a Gandhian Perspective),Himalaya Publishing House, Bombay p. 309.

4

Taluka Model for India's Sustainable Development*

Anil K. Rajvanshi

1. Energy intensity in the Western Model

The energy situation in most developing countries is quite alarming. Energy is the basis of all activities. From it flow activities in agricultural, economic and social areas. Without adequate energy, the development of these countries is jeopardized resulting in economic stagnation and hence in tremendous internal upheavals. Consider the following facts:

1. In 1995-96, India imported about Rs. 40,000 crore worth of petroleum products. The petroleum import bill was 25% of the total export earnings. The demand for petroleum products is increasing at the rate of 7-8% per annum and with increased economic growth the rate will increase further (Sarma EAS 1997). It is estimated that in 2001-

* Originally published in Current Science, Bangalore. March 2002.

2002 India will be importing petroleum products worth Rs. 70,000 crore (Anupama Airy 2000).

2. In 1996, the electricity shortfall in India was estimated to be 15,000 MW and the Government of India does not have money to install this additional capacity. Even if this capacity is somehow added, there are estimates that half of the population in rural areas will not have access to electricity. India requires about 140,000 MW of additional capacity by the year 2010, with an estimated outlay of about Rs.5,50,000 crore. Because of tremendous shortage of electricity, industrial growth and general life in the country is seriously affected (GOI 1995). Moreover with any problems in the national grid, rural areas are affected the most, since the state electricity boards provide urban areas with electricity on priority basis.

3. In the ghettos of Delhi and Surat (the twelfth largest and the fastest growing city in India with a population of about 2 million) about 500 people died of dengue fever in 1996 and of plague in 1994, respectively. This was a direct consequence of extremely unhygienic, filthy and overcrowded conditions prevalent in the two cities. The ghettos are composed of migrant labourers from rural areas. The plague epidemic had a very negative effect on foreign investment in India (Shah. G. 1994)

4. In Mumbai, in 1992, about 400 people died and property worth crores of rupees was looted and destroyed as an aftermath of destruction of the Babri mosque located 2000 km away in a remote town of Uttar Pradesh. The carnage had little to do with the destruction of an ancient religious

structure, but was due to a release of pent-up emotions of a population which is mostly made up of migrants from rural areas and who live in overcrowded and increasingly difficult conditions. The events in Mumbai (the commercial capital of India) had a very negative effect on international and local investment (Engineer A.A. 1993). The effects are felt even today.

5. Between 1950 and 1995, the Government of India spent Rs.50,000 crore on surface irrigation projects, including storage facilities. Till today only 50% of these irrigation facilities, built at such an enormous cost, are being properly utilized. Hence most of the country as usual goes through the cycle of floods and droughts. Besides, the increased use of inorganic fertilizers and pesticides to sustain Green Revolution is reducing the fertility of land, thereby compounding the land-water management problem (Vohra B.B 1996).

6. Developing countries are spending between 2 and 8% of their GNP on medical costs related to declining environment. Thus in India, the number of premature deaths in cities due to environmental pollution is 52,000/year and the number of hospitalizations (due to asthma and other lung-related diseases) was 25 million last year. These casualties cost India about Rs. 4600 crore/year, which is equivalent to the cost of adding 1150 MW electricity to the grid every year (Kumar Preti 1997).

We feel that these events are a direct consequence of a lopsided development model that developing countries like India have been following and which is leading to an undercurrent of economic discontent. The model is based on a 50-100-year-old model of the Western countries, which includes centralized energy production, development of megacities at the expense of rural areas and the unsustainable husbanding of land. This development model has led to high levels of unemployment and poor quality of life in rural India and large-scale exodus of the population to big cities. This exodus is the result of lack of sustainable agriculture in rural areas.

Agriculture is mostly dependent on energy. Lack of energy is therefore the single-most important reason for decline of agriculture-based activity and hence the economic activity in rural areas. A sustainable food and energy strategy for rural areas will therefore create new economic activity and can stem the desperate exodus to cities. With an ever-increasing unmet demand for goods and services, because of economic reasons, a great chasm is developing between haves and have-nots, which is resulting in conflict and a general unrest in the country. The present slowdown in the Indian economy is also creating large-scale unemployment and could further create frightening scenarios of social instability, if timely correction is not made.

It can also be argued that the above situation and events have come about because of mismanagement by and corruption in the Indian Government. But it is our belief that the centralized big-government model in developing countries inherently leads to corruption and mismanagement.

The increase in demand for goods has also led to a sharp increase in energy usage, both in urban and rural areas. With increased penetration of electronic media, the citizens of developing countries aspire for quality of life available in developed countries. Sometimes one wonders whether the wasteful western quality of life is better and desirable. For example, the US alone is contributing 30%

of global greenhouse gas pollution (World Resource Institute). However, if all the people in developing countries like India and China (40% of mankind) have energy consumption similar to that in the US or Europe, then it will have a disastrous effect on the world economy and environment. Thus there are estimates that oil energy consumption in developing countries could surpass that in developed countries within 20 years (Hat field, C.B. Nature 1997). This will create great conflict among nations and it is quite possible that in future the wars will be fought over energy resources. There is, therefore, a need for an alternative development model based upon renewable energies, which is decentralized and takes into account the aspirations of the rual population.

Historically, it has been shown that the quality of life is proportional to the per capita energy consumption. Energy consumption of a country can be broken into two parts – the cumulative energy consumption $E1= \int Ec\, dt$, where Ec is energy consumption of the country at any point in time and E1 is the energy consumption per capita per year. E1 goes in building infrastructure like roads, bridges, power plants, communication networks, etc. During the early and middle parts of this century, developing countries because of historical reasons (most of them were colonized), had very little of E1. Thus it is difficult for them to reach the US or European quality of life, even if E1 somehow becomes available. Since the lifestyle in western countries is unattainable, we should try to develop an alternative lifestyle in India. I think a lifestyle based on the maxim of 'simple living and high thinking' is a possible choice. Thus our ancient philosophical thought should be used to temper our greed for resources and energy. Gandhiji showed that with minimum needs and energy he was capable of producing the highest quality of thought. This has also been the tradition of our great saints (Rajvanshi A.K 2001). The

Gandhian model may be difficult to follow, but it shows the way towards low energy development strategy.

In India about 75% of the population lives in rural and semi-urban areas. It is estimated that for the next 50 years or so, the major part of the population in India and other developing countries will still be village-based. Hence rather than pumping in huge resources in urban areas where the quality of life is becoming worse by continuing on the present path, it is much better to improve the quality of life in rural areas through an alternative model based upon sustainable growth and renewable energy.

In the past, most development efforts for rural poor have focused on villages. But because of inadequate infrastructure, income-generating capability and economic power, they have become sinks for development funds. There are a large number of examples the world over where well-meaning development efforts in small villages have not yielded the desired results. Villages are small but they are unsustainable. Cities in developing countries on the other hand may have rapid growth and development, but they have an ugly growth pattern. Therefore a middle path of a taluka-based development model is being proposed for sustainable rural society.

2. What is a Taluka?

A taluka is an administrative block generally comprising about 90-100 contiguous villages, with a small town as its headuarters. On an average 8 to 10 talukas make up a district. For example in Maharashtra there are 30 districts and 236 talukas. The total population of a Talukais is in between 200,000 and 250,000. The town population is about 50,000. Data on commercial energy usage show that on an average a taluka consumes about

10-15 MW of electricity and about 10-15 million litres/year of petroleum products (GOI 1995). There are about 3342 talukas in India. The major economic activity in a taluka is primarily agriculture-based.

Since the geographical boundaries of a taluka are fixed, it can be thought of as a closed biomass and rainwater basin. It is the thesis of the author that a taluka can produce a majority of its demand of food, fuel, fodder and fertilizer from the natural resources and agro-based material available in it and hence the development can be truly sustainable. For some talukas that do not have sufficient biomass, other sources like solar and wind can be used to produce energy.

3. Why a Taluka-based Model?

Societies are living and dynamic structures. In an evolutionary process, they can be thought to follow the laws of a natural living system.the hallmark of evolution of a dynamic system is its size reduction, increase in energy usage efficiency, increase in complexity, possession of critical mass, and its 'punctuated equilibrium' with its surroundings. In the 'punctuated equilibrium' phase, the system stabilizes for a certain time (Per Bak 1994). One of the crucial conditions for the evolution of a dynamic system is the availability of critical mass. The critical mass enables the system to process materials and energy through it and hence allows it to grow. If the critical mass is not available, the system does not grow and dies-off.

Societies can also be thought to be like Prigogine's dissipative structures (Prigogine 1980). For example, a convection cell in a body of water heated from below is a dissipative structure and is energy-dependent. The resulting shape of these structures therefore depends on the quality and quantity of energy passing through them (Prigogine 1980). The systems possessing a critical mass grow with energy input and go through a 'punctuated equilibrium' phase after which they become unstable and collapse into smaller systems. These small systems then coalesce through time and again form a critical mass and the cycle continues.

However for the societal systems to grow in a sustainable manner, certain conditions have to be fulfilled. Thus sustainable systems can be compared to a chair (Casti Francisco 1980). The four legs of this chair can be thought to be made of four activities: Energy, Economic, Environmental and Equity (social/cultural issues). All of them have to be of equal size for comfortable sitting and interconnected to provide stability. The base (seat) has to be of right size. Too big a base will make the chair sag and too small a base will make it unstable. Correct base size can, therefore, be thought of as the critical mass.

It is our thesis that because of its population size and its fairly developed infrastructure, a taluka has the ability to form a critical mass for a sustainable society for developing countries. With proper use of its agricultural and narural resources, it can produce food, feed and fertilizer in a self-reliant, environmentally sound and economically attractive manner. Hence it can provide the four legs of the chair for sustainable development. As the energy and other resources available are decentralized in nature, a taluka can form an appropriate 'dissipative structure' and can remain in 'punctuated equilibrium' phase.

From the above evolutionary model it can also be conjectured that in future, with the increasing use of renewable energy, all societies will evolve to be decentralized, high technology-dependent and village-based. Similarly, the mega-cities will break into smaller sustainable units. India is already a village-based decentralized society. Hence, instead of following the mega-city-based model, it is better to arrest this trend by introducing high-technology systems in the taluka. These high-technology systems may include internet connectivity, desktop-manufacturing units, and micropower production systems like microturbines and fuel cells.

4. Taluka Model

India produces in its talukas 400 million tons/year of agricultural residues which theoretically can produce 53,000 MW of power through biomass-based power plants (GOI 1995). This power is 70% of the total amount available in the country at present from all other sources. Not only can these residues produce adequate power to supplement existing power production, but husbanding this resource properly can also produce adequate animal feed and fertilizer. With increasing food production, the quantity of agricultural residue will also increase. Its judicious use will improve the rural economy and the quality of land. However, this agricultural residue is spread all over the country and is dispersed. This points towards decentralized power production systems.

Besides producing power, the challenge is also to maintain high quality and productivity of land so that food, animal feed, fertilizer and fuel could be produced in a sustainable manner from it. For this, water and soil conservation has to be implemented. It is possible to achieve this by rainwater harvesting and by planting trees and grasses and general management of biomass resources in talukas. As the economic returns will be directly dependent on the increased biomass production, the landowners in a taluka will take up such measures readily. The strategy will also help increase the income of the farmers (since they will get money from residues which are presently wasted), will provide jobs for labourers in each taluka to collect residues and will create employment in other biomass-based industries. It is estimated that each taluka can create about 30,000 new jobs from such activities (Rajvanshi 1995).

Following this approach in energy self-sufficient taluka model was developed (Rajvanshi 1995). This model was developed for Phaltan taluka. However we feel that this methodology can be easily used for other talukas in the country. The strategy for taking care of energy needs was based on biomass resources. Based upon the historical data of energy needs for Phaltan taluka (Rajvanshi 1995) it was found (as of 1995) that in the year 2000, it would require about 13 X 10^8 MJ of electricity and about 26 million litres of petroleum products (diesel, petrol and kerosene; (Rajvanshi 1995)). It was established that all this energy can be easily met by biomass-based power plants, production of ethanol from sweet sorghum and from existing distilleries, and pyrolysis oil production from agricultural residues and energy plantations. Electricity from biomass-based power plants would replace the MSEB- supplied electricity, while ethanol and pyrolysis oil would replace the liquid petroleum products. The technology for producing all these products already exists (Dunn Seth 2000 and Weinberg, Carl J. - 2001). The details of the strategy are given in Rajavanshi (Rajvanshi 1995). This study also showed that with a capital input of Rs.300 crore, phaltan taluka can produce wealth of Rs.220 crore/year and provide employment to about 30,000 people year-round.

This study became the basis of a national policy on energy self-sufficient talukas and was adopted by the Government of India in 1996 (ref. 11). As a part of this policy, presently all the states in India are collecting data on availability of biomass residues in their talukas. This study, therefore, showed that it is possible to provide all the energy needs of a taluka from its own resources, thereby pointing towards sustainability.

One of the tragedies of rural areas in India and other developing countries has been the lack of production of value-added goods. This has resulted in very little remuneration to the farmers and hence the depletion of rural wealth. We feel that a taluka provides a critical mass for production of agro-based and value-added products. With availability of power and raw materials (agriculture-based), fertilizers, chemicals, processed food products, etc. can be produced. With smart 'bench-top' production facilities available in future, it may be possible to produce substantial amounts of locally consumed items. This will further help in increasing the wealth of a taluka and in creating extra –employment. Recently, micropower projects like gas-based microturbines and fuel cells are becoming available (Dunn Seth 2000 and Fairley, Peter 2001). They will further usher in an era of efficient small-scale manufacturing facilities. Identification and evaluation of such cutting-edge technologies for both agro-based industries and consumer products will help talukas leap-frog into the modern age.

5. Technological issues

There are some other issues that need to be tackled before the taluka model can become truly sustainable and self-sufficient in energy and food production. They are transportation, water supply, environmental pollution, and fertilizer production.

(a) Transportation

The Phaltan taluka study showed that ethanol and pyrolysis oil production can take care of the historical demand of transportation for phaltan taluka. However, this will fuel the already explosive growth of two-wheelers and three-wheelers. An alternative to the existing vehicles is electric cycle-rickshaws (Rajvanshi A.K. 1999-2000). These are 40% more efficient than existing petrol and diesel three-wheelers and are also environmentally sound transportation systems. The electric rickshaw can easily take 2-3 passengers at 30-35 km/h and can go up to 60 km with one battery charge (Rajvanshi A.K. 1999-2000). It is our belief that these vehicles can easily provide the public transport system for talukas (20-25 km radius travel). For inter-taluka travel, ethanol and pyrolyses oil fuel can be used to run the existing fast-moving vehicles like two – and four-wheelers and also help in reducing environmental pollution. Historically, it has been shown that the structure of towns and cities is mostly guided by the transport system. It is our belief that with electric cycle-riskshaws, the size of existing taluka towns can be maintained.

(b) Water supply

A large number of talukas in various parts of Gujarat, Rajasthan, Maharashtra, Andhra Pradesh, etc. have woefully inadequate water supply. This greatly reduces the agricultural activities besides creating conditions for water-borne diseases to spread. The government naturally has gone for mega irrigation projects, which have not helped the cause (Vohra B.B. 1996). The time has come to think of private, decentralized water utilities. This will include rainwater harvesting and treating and recycling used water. Just like the power utilities, one can think of water utilities in a taluka. Anecdotal data suggest that rural people are ready to pay the necessary price for assured and good supply of water. There will still be pockets of resistance for paying for water (which in most places is free and hence wasted), but that resistance can be overcome by the quality of water supply. Water on demand is a luxury in most areas of India and hence its availability can ensure proper payment. Rainwater harvesting can create good supply of water for both agriculture and household uses. Our data showed that rainwater harvesting in Phaltan taluka can yield 4 to 5 times more water per year than the existing canal supply (Rajvanshi 1995). This water can be collected in 3000 check dams of about 1 ha size and can supply water, both for irrigation and household purposes in Phaltan taluka (Agarwal, Anil and Narain Sunita (eds) 1997). The cost of water from such a supply will come to 1 paisa/litre. The Nira Right Bank Canal is the main source of water for both irrigation and water supply for Phaltan taluka. A private utility in a taluka can manage this easily compared to the corrupt public system. There are a good number of examples of cooperative society-managed water utilities which are coming up in India and their examples can be followed for talukas (Fernadez, Aloysins P. 1998 and Kakade B.K 200). With increased water supply there will be a tremendous increase in agricultural production and consequently in availability of agricultural residues, thereby helping both power and fertilizer production in talukas.

(c) Environmental pollution

Environmental pollution in taluka areas is normally from three sources: (i) Agroprocessing industries like food processing, distilleries, etc.; (ii) vehicular pollution, and (iii) sewage. Vehicular pollution can be taken care of by use of ethanol and pyrolysis oil in existing vehicles and with the use of battery-powered vehicles for shorter distances. Agro industries produce tremendous pollution in rural areas and destroy the water and land resources by their effluents. In Phaltan taluka there is one distillery of 30,000 1/day capacity, which produces about 450,000 1 of effluent (Rajvanshi 1995). With an average COD (chemical oxygen demand) loading of 100,000 mg/1 in the effluent, its treatment can put tremendous pressures on water supply. Various technologies like solar detoxification of effluents are becoming available and can be used (Rajvanshi A.K 1999). Here again the role of water utilities becomes important. The effluents can be treated and made available to farmers as irrigation water. Similarly, sewage treatment can also come under the umbrella of water utilities.

(d) Fertilizer production

Availability of organic fertilizer is extremely important to maintain fertility of the soil and hence sustainability of land. With almost all the agricultural residues taken for energy generation, the fertilizer issues can become critical. However, there exists enough potential for making fertilizer from night-soil and composting of weeds and vegetable waste so that the possibility of fertilizer issue to be solved. Our study showed that enough night-soil and dung (from draught animals, poultry and sheep/goat) exists and it can be used with unutilized biomass (weeds, grasses, etc.) to produce excellent fertilizer (Rajvanshi 1995). Also, the increased agricultural activity (because of availability of water) will create more residues, which can go for fertilizer production. Technologies also exist whereby these materials can be composted in fast reactors (Cnevas, Virginia, C. 1993). With the availability of power in a taluka, it is felt that the production of organic fertilizer can become a major industry. Farmers presently sell raw dung in rural Maharashtra at a good profit. With the processing of this dung, remuneration to the farmers can increase further. There will nevertheless be a competition for agricultural residues between the power plant and the fertilizer factory. However, we feel that the market forces will ultimately decide their allocation.

7. Policy Issues

The following policy issues will have to be addressed before the above scenario can become a reality:

(a) A policy decision will have to be made by the Government of India to set up a Taluka Development Corporation and invite private-

sector participation in setting up power and water utilities in talukas. A partnership among the corporate sector, local NGOs and the government can be a new paradigm for rural development.

(b) A policy will also have to be formulated so that the corporate sector will not only produce power/water, but will also be allowed to carry out its distribution. Most of the independent power projects have been bogged down by the disputes regarding distribution. Only possession of distribution rights will allow the utilities to make money and give good service.

(c) Since both power and water production is from renewable sources (biomass and rain), existing norms, tax benefits and soft loans applicable and available to renewable energy sources should be made available to the corporate sector involved in the taluka programme.

(d) Policy decisions will also have to be made by municipal corporations/bodies of taluka towns to allow only environmentally sound vehicles to ply within the town. Since the area of a taluka and the number of vehicles running in each taluka are small, it may be possible to manage this issue.

It is our thesis that in a democratic society like India, sustainable taluka development will decentralize economic and hence political power. Decentralization of economic and political power is the best bet against economic deprivation, corruption and unaccountable ruling elite and can be the engine for internal peace, stability and development of a compassionate society. It is my belief that development and democracy work best in a decentralized power structure, a message that was constantly preached by Gandhiji. I also feel that the taluka plan has the potential of producing a sustainable society for one-fifth of mankind (India'a population) and in the process can show the world a new way.

One of the great strengths of India is that the majority of its people can be satisfied with a few material comforts. This strength can become useful in the paradigm outlined in this paper. In a democratic set-up, one cannot force the population into a certain lifestyle. But the existing traditions, norms, strengths, etc. can be used to guide the society into sustainable living. We hope this paper will help start a debate on this issue.

REFERENCES

1. Sarma, E.A.S., pers, commun., Ministry of Power, Govt. of India, October 1997.
2. Anupama Airy, Indian Express, 1 September 2000
3. Power Map of India 1995, Central Board of Irrigation and Power, Government of India, New Delhi, 1995.
4. Shah, G., Economic and Political Weekly, 1994, vol.XXIX, pp.2671-2676.
5. Engineer, A.A., Economic and Political Weekly, 193, vol. XXVIII, pp.81-85.
6. Vohra, B.B., RGICS Paper No. 35, Rajiv Gandhi Foundation, New Delhi, 1996, 0.46
7. Kumar, Priti, Down to Earth, 1997, 6, 29-43.
8. World Resource Institute, USA, http://WWW.org/climate/contributions_map.html
9. Hatfield, C.B., Nature, 1997, 387,121.
10. Rajvanshi, A.K., Acceptance Speech for Jamnalal Bajaj Award 2001, delivered at Mumbai on 6 November 2001.
11. Task Force Report, Ministry of Non-conventional Energy Sources, Government of India, New Delhi, March 1995.
12. Per Bak, etal., New Sci., 1994, 141, 36-39.

13. Prigogine, Iiya, From Being to Becoming, W.H. Freeman and Company, San Francisco, 1980.

14. di Casti, Francisco, Nat. Resour., 1995, 31, 207.

15. Rajvanshi, A.K., Economic and Political Weekly, 1995, vol. XXX, pp. 3315-3319

16. Dunn, Seth, Renewable Energy World, 2000, 3, 80-89.

17. Weinberg, Carl, J., Cogeneration and On-Site Power Production, 2001, 2, 49-64.

18. Fairley, Peter, MIT Technol. Rev., 2001, 104.

19. Rajvanshi, A.K., Human Power, Winter 1999-2000, No.49, pp.15-18.

20. Agrawal, Anil and Narain Sunita (eds), Dying Widsom, Centre for Science and Environment, New Delhi, 1997, p.321.

21. Fernandez, Aloysius, P., ILEIA Newsl., 1998, 14, 12-13.

22. Kakade, B.K., Leisa India, 2000, 2, 18;40.

23. Rajvanshi, A.K., Final Project Report submitted to MNES, New Delhi, June 1999, p.63.

24. Cuevas, Virginia, C., ILEIA Newsl., 1993. 9, 11-12.

25. Moorty, V.K., LEISA India (suppl.), 1999, 1, 12-14.

5

Drought Management and Sustainable Development*

H.P.Singh

1. Introduction

Drought is a phenomenon of temporary negative deviation in environment moisture status. The actual rainfall often falls much below the 'normal' expected on a long-term basis because of the inherent variable character of the monsoon. This results in drought, which is manifested in terms of crop failure in drylands and depletion in surface and groundwater resources. The agricultural drought is therefore of particular concern in dryland regions. The consequence is large-scale human migration and loss of livestock and human lives due to scarcity of water, food and fodder(Oliver and Fairbridge, 1987).

State intervention to alleviate drought situation dates back to the year 1880,when the first Famine Commission was appointed by the then British Empire, Setting up of

* Keynote Address at the National Seminar on the Subject at S.K. University. Ananthapur, A.P. September 14-15, 2001.

this commission had its roots in the recurring droughts which the country faced from 1860 onwards. Research in dryland farming was initiated as early as 1923 at Manjari near Pune. Following that in 1933-35, the then Imperial Council of Agricultural Research (now Indian Council of Agricultural Research, or ICRA) sponsored a Dryfarming Scheme at five centers viz., Solapur, Bijapur, Raichur, Hagari and Rohtak. Setting up of Soil and Water Conservation and Training Institute at Dehradun in 1954 and Central Arid Zone Research Institute (CAZRI) at Jodhpur in 1959 were perhaps the first major initiatives made in independent India to address the problems for soil and water conservation and rainfall farming. It was in 1970 when an All India Coordinated Research Project for Dryland Agriculture (AICRPDA) was instituted by ICAR at 22 centres across contrasting agro-climatic regions of the country to conduct research in dryland farming in an organised and structured framework. In 1983, an All India Coordinated Research Project on Agrometeorology (AICRPAM) was started to give further impetus to dryland research by understanding and defining the crop growth related weather factors. The modest beginning of AICRPDA led to the establishment of a full-fledged research oraganisation-Central Research Institute for Dryland Agriculture (CIRDA) in 1985 at Hyderabad. The chief mandate of CIRDA is to embark upon lead research in dryland agriculture, leaving location specific problems and their solutions to AICRPDA and AICRPAM. Almost coinciding with the inception of AICRPDA, International Crops Research Institute for the Semi-Arid Tropics (ICRISAT) was also established at Hyderabad in 1972.

Following mid-term appraisal of the Fourth Five-Year Plan, Rural Works Programme promulgated in 1970-71 was redesigned as Drought Prone Area Programme (DPAP). Similar to DPAP, a Desert Development

Programme was started in 1977-78. In mid 1970s, Integrated Dryland Development Project (IDDP) was initiated with the purpose of transferring the benefits of research to the farmers. Almost at the same time (1983-84), a scheme namely "Pilot Project for Propagation of Water Conservation/Harvesting for Rainfed Areas on Watershed Basis" was conceived. This project is also known as Model watershed Programme was spread across 47 sites in 16 states. CIRDA provided technical back stopping to 30 Model Watersheds. Encouraged by the gains shown by the Model Watershed programme, Ministry of Agriculture conceived a massive national effort on stabilizing and improving the quality of agriculture in rainfed areas. National Watershed Development Project for Rainfed Areas (NWDPRA) was launched in 1987-88. Apart from the internal support, a number of watershed projects have received external funding from agencies such as World Bank, DANIDA, EEC, ODA, FRG, etc.

2. Causes of Drought

The root cause for deficit rainfall that results in drought is the widespread and persistent atmospheric subsidence arising from general circulation of the atmosphere. Recent studies on interactions between global circulations and drought showed that the *El Nino* phase of the Southern Oscillations (ENSO) contributes substantially to summer droughts. The frequency of drought is also influenced by climatic changes as a result of increased concentration of the atmospheric carbon dioxide (CO_2), methane and nitrous oxide. The Inter-governmental Panel on Climatic Change (IPCC) of the World Meteorological Organisation projected an increase in atmospheric temperatures of 0.1 to 0.3°C by 2010 and 0.4 to 2.0°C by 2020 in South Asia that may result in a decrease in cereal production by 5 to 15% in the region (Houghton *et al.*, 1990). Also, the extensive deforestation in vogue since centuries has altered the hydrologic cycle thus enhancing the incidence of droughts in several countries in the region.

3. Frequency of Droughts

A study of moderate and severe droughts that occurred in India indicates that most areas, except small pockets in North-Eastern India and Kerala, have been affected by drought at one time or the other (Anonymous, 1994). Based on historical records, Jaiswal and Kolte (1981) reported 120 drought or famine-like incidences in one or other part of the country between 1291 and 1979. The 20th century alone experienced droughts of varied intensities occurred during 28 years in India (Venkateswarlu, 1997).

4. Impact of Droughts

Agricultural drought leads to loss of crops, malnutrition of human beings and cattle, land degradation, loss of other economic activities, spread of diseases and migration of people and livestock (Kulshrestha, 1997). Droughts adversely affect not only the food security at the farm level but also the national economy and overall food security.

The duration of availability of water in surface water bodies reduces significantly during drought year. The groundwater table declines and the shallow wells dry up. Sometimes, the concentration of toxic elements such as arsenic, fluoride and nitrate are increased. In deep wells concentration of salts increases due to lowering of water table. The poor people suffer the most since they own shallow wells and cannot afford to deepen them.

Droughts result in mortality and reduced productivity of livestock. Driven by enhanced livestock pressure due to depletion of forage resources, overgrazing and indiscriminate cutting of vegetation take place leading to land degradation. This is followed by distress sale of cattle and even small ruminants. Migration occurs leading to uncontrolled grazing and overgrazing, and thus triggering land degradation in other areas.

Recurring droughts bring about changes in the nature and extent of the socio-economic values and attitudes of the people (Purohit, 1993). Rise in prices, concentration of charity, diminution of credit and consequently enhancement of the rate of interest on loans, reduced grain trade, increase in petty crimes, unusual migration of the people along with their herds, etc., have been some of the most common outcomes. The agricultural sector fails to provide basic employment to rural workers thus resulting in migration, underemployment and creation of slums in the cities. Rural women are overburdened with additional work to earn through relief works. Poor quality drinking water causes several diseases leading to high infant mortality. Migration and taking infants to work also leads to increased child mortality. High morbidity in women and children has been common due to low intake of calories, much below the energy spent for hard labour in relief works.

The entire society is adversely affected due to rise in prices, additional taxation, etc., as a consequence of drought. However, farmer is the greatest sufferer who directly bears the brunt in terms of loss in production.

The impact of drought is not just a temporary adversity or a calamity. The relief measures, imports, foreign assistance and taxation on the middle class of the society to meet the food needs are merely national attempts to address to the secondary impacts of drought. The basic adverse impact of drought is obviously the continuing land degradation or desertification in vulnerable areas, which if continued, can become irreversible. Obviously, there are many direct factors too leading to land degradation. Yet, since drought has a direct impact on agricultural production, any effort aimed at the control of land degradation and protection of natural resources, would substantially mellow down the adverse impact of drought on agricultural productivity through better environment on one hand and improved soil quality (resilience for tolerance of moisture stress) on the other.

5. Drought Management – The Key Players

Drought is a natural disaster with serious and long term socio-economic implications. It is therefore vital to develop appropriate measures to overcome it. They are currently being implemented by the following sectors:

(a) Government Sector

- Relevant policies at the national, regional and district levels,
- Rural development infrastructure, and
- Input supply, marketing and farm advisory services

(b) Non-government sector

- NGOs
- Rural institutions, local self-governments
- Private sector
- Philanthropic organizations
- Community codes (tribes, herders), and
- International aid agencies

(c) Research and Development institutions

- Effective rainwater and soil management by linking on-stations and on-farm research

- Weather forecasts
- Contingency crop planning/mid-season corrections and
- Alternative land use systems

Research and development (R and D) in the areas of agro-meteorology, dryland farming and hydrology have contributed substantially to the knowledge base for drought management through weather forecasts and advance planning to meet emergencies. This shift in R and D strategy has had to some significant impact.

In India, where drought has been endemic for the past 150 years, a fairly organised management system to tackle it has emerged. However, the steps taken in the early stages were essentially adhoc in nature. Relief work was confined to providing employment to the distressed population without any long-term perspective. The launch of DPAP has its impact in dealing with the infamous droughts of 1987 and 1999-2000.

During the past three decades, major research efforts have been made to improve the productivity of rainfed areas in India and other countries of the region, with the aim of circulating the adverse consequences of drought. Relevant agricultural practices such as suitable crops, improved varieties, modern tillage and seeding practices, soil and rainwater conservation, water harvesting, fertilizer usage, weed control, alternative land use systems and plant protection have been developed through intensive and location specific research efforts. However, farmers, especially the small ones who form the bulk of the stakeholders have not adopted many of them to conserve natural resources (soil and water).The integrated watershed management approach, which is the core strategy of the national program to develop drought-prone areas in India, has not had the desired impact. The following factors among others, are responsible for this setback:

(a) Technology bias on biophysical issues (lack of appreciation of farmers conditions, their priorities and resources)

(b) Poor top-down extension strategy

(c) Lack of on-farm research in rainwater harvesting and watershed management

(d) Excessive reliance on new crop varieties (Lack of appreciation of farming system perspectives and insufficient diversification of production systems)

(e) Inadequate rural infrastructure

6. Drought Management-New Approaches

In view of the formidable task involved in drought management, a great deal remains to be done to tackle the problem. Projections for the next two decades must be considered, and new approaches and strategies adopted to meet the challenge.

7. On-Farm Research

On-farm research is underway in India since the mid-1970s. However, its focus is primarily on demonstrating or, at best testing the results obtained at research institutes and agricultural universities. Virtually no attempt has been made to tailor them to the needs of farmers. Therefore, once the projects were completed, the farmers reverted to their original practices. This was the case in many pilot projects, including many of the model watershed ones (46 in total) implemented in various agro-ecological regions in India during the 1980s. Hence, technologies suited to the farmers' socio-economic conditions and the indigenous environment can only be adopted if on-farm research is conducted with the participation of scientists, extension workers and farmers as a team.

8. Farming Systems Perspective

Farming systems in drylands are by and large complex and charecterised by several environmental and socio-economic variables. Addressing only one of these components, e.g. crop variety or fertilizer use does not generally result in a dramatic increase in productivity. Mixed farming-crop production and animal husbandry – for risk aversion, remains the mainstay of subsistence farming.

Planning farming systems research needs an understanding of current farming practices. The following four sets of information are needed to initiate such research in real field situations:

(a) Socio-economic conditions of the people, their perceptions, priorities and levels of education

(b) Natural resource conditions

(c) Technology (research information) developed at the research centers and

(d) Infrastructure (market and input issues) (Singh, 1997)

In irrigated areas, a synergy of production components (viz.improved variety, water management, fertilizer use and plant protection) usually results in a quantum leap in productivity. Farmers get impressed and readily accept the new technology. However, in rainfed areas, such synergy could at best only operate at a very low level. Water, which is the most important input, is an uncertain component. Fertiliser is seldom used because of inherent risks. Given this scenario, it is difficult to convince farmers to adopt cost intensive farming methods.

Crop cultivation alone cannot sustain dryland farming. All components of production must be integrated. Only this way, it is possible to achieve an optimal system that can increase productivity in rainfed areas.

9. Farmers' Participation in Technology Development

In the past, farmers in rainfed areas have, by and large, ignored technological advancements in agriculture. Pretty (1995) developed the following set of typologies regarding their participation in development programmes:

- Enhancement of natural resource base is a must to realize this end or goal;
- Manipulative participation;
- Passive participation;
- Functional participation;
- Interactive participation;
- Self-mobilisation.

Most extension efforts have hitherto been oriented towards the first four types. However, a methodology to include the following additional aspects may be appropriate to involve farmers in overcoming drought.

- Include them in resource appraisal;
- Conduct demonstrations to arrest land degradation and water and soil loss with such tools as the portable rainfall simulator;
- Interact with them to obtain their perceptions on: (i) drought management issues, (ii) watershed and its relevance; and (iii) sustainability of rainfed farming;
- Identify and list indigenous technical knowledge so that it can be utilized.

Constant interaction may eventually lead to voluntary farmer participation or self-mobilisation. This should be the strategy for technology transfer in rainfed areas in the next decade.

10. Grass root Extension System

The Panchayat Raj Institution can be organised to cater to gross roots extension needs. The Self-Help Groups (SHGs) approach has proved successful and is now taking shape as a movement in many states in the country. User groups and village volunteers' concepts are also being implemented with some success. These positive signals can be employed and consolidated to assist encourage the village local self-governments system evolve into a community organization. This may eventually lead to a "save and nourish your own land for sustained productivity" model. Such an institution at the grass-root level can be supported by the country's R&D program.

11. Consortia Development

At present a multitude of government institutions, NGOs and private sector/corporate organizations are working towards improving agricultural productivity in drought-prone areas. These efforts are handicapped for want of skilled manpower and exposure to the latest research technologies. It is therefore necessary to adopt a consortium approach to exchange knowledge and experience with a view to solving problems in the right perspective. Each agro-ecological region or sub-region must establish a consortium of its own to control land degradation and improve farm productivity. The research organization in the region may be the focal point of activity.

12. Early Warning, Drought Monitoring and Decision Support Systems

Rainfall distribution and its quantum are the two key factors that determine crop productivity. Weather forecasts can be broadly classified into three categories viz (1) short range (validity of upto 3 days), (2) medium range (validity from 3 to 10 days), and (3) long range (validity from 10 to 30 days). Early warning is given by the meteorological department in many countries and relayed through the press, radio and television. The latest technological innovations to monitor droughts include remote sensing. Monitoring of spatial drought conditions (at block level) in a few villages in Rayalaseema, India using satellite data was reported by Jayaseelan *et al.*,(2001). The threshold Normalised Difference Vegetation Index (NDVI) was compared with moisture deficit values to assess the extent of aridity in affected areas.

Management of mid-season and terminal droughts is important as it impinges on productivity. Various methods have been devised but they could not be applied because of lack of Early Warning System (EWS) on the onset of dry weather. Medium range weather forecasts are now in use in India as a form of EWS to control diseases and pests. These, together with recommended practices to alleviate aridity can help to arrive at optimal decisions for drought management.

13. Contingency Crop Planning

Several technologies have been developed and tested to enhance crop production under adverse weather conditions. Often, variable rainfall distribution poses a constraint. Therefore, every cropping strategy should be based on water availability from year to year. The contingency crop plans during times of rainfall deficiency are given below:

- Normal monsoon season followed by inadequate rainfall: If the latter occurs after planning, mid-season corrections such as reduction in plant population (thinning), use of green material as fodder or for organic recycling, spraying, anti-transpirants (e.g., atrazine, borax, kaolin), weeding and soil mulching can be adopted to overcome water shortage.

- Late monsoon season followed by normal rainfall: Here, the crop growing period is between 40 to 90 days. The selection of short duration varieties is important to suit arid conditions and accommodate the late onset of rain. Pulse and oilseed planting is recommended. Fodder and mustard can be grown after the seasonal crop harvest to make use of late rainfall.
- Late monsoon season followed by inadequate rainfall: Leguminous crops and oilseeds perform better under such conditions. They mature in a short period and give reasonable yields.
- To minimize risk and avoid complete failure, mixed cropping is advisable, in case the rainfall pattern is not suited to any specific crop.

The recommendations can be made following a comprehensive analysis of location specific situations through early warning and correct decision making.

14. Integrated Watershed Management

The watershed is the most appropriate ecological area unit for efficient and homogenous management of land and water resources in any arid terrain. A suitable watershed area can be selected for purposes of easy implementation. Based on the detailed survey of resources, such as land capability, a combination of conventional and participatory approaches and technological options with respect to soil and water conservation, rainfall harvesting, agroforestry, and livestock management can be adopted to minimize the risks caused by drought. This approach ensures planning based on available water, its priority use and the preparation of an integrated action plan to exploit natural resources, after taking into consideration the capacity and the socio-economic status of the rural people.

The central objective of watershed management is to conserve soil and water for sustainable production in rainfed areas. The first task for soil management is to reduce erosion by controlling runoff. The next is to conserve the rainwater for plant, domestic and livestock needs. In this context runoff control can be implemented in the following two stages:

- Retain the bulk of rainwater within field, subject to available soil and water storage capacity that is in situ water harvesting, and
- Divert excess water for
  - ❐ Storage in village pond, augment recharge of deep groundwater
  - ❐ Recharge shallow aquifers, and
  - ❐ Storage in farm ponds

Maintaining an adequate supply of rainwater to the village pond is the first priority as this is a common property resource utilized for domestic (E.g., washing) and livestock consumption. Recharging shallow aquifers is the next best option as they are owned by a large number of farmers. Recharging groundwater is possible only in wetter areas and those with adequate catchment. When recharging aquifers is not possible in the absence of water bearing rocks, the farm pond remains the only option to conserve excess runoff. It can be used to serve both the community and individual farmer. The latter is the easiest as it eliminates sharing costs (labour inputs). Small ponds owned by individual farmers merit greater attention.

15. In Situ Rainwater Harvesting

This is vital factor in drought control. The principle here is to reduce runoff to facilitate either greater water intake in the soil or direct it to the planting by modifying land configuration to enhance its storage in soil. Extensive research efforts in this area begin in India in the 1930s and intensified during the last three decades. They resulted in the development of several useful technologies. Field and contour bunding, riding and keyline and contour cultivation and vegetative barriers have in the past enhanced in situ soil storage of rainwater.

16. Village Ponds and Farm Ponds

The former is larger and can serve as reservoirs to mitigate the scarcity of drinking water particularly for livestock and to provide for daily needs of villagers such as washing, cleaning and bathing. Here water is available from two months to a year after the wet season depending upon the catchment's characteristics, runoff volume and its utilization. Heavy sedimentation, high evaporation, seepage losses and pollution limit the utility of these ponds.

Normal farm ponds are for pre-sowing, protective irrigation and livestock consumption. The scheduling of limited water supply and setting priority for its allocation are important considerations. The first task is to reduce conveyance and evaporation and to direct water to the root zone. One supplemental/life saving irrigation of 20 mm at the most critical stages of crop growth during prolonged drought can increase the grain yield by 30 to 80% (Venkateswaralu, 1981).

The pond size of 10.5 m * 3 m * 4 m = 126 m^3 is adequate to provide life-saving irrigation of 20 mm to 0.5 ha of cropped land. This includes water loses of upto 26 mm due to evaporation and seepage. The reason for the abnormally small width is to make I practical for covering the pond with locally available material such as stone slabs and thatched blocks across the length to check water loss via evaporation.

Prior to the advent of the watershed concept, rainwater storage in drought-prone areas were by traditional means, i.e. rainwater collected from rooftops and underground cisterns were used to store runoff from natural or constructed catchments. In the past, these methods have met the drinking needs of the rural people, especially those in remote areas. For the present, these sources are used primarily for livestock consumption, washing, cleaning, etc. and also for nurseries or trees planted in the vicinity of backyards.

17. Crops, Varieties and Cropping Systems

The prevailing cropping system may not necessarily be the most suitable one. Farmers grow certain crop either for convenience or by tradition. Their first priority is to produce food for the family and livestock. This needs to be balanced with the requirements for natural resource management on the one hand, and socio-economic and market demands on the other. Alternative crops and varieties for different periods of sowing, together with those that are suitable despite any delays in sowing or resowing and yet can sell globally need to be identified.

18. Soil and Crop Management

Different land configurations to prevent runoff have been discussed earlier. Other major aspects that may merit attention are tillage and the control of surface evaporation.

(a) Tillage

It has a marked influence on soil and rainwater conservation and makes the soil surface more permeable to water intake. Deep tillage (5-30 cm) breaks the hard layers, facilitates faster penetration of rainwater and enhances the root system. The subsoil resources are thus utilized more efficiently. Off-season or pre-rainy season tillage also has a visible impact on rainwater intake and weed control, besides improving soil moisture content or off-season planting.

Excessive tillage however is not recommended. It accentuates wind erosion in sandy soils and does not permit build-up of soil organic matter. Therefore, minimum tillage together with organic waste recycling is best to support a good crop stand. This may also lead to an increase in organic matter due to reduced exposure to high atmospheric temperature.

(b) Surface Mulching

It can help conserve soil and rainwater. Studies in various locations in India demonstrated its usefulness in reducing water loss from the soil surface. It also significantly lessens runoff from cropped fields and assists in weed control. However, it is generally not popular with farmers due to operational constraints. In mixed farming, using straw as mulch adversely affects the fodder supply. Organic waste material can be utilized as surface mulch instead. This practice is feasible in tree crop areas where only the planting basin needs to be covered.

Work has recently begun on green material soil or land cover, i.e. to combine mulch and manure in different locations in India. After planting. *Gliricidia* and *Leucaena* branches/loppings are used as cove and incorporated in the soil following canopy development. Encouraging results from this practice have been reported (Singh *ed al.*1998).

(c) Integrated Nutrient Management

Good soil quality is vital for plants to withstand the dry weather. It can be realised by adopting integrated nutrient management (INM), which is the key to maintaining and sustaining soil productivity. Extensive studies conducted at research and on-farm stations have shown the importance of farmyard manure (FYM), composted organic wastes, and add bio-fertilizers in supplementing the nutrient requirements of crops and providing stability to yields under rainfed condition (Singh *ed al*, 1999; Venkateswarlu and Wani 1999).

The availability of FYM in sufficient quantities for field crop planning is a major hindrance to its widespread adoption. Thus, alternative sources such as green leaf manure eg. Loppong of *Leucaena* or *Gliricidia* and crop residue have been evaluated at a number of locations in India. Recent studies recommended fertilizer application of 20 kg N/ha supplemented by green leaf and land cover.

Composting of organic waste can substantially contribute towards maintaining and upgrading soil quality. Its quality rises by several folds but the benefits remain the same or slightly better than FYM. The additional cost of composing it with FYM is negligible. It has been reported that termite infestation is greatly reduced when compost is used instead of FYM. The organic matter build up from the latter provides resilience to withstand stress.

19. Alternative Land Use Systems

Data from several locations in India indicated that annual crops cultivated on land capability class IV and above are prone to drought. The soils here are better suited for perennial grasses, legumes and woody trees. Agro-forestry, which *includes silviculture*, *horticulture*, *hortipasture* and *silivipasture* can be successful alternatives. Less arable land can consider adopting them and integrating livestock with crops to attain a viable production system.

Silivipasture is ideal for rehabilitating marginal or degraded lands. A perennial tree crop such as *Leucaena leucocephala* is planted either with *Cenchrus ciliaris* or *Stylosanthes hamata*. Such pastures can support upto 6 sheep per hectare on a continuous basis without the need for any supplementary feed, while native pastures can support only 2 sheep per hectare. Ley farming is another approach where a legume or a non-legume forage crop is rotated with food grain crops. This system improves soil quality besides providing fodder.

In view of the long gestation period of tree crops, number of bushes such as henna, curry leaf and annette have been evaluated at CIRDA and found to be remunerative both as pure crops and as intercrops with short-duration pulses (greengram and blackgram). Network research carried out in India revealed that alternative land use involving perennials (tree/crop. Grass shurb or a combination of both) has advantages and can conserve natural resources and increase productivity. Some of the advantages of planting them are as follows:

(a) Provide permanent vegetative cover to the soil or land surface and thus substantially control erosion caused by both runoff and wind

(b) Improve the microclimate for crop growth

(c) Provide good quality green fodder, which is in short supply to support livestock. Thus the integration of livestock farming with arable cropping is highly recommended.

(d) Protect the environment and upgrade soil quality through their deep root system.

(e) Enhance organic matter by recycling biomass into the soil

(f) Reduce runoff, surface evaporation and weed growth and improve eater use efficiently when

lopping from the trees is spread on the soil surface for recycling

(g) Provide fuel, timber and minor forest products (e.g. gum) and thus lessen the farmers' dependence on forest reserves.

(h) Supplement the diet of poor farm families by giving the necessary vitamins and minerals and thus enhance their nutrition needs.

(i) Generate much needed cash when aromatic and industrial value plants are grown

(j) Support the development of soil microbe

(k) Generate employment throughout the year for farmers (when the agro-forestry system together with livestock husbandry and water harvesting are established) and thereby substantially increase their income level.

20. Conclusions and Recommendations

With a growing human and livestock population, the pressure on cultivated land in drought-prone rainfed areas will undoubtedly increase in the foreseeable future. The constant rise in demand for food grains will in all probability force farmers to encroach on marginal lands and thus accentuate the problems of land degradation. Despite a slowing down in livestock numbers, the shrinking forage resource is likely to result in a huge demand-supply gap for both green and dry fodder due to the expanding area under food and non-food crops. Although definite trends are not available, fears exist that the predicted change in climate may cause global temperatures to rise and thus accelerate the frequency and intensity of droughts. Consequently, deterioration in soil quality, and vulnerability to crop losses during dry seasons may become more pronounced. Further, to meet the projected demand for food and fodder, intensive land use is likely to occur in rainfed areas in the years ahead. The ability to meet such predictions without further degrading the already fragile land will be a major challenge in the years ahead.

The scenario is complicated if one goes by the projections on farm size for the coming two decades. It is estimated that its average in rainfed areas in India will decrease by 100% from the present level by the year 2020. Such tiny holdings will not only constrain partial mechanization, but may also limit the livelihood of the rural populace.

Rapid trade globalisation is giving new dimensions to small-scale farming. Hence, focus has to be on products and their quality in which a country or community has the competitive edge.

Strategies to combat drought should address food security both at the national and the farm level. Programs and policies to overcome it should aim at improving the per unit area of production as well as the quality of produce and, at the same time, reduce production cost by adopting practices such as integrated pest management. Achieving sustainable production in unproductive areas brings about profitability and the enhanced income will increase the purchasing power of their inhabitants and enable them to attain food security. In India, presently there is a reserve stock of 60 million tons of food grains. But million of people do not have access to this surplus due to lack of purchasing power.

The following activities may merit consideration when formulating national action plan to combat drought and for sustainable development.

- Characterise in detail the nature of droughts, their types and frequency based on past weather records, any strengths and weaknesses, opportunities and/ or dangers that emerge, and analyse the agro-ecological environment

- List indigenous technical knowledge for drought management
- Study current farming systems and available technologies for drought mitigation and the extent of their adoption and examine gaps in research and technology development
- Identify agro-ecological sub-regions affected by droughts; prioritise problems and areas for allocation of resources
- Implement grass root extension system
- Develop consortia on drought management
- Structure on-farm research and farmer participation in the technological development of farming systems, and
- Program development with focus on short, medium and long term intervention and examine policy issues.

REFERENCES

1. Anonymous. 1994. *Report of the Technical Committee on Drought Prone Areas Programme and Desert development.* Ministry of Rural Development, New Delhi, India.
2. Houghton, J.T., Jenkins, G.I. and Ephraums, J.J. 1990, Climate change. *The IPCC Scientific Assesment*, WMO/ UNEP. Cambridge, UK.
3. Jayaseelan, A.T., Suresh Babu, A.V., Chandrashekar, K. and Rupenkumar, G.V. 2001.IRS/WIFS data use for 1999 droughts in Rayalaseema districts of Andhra Pradesh, India. In: *Remote Sensing and Geographical Information Systems*(ed. I.V. Muralikrishna), B.S.Publications, Hyderabad, India pp 61-66.

4. Kulshrestha, S.M. 1997. *Drought Management in India and Potential Contribution of Climate prediction*. Joint COLA/CARE Technical Report No.1, Institute of Global Environment and Society,Calverton.

5. Oliver, J.E and Fairbridge, R.W. 1987. *The Encyclopedia of Climatology*. Van Nostrand Reinhold Co., New York, USA.

6 Pretty, J.N. 1995. Participatory learning for sustainable agriculture.*World development* 23(8): 1247-1263.

7. Purohit, M.L. 1993. Socio-economic aspects of drought and desertification. In: *Desertification inThar, Sahara and Sahel regions*. Scientific Publishers, Jodhpur, India, pp. 205-218.

8. Singh, H.P. 1997. Role of farm research and farming systems perspective in sustainable development of Thar Desert. In: *Desertification and Control in the Arid-Ecosystem of India for sustainable Development* (eds S. Singh and A. Kar), Agro-Botanical Publishers, New Delhi, India. pp. 380-386.

9. Singh H.P., Sharma, K.L., Venkateswarlu, B. and Neelavani, K. 1998. Prospects of Indian agriculture with special reference to nutrient management under rainfed ecosystems. In: *National Workshop on Long term Soil Fertility Through Integrated Plant Nutrient Supply System*. Indian Institute of Soil Science, Bhopal, India.

10. Venkateswarlu, B. and Wani, S.P. 1999. Bio-fertilizers: an important component of integrated plant nutrient supply in drylands. In: *fifty Years of Dryland Agricultural Research in India* (eds H.P.singh, Y.S.Ranakrishna,K.L.Sharma and B.Venkateswarlu), Central Research Institute for Dryland Agriculture, Hyderabad, India, pp.379-394.

11. Singh, H.P., Sharma, K.L., Venkateswrulu, B. and Neelavani, K. 1999. ferilizer use in rainfed areas: Problems and Potentails *Fertilizers News* 44(1): 27-38.

12. Venkateswarlu, J. 1981. Maximization of crop production in dryland. *Indian Journal of soil conservation* 9(1): 124-140.

13. Venkateswarlu, J. 1997. *Sustainable crop production. In: Symposium on Recent Advances in Management of Arid Ecosystems.* Arid Zone Research Association of India, Jodhpur, India.

Part—II

SECTORAL DEVELOPMENTS

6

Agricultural Growth, Employment and Poverty:

*A Policy Perspective**

R. Radhakrishna

1. Introduction

Agriculture dominates change in India through its causal links with factor and product markets. It employs 60 per cent of the labour force and contributes 26 per cent of the gross domestic product. In the poorer states, its contribution to the domestic product is close to 40 per cent. Low productivity in agriculture has led to the concentration of the poor in this sector. Due to the sheer size of the agricultural economy and the importance of its major products (cereals) in the diets of the poor, gains in agriculture productivity have significant potential impact on poverty. Theoretically, it is possible to reduce poverty as well as expand the domestic market for industry by raising labour productivity in agriculture and spreading its gains among the low-income groups. Modelling of the

* Presidential Address at the 43rd Annual conference of ISLE, published in EPW, 19th January, 2002.

linkages between agricultural and industrial growth has shown that a 10 per cent increase in agricultural output would increase industrial output by 5 per cent and urban workers would benefit by both increased industrial employment and price deflation [Rangarajan 1982; De Janvry and Subba Rao 1986]. However, there is an asymmetry of adjustments in the demand for and supply of agricultural goods. An increase in non-agricultural production would lead to an immediate increase in demand for intermediate and final agricultural goods whereas supply-side adjustments involving re-allocation of resources and net additional investment for capacity expansion take a much longer period [Strom 1992]. There is a widely held view that in a large country like India, the demand stimulus for industrialisation would come mainly from agriculture with less social and economic costs.

Interdependencies in food and labour markets are important for the development process. An upward shift in the food supply curve would simultaneously result in an upward shift in the labour demand curve. The magnitude of the interdependence depends on the technique of production causing the shifts in the food supply curve. Similarly, an upward shift in the labour supply curve shifts up the food demand curve. The extent of interdependence between forces of labour supply and food demand depends on the employment-output elasticity and the income elasticity of demand for food. The recent estimate of the employment-output elasticity in agriculture is around 0.5 income elasticity of food is in the range of 0.55-0.60 and that for cereals is 0.25-0.30. The other important inter-dependency, which plays a crucial role in inducing indirect employment, is that between food and other sectors through demand linkages. Since food accounts for a major share in the budget of the poor and any reduction in the food price leaves a significant proportion of income for other items, a lower food price stimulates employment in industrial and service sectors. On the other hand, an increase in the food price would increase the wage costs of industrial products and hence the prices of industrial products. In the absence of adjustments through exports, it would result in demand deficiency. Clearly, the most favourable situation in India is one in which labour demand outpaces its supply and food supply outpaces its demand.

Wage rates cannot fall below a certain minimum determined by the costs of subsistence living and the labour supply curve turns elastic at the subsistence wage rate. Demographic pressure cannot push the wage rate below the subsistence level. People would be willing to starve rather than work unless the energy expended in physical work is compensated by the energy provided by food [Seckler 1982]. Foodgrain price usually determines the subsistence wage rate in agricultural as well as in the urban informal sector since foodgrains account for about four-fifths of the calorie intake of the poor. Clark and Haswell, in their survey on agricultural wage rates in subsistence economies, observed that the rural labourer, however poor, does not take up a day's work for less than 3 Kg grain equivalent. The subsistence wage rate in a poor country is more than its marginal product, which constrains the availability of agricultural surpluses for industrialisation.

Both cost-reducing as well as labour-absorbing technical progress in agriculture and expansion of the non-farm sector are essential for development in a country like India. If rural non-farm and urban informal sectors grow at a sufficient rate, they can absorb the surplus labour and surplus food. If they grow at a lower rate, the terms of trade turn against agriculture, and consequently, agricultural incomes are depressed. In practice, price fall is moderated either by increasing buffer stocks or by expanding wage employment programmes. On the other hand, if agricultural production lags behind demand, it leads to an increase in food prices, and thereby to an increase in nominal wage rates of industrial workers, which, in combination with higher prices of agricultural raw materials, contributes to cost-push inflation. The performance of the non-agricultural sector is, therefore, harmed by too high as well as too low levels of agricultural prices, which is the razor's edge characteristic of agriculture [Alagh 1991].

The virtuous cycle between agriculture and non-agricultural enterprises plays a strategic role in providing employment opportunities in rural areas [Mellor 1978; Stern 2001]. The countries that made substantial progress in poverty reduction, created off-farm opportunities [Stern 2001]. There has been a spurt in the growth of non-farm enterprises in the Chinese countryside after liberalization around the late 1970s where off-farm employment grew at a rapid rate of 12 per cent per annum, currently employing 31 per cent of the rural labour force [Stern 2001]. As such, rural enterprises can become both an engine of growth as well as major contributor to the reduction of rural poverty. There is a widely held view that in India, the potential for labour absorption is high in agro-based industries, small and medium industries and the rural services sector. Most of these activities are highly labour-intensive and provide employment opportunities for the semi- and unskilled rural labour and semi-skilled urban labour force.

In the ongoing globalisation process, production and demand patterns undergo significant change. While better-off farmers produce high-value products for exports and for the affluent segment of the domestic market, the small farmers are likely to grow crops mainly to meet domestic food needs. Small and medium industries in the rural and semi-urban areas produce consumer goods to meet the needs of the lower strata of society. Some of the workers of small farmer households may be employed in non-farm activities either full or part-time. When non-farm activities provide stable sources of income to small farmers they can take the risk in opting for high-value crops with high risk. Income diversification of farm households and the insurance role of non-farm activities would strengthen the viability of small farm economy. Another way of achieving this is by contract farming, which facilitates the integration of small farms with agro-processing companies, which extend technical expertise and financial support to the farmers to grow high value-added crops. Historically, contract farming has been a standard practice in the Indian sugar industry. However, there is a need for contracts to be formal under a regulatory authority. Among the developing countries experiencing growth without worsening of inequalities, Vietnam is an example where poor rice farmers benefited from rapidly growing exports of rice and garments and footwear, etc, produced by small enterprises. Here, the link between exports and poverty reduction is very strong. The important requirement is the proper mix of policies and programmes in the rural sector. In the absence of upward mobility, growing aspirations of the lower strata lead to social discontent.

2. Agrarian Reforms

In the pre-green revolution period, from1950-51 to 1965-66, the main policy thrust was on agrarian reforms as well as modernizing agriculture though largescale investment in irrigation and power and creation of other infrastructure such as credit institutions, regulated markets, roads and extension as also research institutions. Immediately after independence, India abolished intermediary landlordism (Zamindari system), giving occupancy rights to 20 million statutory tenants, facilitating modernisation of agriculture, Dantwala (1986) argued that the "abolition of zamindari and similar intermediary tenures, which were highly inequitable and oppressive, was a progressive measure. Its abolition, covering some 40 per cent of the cultivated area, even with the shortcomings, must be considered as an improvement in agrarian relations. "Tenancy laws were enacted in almost all states with the objective of providing security of tenure, regulating rent and conferring ownership rights on cultivating tenants. Since a major proportion of tenanted land was under better off owner-cum-tenants and only a small proportion was under a large number of poor small tenants, tenancy laws helped the lot of bigger cultivators more than the small [Rudra 1978]. Simultaneously, ceilings on landholdings were imposed in the early 1950s and the surplus of land was taken over and distributed among the landless. The 1950s ceiling legislation was further amended in the early 1970s, making it more progressive. Implementation of land ceiling laws was equally disappointing. As a result of the implementation of the land ceiling since the 1950s, a total of 3.01 million hectares(mha) of land was declared surplus, nearly 2.31 mha (less than 2 per cent of the cultivated land) was taken over and 1.76 mha was distributed among five million beneficiaries, half of whom were SCs and STs. The small magnitude of the declared surplus was due mainly to poor legislation with large number of loopholes [Dantwala 1986]. Thus, the opportunity for a more equitable distribution of land was missed. However, the abolition of intermediaries and imposition of ceilings on landholdings had, over time, contributed to the growth of capitalist farming and arrested the concentration of land ownership. It is widely held that restructuring of land relations is a measure of great significance to the rural poor. The protection and enlargement of control and command over land are crucial issues for the poor. It is estimated that all efforts taken together including Bhoodan and distribution of government wasteland accounted for less than 10 per cent of the cultivated land [Sankaran 1994]. It may not be possible that all the rural poor can be accommodated but there is scope for utilizing the wasteland for providing access to the poor and also eliminating the biases against the poor in land relations. The desire to possess land is strong among the poor as ownership of land denotes one's social status.

In the mid-1960s, policy emphasis had shifted from institutional to technological factors. The green revolution, which is associated with high-yielding variety of seeds, ushered in a new phase of agricultural upgraded modernisation. There had been a steady stream of technological innovations contributing to yield improvements in wheat and rice. The advances in chemical fertiliser technology gave a central place to fertiliser in transforming crop production. Cost-reducing technologies led to rapid expansion of tubewell irrigation. There had been a shift towards owner cultivation from tenant cultivation, leading to a sharp decline in tenancy. The overall process of growth had widened the labour market in agriculture, animal husbandry, transport, petty trade, small industries and construction. Wages doubled in the green revolution regions compared with those in other regions. The green revolution triggered the first large-scale rural to rural migration in India, where in the poorly paid under-employed labour in rainfed marginal environments started migrating to green revolution regions. Such migrations contributed to some increase in wages in some of the under-developed regions which supplied the labour. However, the process of labour market adjustments through inter-regional migration seems to have come to an end with the spread of farm mechanisation in the green revolution regions.

In the post-reform period, policy emphasis has shifted to liberalising trade in agriculture. In the beginning, economic reforms bypassed agriculture in terms of direct reforms, except with trade liberalisation and relaxation of some export controls over agricultural products. However, subsequent currency devaluation, a shift towards floating exchange rates and reduction in industrial production have had indirect effects on the agricultural sector. With the establishment of WTO on January 1,1995 and India becoming its member, all quantitative restrictions (QRs) were dismantled by the end of March 2001. It is argued that these policy shifts would provide an opportunity for our farmers and agro-based industries to tap world markets.

There have been moves for relaxing the ceiling on landholdings. Given the poverty of small and marginal farmers, with the market price offered they can be ousted from farming enterprise. Since there is no evidence of increasing returns to scale in Indian agriculture, there is no case on efficiency grounds for doing away with the existing ceilings [Rao 1994]. However, it would be necessary to remove legal restrictions on the lease market for agricultural land as well as to facilitate the augmentation of operational holdings of small and marginal farmers [Murty 1998], Contract farming can, to some extent, overcome the constraints of land ceiling without any change in ownership of land. The Asian experience suggests that the impact of post-liberalisation growth on poverty reduction is greatest in situations where land reforms have been implemented and a high priority has been accorded to physical infrastructure and human resource development [Rao 1996].

3. Growth Performance of Agriculture

India's agricultural growth reveals two distinct phases during the pre-reform period: Pre-green revolution period and post-green revolution period. The first phase, from the beginning of planning to the mid-1960s, was characterised by severe imbalances between the demand for food and its domestic supply. In the post-green revolution period, from about the mid-1960s to the close of the 1980s, the country achieved near self-sufficiency in food and food security. The later phase warrants further subgrouping: the 1970s characterised by the emergence of intra and inter-regional and inter-crop imbalances in crop yields, and the eighties, when yields of crops like rice, oilseeds and pulses registered high growth, especially in the backward regions. The latter period marked a turning point in terms of regional spread of agricultural growth and diversification of agriculture. Even the states with high incidence of poverty – Assam, Bihar, Madhya Pradesh, Orissa, Rajasthan, Uttar Pradesh and west Bengal – registered significant improvement in crop yields, thus contributing to decline in poverty. During this period, two types of shifts took place in rural production: intra-agricultural crop production shift from cereal to non-cereal crops such as oilseeds, vegetables and fruits, and a shift from crop production to non-crop sectors such as animal husbandry and dairying.

Growth of foodgrain production accelerated to 2.9 per cent during the 1980s. Its supply outstripped effective demand, leading to bulging buffer stocks. The transition from scarcity to surplus is a matter of tremendous importance, as it enabled India to overcome the problem of concomitant political pressures associated with food aid during the periods of previous food crises. However, the growth rate decelerated to 1.8 per cent during the 1990s. What is disquieting is that the annual growth rate of foodgrain production was lower than the historical growth rate and barely kept pace with the population growth rate. Ironically, even at this slow growth of foodgrain production, its supply outstripped its effective demand and the 1990s witnessed a rapid further increase in the buffer stocks held by the government, whose disposal has become a cause for concern apart from increasing the cost of food management. Paradoxically, the relative cereal prices, which had declined in the 1970s and 1980s, reversed their trend and registered a rise in the 1990s amidst ever increasing buffer stocks. Moreover, in high inflation years, cereal prices rose even higher [Ravi 2000]. An increase in cereal price significantly reduces the calorie intake of the poor as it is sensitive to cereal prices. Not surprisingly, the upward trend in the relative price of cereals in the 1990s coincided with a slowdown in the decline in poverty. The overall annual growth rate of agriculture declined to 3.6 per cent during the 1990s from 3.9 per cent during the preceding decades and that of its allied sectors declined to 3.7 per cent from 4.2 per cent during the corresponding periods.

Despite favourable terms of trade for agriculture and normal south-west monsoon, growth of food production has been sluggish during the 1990s, and the process of diversification of agricultural production from coarse cereals to oilseed crops in rainfed areas has slowed down. These trends may be attributed to: (1) a decline in public investment in agriculture since the early 1980s (the annual growth rate being 1.9 per cent during the 1990s compared with 4.0 per cent during the 1980s) which slowed the expansion of irrigation, (2) low public investment in R and D (0.5 per cent of agricultural GDP as against the norm of 1 per cent recommended by the ICAR), affecting technological progress, (3) decline in the annual growth rate of fertilizer use from 7.8 per cent during the 1980s to 4.3 per cent during the 1990s (4) deceleration in the annual growth rate of area under high-yielding varieties from 4.9 per cent during 1980s to 2.8 per cent during the 1990s (5) fall in soil fertility due to intensive cultivation and wheat-rice rotation year after year in the north-western region and (6) over-exploitation of groundwater due to unregulated expansion of tubewells. More than a decade of high growth in food production has led to complacency among policy-makers which led to slackening of investments in agricultural research, irrigation and rural infrastructure that would provide productivity growth in the crop sector. However, one consoling development is the compensatory rise in private capital formation in agriculture during the 1990s compared with the earlier decades –the annual average growth rate of private gross capital formation in agriculture was 8.1 per cent during the 1990s compared with –0.1 per cent during the 1980s and 7.2 per cent during the 1970s [Rao and Jeromi 2000].

4. Rural Employment Trends

Of the 397 million people in the labour force in 1990-00, 388 million were employed and 9 million (2.2 per cent) reported unemployed during the greater part of the year. The primary sector-agriculture, animal husbandry, fisheries and forestry- employed 238 million (60 per cent) of the workforce, unorganized non-agricultural sector 133 million (33 per cent) and organised sector 28 million (7 per cent). Employment in the organised sector increased slowly from 24 million in 1983 to 28 million in 1990-00. Evidently, unless some spectacular changes occur, the organised sector's share in the absorption of additions to the labour force will have to be absorbed in the unorganized non-agriculture sector as agriculture is already overcrowded.

The composition of employment (self employment, regular salaried employment and casual employment) has been changing. While self-employment is on the decline, casual employment is on the rise. The share of self-employed in the rural workforce declined from 62 per cent in 1977-78 to 56 per cent in 1999-00, while the proportion of casual labour increased from 30 per cent to 37 per cent. Regular employment marginally declined from 7.8 to 6.7 per cent during the same period.

Though the usual principal status unemployment rate at 1.96 per cent in 1999-01 is not a serious concern in rural India, current daily status unemployment rate at 7.21 per cent is high. Unemployment among educated youth (15-29 years) has been high. The usual status unemployment (1999-01) among rural youth with secondary education and above is estimated at 23 per cent. What is of particularly serious concern is unemployment among educated females in rural areas which is about three times more than that of their male counterparts, presumably due to limited chances open to them for migration to urban areas to secure employment.

During the past two decades there have been some perceptible trends in the structure of rural employment. The share of agricultural sector in the rural workforce declined from 83 per cent in 1977-78 to 76 per cent in 1999-00 while that of rural non-agricultural sector increased from 17 per cent to 24 per cent over the same period. The annual growth rate of work-force in agriculture was 1 per cent during 1977-99 while the same in non-agriculture sector was 4.3 per cent during 1977-88 and 2 per cent during 1988-2000. Non-agricultural rural households are gradually withdrawing from cultivation to concentrate on the main non-agricultural occupations in agriculturally-developed states. As a result, the proportion of rural households receiving incomes from cultivation fell from 62.4 per cent in 1987-88 to 57.1 per cent in 1999-2000. Employment diversification occurred even in some semi-arid regions wherein toddy tappers and shepherds reverted to their traditional occupation from casual labour in agriculture [Krishnaiah 1995]. The shift of workforce from agricultural to non-agricultural activities was shown to be an outcome of growth rather than a "distress" phenomenon [Vaidyanathan 1994]. Expansion of rural non-farm sector has been influenced by growing commercialization in the rural economy. Employment potential of the non-farm sector appears to be directly related to commercialization of agriculture. This is normal pattern of development and, in fact, the process has been very slow in India.

The pace of change did not accelerate during the post-reform period as anticipated, total rural employment growth rate declined from 1.57 per cent per annum during 1977-87 to 1.15 per cent during 1987-99; rural non-agricultural employment growth rate declined from 4.32 per cent to 2.06 per cent; while agricultural employment rate remained around 1 per cent during the pre- and post-reform periods (1977-87 and 1987-99). Slowdown in the growth of rural non-farm employment seems to have contributed to the decline in the growth rate of rural employment. An entirely new trend of shifting non-farm activities and wholesale trade from rural to urban areas seems to be emerging in India [Bhalla 2000]. The underlying factors behind this phenomenon and its likely impact on the rural economy have yet been little understood.

5. Agricultural Wages

In spite of sluggish growth of rural employment during the 1980s, real wages increased. This could be due to both expansion of employment in non-agricultural activities such as construction and services [Bhalla 1991 and Rao 1994] and implementation of public employment programmes. Real wages improved in the post-reform period despite deceleration in agricultural productivity and slowdown in the rural non-farm employment. The growth rate of daily real wage earnings of rural male agricultural casual labour increased from 1.36 per cent during 1987-93 to 2.80 per cent during 1993-99 and that of their female counterparts increased from 2.34 per cent to 2.94 per cent during the same period. The rising real wages led to labour substitution in irrigated agriculture and made rainfed farming unremunerative.

There has been a debate whether slow growth of agricultural employment was consequence of increasing wages. Bhalla (1993) feels that there was a significant reduction in man-days per hectare due to mechanization adopted partly in response to rising real wages from mid-1970s, and partly to meet time schedules in sowing and harvesting in crop cycles and the availability of concessional farm machinery loans. Econometric studies revealed a decline in labour demand due to an increase in real wage: a 1 per cent increase in real wage would reduce labour demand by 0.4 per cent in rice cultivation, 0.35 per cent in wheat and 0.14 per cent in maize [Kumar 1998].

A balanced assessment of the factors responsible for rising wage rates during the 1980s and the consequent decline in rural poverty highlights high agricultural growth, opening of rural non-farm activities, provision of public employment programmes on a large scale, and union interventions in the labour market [Kannan 1998, Narashimha Reddy 1998, Sharma and Kumar 1998]. In the poorer rain-fed areas in which agriculture stagnated during the 1980s, real wage improvement as well as reduction in poverty could be attributed to the expansion of employment programmes and political mobilization of labour by the unions. It is a moot question whether such improvement can be sustained in the absence of agricultural growth. It is only when rising labour productivity is accompanied by the opening up of employment opportunities in the rural non-farm sector, as happened in some regions in the 1980s, that the trickle-down effect would be stronger. While an improvement in labour productivity would create enabling conditions for higher wages, it is the bargaining power of labour which translates the productivity improvements into higher wages.

6. Labour Market Concerns

Some worrisome trends in the labour market which have persisted since the beginning of planning are inadequate growth of productive employment in rural areas, casualisation of a mass of rural workers without safety net, feminisation of agricultural labour with low wages and persistence of child labour. In dryland areas, a continuing bias against females in the labour market persists. Also, in these areas, many agricultural labourers are under-employed and wages paid are very low, much lower than the minimum wages. Ordinarily, one would not be willing to supply labour for less than the minimum wage, when one knows that under the law one is entitled to get minimum wage. But a person is forced to work at less than the minimum wage rate out of compulsion arising from hunger and poverty.

Incidence of child labour is high in India and the estimated number varies from 17.5 million to 44 million (ILO). It is estimated that one-third of the child workers in Asia are in India. What is disquieting is that number of child workers in the labour force is increasing in India while it is declining worldwide. The largest number of child workers is engaged in agriculture. Child employment benefits the employer but adversely affects poor as a class although it may supplement the income of the household supplying child labour. The poor are made worse off as employment of children brings down the wage levels. It is a paradox that high levels of adult unemployment coexist with high incidence of child labour in India.

The number of interstate distress rural migrant workers is estimated to be around 10 million [Sankaran 1994]. Green revolution significantly increased remunerative wage employment in pockets of assured irrigated areas while employment opportunities nearly stagnated in the vast rain-fed semi-arid areas. In the latter areas, wages are low, underemployment of workforce is rampant and incidence of child and female labour is high. Low wage rates, coupled with underemployment, are causing interstate distress migration of farm workers from dryland areas of Bihar, Orissa, Chattisgarh, Andhra Pradesh (Mehboobnagar district) and Tamil Nadu (Salem district). Rural migrant workers are preferred by the employers even in areas of abundant labour supply because of greater control that can be exercised by them over the migrant labour without regard to any social responsibility (ibid). A graphic sketch of the miserable plight of interstate migrant labour is drawn by Sankaran (1994). He observes that "the time they spend in their own villages aimed at keeping them alive until the next recruiting season, often with the help of advances of money by the recruiting agents and while on migratory work the time is spent on keeping them alive until they return to the village".

7. Public Intervention

Government legislations such as minimum wage, social security legislation and social institutions (for example, labour unions) have been in existence in India to protect labour. They have been improving wages and socio-economic position of the poor and the underprivileged sections in the labour markets [Kannan 1998, Reddy 1998, Sharma and Kumar 1998]. Labour unions in Kerala were pioneers in India in achieving minimum wages, 8-hour work-day and abolition of some other forms of exploitation even before the time of state formation in 1956 [Kannan 1998]. Labour mobilisation in Bihar since early 1970s raised their wages as well as socio-political consciousness, and improvedtheir socio-economic conditions [Sharma and Kumar 1998]. Some NGOs in Andhra Pradesh were successful in mobilizing agricultural labour against the powerful landowners, moneylenders, traders and contractors to secure better wages with their new-found bargaining power [Reddy 1998].

The central government, over the years developed a wide spectrum of employment programmes to create additional employment during drought years. However, their contribution was small compared with the magnitude of unemployment. The contribution of all employment programmes, including urban programmes, to total employment has been just about 2 per cent. Employment programmes in the past were not integrated with the development of agriculture and rural infrastructure. While they provided residual employment, they did not enhance the labour absorbing capacity of the rural economy. Delivery systems of these programmes have remained essentially top-down ventures heavily dependent on inept bureaucracy. Though huge sums were spent on these programmes over time, their qualitative achievements in terms of decentralized decision-making, people's participation, and creation of durable assets were rather disappointing.

Among the employment schemes, the Maharastra Employment Guarantee Scheme (EGS). which provides every adult a statutory right to get guaranteed employment for unskilled manual work and to receive wages, has been more successful in generating additional purchasing power among the poorest by providing gainful employment on local public works during drought years. The programme is self-targeting as only poor, particularly female workers turn up for manual work. The EGS enabled the poor to survive with dignity and avoid abject poverty. However, its implementation is saddled with over-bureaucratisation and excessive centralisation, with an almost complete absence of people's participation.

8. Trends in Poverty

During the 1990s, the slowing down of rural employment growth and slowdown in the growth momentum of rural non-agricultural activities appear to have affected the pace of decline in rural poverty and widened rural-urban disparities. We shall review the trends in total expenditure data of the past three decades (that is, 1970-71 to 1998), based on the detailed study of Ravi (2000).

Rural per capita total expenditure (PCE) per month at 1990-91 prices, which was Rs.158 in 1970-71, increased steadily to Rs.213 by 1989-90 and declined sharply by 5 per cent to Rs.202 in 1990-91.During the 1990s, it fluctuated at Rs 202-214, except in 1997 when it reached the highest level of Rs.235. Its annual trend growth rate fell to 1.2 per cent during the 1990s from 1.5 per cent during 1970-89. In contrast, there has been acceleration in the trend growth rate of the same in urban areas where annual growth rate was1.45 during 1970-89, which almost doubled to about 2.8 per cent during the 1990s. Clearly, rural-urban disparities have widened during the 1990s. During 1970-89, the rural-urban differential expressed as a ratio of the urban PCE to that of the rural, increased at a moderate rate of 0.1 per cent per annum, which accelerated to 1.6 per cent during the 1990s.The benefits of better income growth during the 1990s seem to have benefited the urban areas more than the rural, thus aggravating the rural-urban divide. This is in conformity with the finding that employment growth during the 1990s was concentrated in urban areas [Bhalla 2000].

Expenditure inequality widened in both rural and urban areas, though statistically not significant in rural areas. The Gini coefficient estimate of urban consumer expenditure increased at a high rate of 1.4 per cent per annum during the 1990s. However, as will be seen, the urban poor also gained substantially since the increase in per capita expenditure more than compensated the adverse effect of rising inequality.

The rural bottom 30per cent experienced a deceleration in the growth rate of their per capita expenditure during the 1990s. In contrast, their urban counterparts had a higher growth rate of per capita expenditure, despite an increase in expenditure inequality. While the growth rate of per capita expenditure of the rural bottom 30 per cent declined from 1.71 per cent per annum during 1970-89 to 1.19 per cent during the 1990s, the same for their urban counterparts increased from 1.44 per cent to 1.70 per cent . Though all the urban classes gained during the 1990s, the top 30 per cent gained the most.

Rural poverty declined at an annual rate of 2.5 per cent during the 1970s and 1980s, most of it during the 1980s and at 0.73 per cent during the 1990s.Poverty levels declined steadily from 57 per cent in the 1970s to 33 per cent in 1989-90. During the 1970s and 1980s, per capita real expenditure of rural households registered a significant increase from Rs.158 in 1970-71 to Rs.213 in 1989-90. Its subsequent sharp fall during 1990-91-1992 had an adverse effect on rural poverty; pushing the poverty ratio again to 44 per cent in 1992. Thereafter, it remained around 40 per cent except in 1997, when it declined to 33 per cent. Since the rate of decline of rural poverty has been lower than the rate of growth of rural population during the 1990s, the absolute number of poor would have increased in the last decade. On the other hand, urban poverty declined at the rate of 2 per cent pa during the 1970s and the 1980s and at 3.05 per cent during the 1990s. The acceleration in the decline of urban poverty is due to the high-income growth achieved during the period of liberalisation, which seems to have percolated to the bottom through the trickledown effect. The decline of urban poverty would have been sharper had there been no worsening of inequalities. The notion that poverty is getting concentrated in rural areas is clear from the preceding analysis. The widening rural-urban disparity in incomes should be a matter of great concern in a country like India.

9. Concluding Observations

Yield improvements and growth of the rural non-farm sector contributed to the diversification of employment opportunities. However, the slow growth of the rural non-farm sector failed to create sufficient jobs to employ the large surplus agricultural labour. Growth of non-farm sector is essential for long-term poverty alleviation. This has been the process of transition towards an industrial economy in many east and south-east Asian countries which experienced sharp reduction in poverty [Baker and Dawe 2001]. Their rice economies experienced significant increase in productivity and hence, real wages and consequent farm mechanization (ibid). The resources saved in rice growing have been channeled into non-rice sectors which contributed to substantial employment expansion. In contrast, there is no such significant shift of resources in India from rice/wheat to other sectors.

Still a large number of rural poor particularly in marginal environment survive at the brink of subsistence, depending on uncertain employment and meagre wages. The real challenge lies in increasing their purchasing power by expanding remunerative employment. This has to be achieved in the face of increasing natural environmental degradation due to population pressure. As the green revolution favoured mainly irrigated areas, future research should be targeted to develop drought-resistant seed varieties benefiting farming in areas with scanty rainfall. Innovations in dryland farm practices such as rainwater harvesting, moisture conservation, intercropping, and adoption of drought-resistant seed varieties are imperative to enhance and stabilise agricultural production in the rainfed areas.

It is widely accepted that India needs an agricultural growth rate of 4.0-4.5 per cent to reduce poverty significantly [Rao and Radhakrishna 1999]. At this growth rate, agricultural development would diversify into dairying, animal husbandry, fisheries, floriculture, horticulture and other areas. This would spur the growth of agro-processing industries in rural areas to meet domestic as well as export demand. Rice and wheat farmers should be induced to look for new sources of incomes in diversified agriculture to compensate the fall in incomes in rice and wheat cultivation. As the world prices of rice and wheat are already lower than their domestic prices and are not likely to fall, the domestic prices of rice and wheat will tend to fall to align with the world prices. Moreover, the world market for rice is very limited and confined to superfine varieties. As the demand for cereals is mainly population-driven whose growth rate is slowing down, it should be prudent to divert resources from rice and wheat cultivation to high-value crops.

Irrigated agriculture has now reached the take-off stage where growth with good spread and coverage can be generated through normal market mechanisms and right policy mix. Since income improvement in these regions is likely to increase the demand for the products of animal husbandry, fruits, vegetable and processed foods, marketing and agro-processing should receive the attention of policymakers. Public spending in irrigated regions should be very selective, facilitative and confined to those critical areas which would supplement private initiative. As the demand for skilled labour is likely to move ahead of its supply in rural areas, support programmes for skill development may be organised in newly emerging activities in response to economic restructuring. In short, a strategy combining promotion of agricultural growth, productive non-farm employment and high levels of social development would be needed to trigger off labour-intensive growth in rural areas.

Poverty alleviation progarammes should go beyond their present minimal concerns of providing protective 'safety nets'. There should be substantial investment in human resource development for enhancing people's inherent earning capacity. Along with this, there should be attempts to create more economic space for the poor by equipping them with assets and skills for livelihood outside agriculture. All this should contribute to the generation of self-reliant employment.

Strengthening of local institutions to empower people, as was done by Anna Hazare in Ralegan Siddhi Village, political mobilisation of people by NGOs and social activists for ensuring statutory minimum wages, and prevention of discrimination in the labour markets as was done by labour unions in Kerala, need to be emulated elsewhere on a much large scale. Else the new economic policies would only benefit the already rich and the privileged and most likely bypass the poor. It needs to be emphasised that the ongoing economic reforms by themselves may not lead to growth with equity. It is desirable that a new set of measures for human development is placed on the national agenda with local institutions and labour unions taking the initiative for their effective implementation.

REFERENCES

1. Alagh, Y.K. (1991): *Indian Development Planning and Policy*, Vikas Publishing Press, New Delhi

2. Barker, R and David Dowe (2001): 'The Asian Rice Economy in Transition: Challenges Ahead', Keynote address, International Prospects of Rice Supply and Demand in the 21st century, International Rice research Institute, Los Banos, Philippines, December 3-5.

3. Bhalla, S. (1991): 'Report of the Study Group in Employment Generation' in *Report of the National Commission on Rural Labour*, Vol. 11, Government of India, New Delhi.

4. Bhalla, S. (1993): 'The dynamics of Wages Determination and Employment Generation', *The Indian Journal of Agricultural Economics*, Vol. 48, No. 3.

5. Bhalla, S. (2000): 'Behind Poverty: The Qualitative Deterioration of Employment Prospects for Rural Indians', Working Paper Number 7, Institute of Human Development, New Delhi.

6. Dantwala, M.L. (1986): 'Agrarian Structure and Agrarian Relation In India' in Dantwala et al (eds), *Indian Agricultural Development since Independence*, Oxford and IBH Publishing Co, New Delhi.

7. De Janvry, A and K. Subbarao (1986): *Agricultural Price policy and Income distribution in India*, Oxford University Press, New Delhi.

8. Kanan, K.P. (1998): 'State and Union Intervention in Rural Labour: A State of Kerala' in R Radhakrishna and Alakh N Sharma (eds), *Empowering Rural Labour in India*, Institute of Human Development, New Delhi.

9. Krishnaiah, M. (1998): 'Labour Institutions in Backward Agriculture' in Radhakrishna, R and Alakh N Sharma(eds), *Empowering Rural Labour in India*, Institute for Human Development, New Delhi.

10. Kumar, P. (2001): 'Agricultural Performance and Productivity' in Acharya S.S and P Chaudhari (eds), *Indian Agricultural policy*, Rawat Publications, New Delhi.

11. Mellor, John W. (1978): 'Food Policy and Income Distribution in Low Income Countries', *Economic Development and Cultural Change*, Vol. 27, No 1.

12. Reddy, Narashima (1998): 'Union Intervention in Rural Labour Markets: The Experience of Andhra Pradesh' in R. Radhakrishna and Alakh N. Sharma (eds), *Empowering Rural Labour in India*, Institute of Human Development, New Delhi.

13. Rangarajan, C. (1982): 'Agricultural Growth and Industrial Perofrmance in India, Research Report33', International Food Policy Research Institute.

14. Rao, C.H. Hanumantha (1994): *Agricultural Growth, Rural Poverty and Environmental Degradation in India*, Oxford University Press, Delhi.

15. Rao, C.H.H and R. Radhakrishna (1999): 'National Food Security: Policy Perspective for India' in G.H. Peter and J.V. Braun (eds).*Food Security Diversification and Resource Management: Refocusing Of Agriculture*, International Association of Agricultural Economics: Ashgate.

16. Rao, V.M. (1996):'Agricultural Development with a Human Face: Experience and Prospects', *Economic and Political Weekly*, June 29.

17. Rao, V.M. and P.D. Jeromi (2000): 'Modernising Indian Agriculture: Priority Tasks and Critical Policies', Study No 21, Department of Economic Analysis and Policy, Reserve Bank of India, Mumbai.

18. Ravi, C. (2000): 'Complete Demand Systems, Welfare and Nutrition: An Analysis of Indian Consumption Data', unpublished Ph.D thesis.

19. Rudra, Ashok (1978): 'Clears Relation In Indian Agriculture', *Economic and Political Weekly*, June 3, 10 and 17.

20. Sankaran S.R. (1994): 'Rural Poor and Public Action: Some Issues', C.V. Subba Rao Memorial Lecture, AP Economic Association, XIII Annual Conference, Nagarjuna University, Guntur, December 10-11.

21. Seckler, D. (1982): "Small But Healthy: A Basic Hypothesis in the Theory, Management and Policy of malnutrition' in P V Sukhatme(ed), *Newer Concepts and Their Implications for Policy*, Maharastra Assciation for Cultivation of Science, Pune.

22. Sharma, Alakh N. and Ajay Kumar (1998): 'Peasant Mobilisation in Bihar: Implications for Rural Labour Markets' in R. Radhakrishna and Alakh N. Sharma (eds), *Empowering Rural Labour in India*, Institute of Human Development, New Delhi.

23. Storm, Servaas (1992): *Macroeconomic Contribution in the Choice of an Agricultural Policy*, Thesis Publisher, Amsterdam.

24. Stern, Nicholas H. (2001): 'Building A Climate for Investment, Growth and Poverty Reduction in India', 16th Exim Bank Commencement Day Annaul Lecture, Mumbai.

25. Vaidyanathan, A. (1994): 'The Employment Situation: Some Emerging Perspectives', *Economic and Political Weekly*, Vol. 29, No 50, December 10.

7

Reforming Rural Non-Farm Sector

S. Mahendra Dev

1. Introduction

The importance of the rural non-farm sector in poverty alleviation and promotion livelihoods is being increasingly recognised. With its share of less than 30 per cent in GDP, agriculture has to bear the burden of more than 60 per cent of the workers. Migration to urban areas is not a solution as towns and cities have their own problems of demographic pressures. To increase wages in agriculture and to shift workers to more productive areas, promotion of the rural non-farm sector is advocated. An increase in rural non-farm employment is one of the main factors responsible for the reduction in poverty in the 1980s.The debate on the trends in and nature of rural non-farm employment (RNFE) has once again assumed importance in the context of economic reforms in the country. At this juncture, it is useful to address the following questions. What is the impact of economic reforms on RNFE? Which

* Published in The Hindu, Chennai, September 3, 2001.

sub-sectors in RNFE have grown during the reform period? Is the growth in RNFE due to 'pull' factors or 'push' factors?

2. Trends in RNFE Growth

Here are some statistics based on national sample survey quinquenniel surveys on employment and unemployment to examine the trends in RNFE. The percentage of RNFE in total rural employment increased from 16.6 per cent in 1977-78 to 18.4 per cent in 1983, to 21.6 per cent in 1993-94 and to 23.8 per cent in 1999-2000.We are not considering the NSS data for 1987-88 because that was a drought year. If we look at the yearly increase in the percentage share of RNFE in total employment it was 0.35 per cent per annum during the reform period (93-94 to 99-00), which is more or less similar to earlier periods. Let us look at the absolute numbers in RNFE. The number of workers in RNFE increased from 36.1 millions in 1977-78 to 44.9 millions in 1983 to 62.98 millions in 1993-94 to 71.52 millions in 1999-2000.The growth rate (compound) in RNFE during 1977-83 was 4.06 per cent per annum while it was 3.28 per cent per annum and 2.14 per cent per annum during 1983-94 and1993-2000 respectively. In other words, during the reform period ('93-94 to '99-00) the growth rate of employment RNFE was lower than the pre-reform period. This is a matter of concern. However, this has to be seen in the context of the low overall growth of employment (around 1 per cent per annum) during the reform period. Ninety per cent of the additional employment during the reform period was due to RNFE as compared to 39 per cent in the earlier periods. What do we conclude? As in the overall growth rate, the growth rate of workers in RNFE declined during the reform period. There is, however not much change if we look at the annual increase in share of RNFE in total rural employment. But, the expected growth in rural non-agricultural sector due to economic reforms does not seem to have materialised. As compared to East Asian experience, the growth in RNFE in India has been much slower.

3. Gender Difference in RNFE Growth

There are, however, differences between males and females in terms of growth in RNFE. In the case of males, the share of RNFE in total rural employment increased from 19.3 per cent in 1977-78 to 28.7 percent in 1999-00 (a 9.8 percentage point increase over 22 years). In the case of females, it increased from 11.8 per cent to 14.6 per cent during the same period (2.8 percentage points increased). During the reform period (93-94 to 99-00), there was 2.8 percentage points increase for males while it was 0.7 percentage points for females. It looks like the growth in RNFE is more a male phenomenon.

4. Sectors that Contibute to RNFE

The second issue is about the sectors that contributed to the increase in RNFE during the reform period. K.Sundaram's paper 'Employment and Poverty in 1990's'(*Economic and Political Weekly)*, August 11-17,2001 provides absolute numbers of employment in rural areas at one digit level. One can derive the shares of sub-sectors in additional employment created during 1993-94 to 1999-00. The additional employment created in the rural non-farm sector during the reform period was 8.54 millions. Out of these, 3.1 millions workers were from the construction sector. In other words, 36 per cent of the additional employment in RNFE during the reform period was due to construction. And 27 per cent was due to manufacturing and repair services (the share of repair services being 5.4 per cent) and 25.5 per cent was due to transport, storage and communication. The contribution of retail trade was 13 per cent while that of hotels and restaurants was only 4 per cent. Thus in rural areas also, there is no fear of India becoming a "restaurant and bar economy". In the case of community and personal services, there was a decline in employment while employment of social services (education and health) increased. The shares show that around 63 per cent of the additional employment was due to construction and transport, storage and communications. It is not clear whether the creation of additional employment in the activities led to improvements in the well-being of the poor.

5. Role of Push and Pull Factors

The related question is whether the growth in RNFE is due to 'push' or 'pull' factors. Sundaram's analysis (in the above mentioned paper) on rural real wages of casual labourers indicate that it is a 'pull' phenomenon. The growth rates in real wages of casual labourers have not declined during the reform period. However, some other indicators such as poverty in rural non-farm sectors given by Sheila Bhalla suggest that it could be a 'push' phenomenon. The numbers show that in the rural areas, the three poorest segments are agricultural labourers, construction workers and manufacturing workers. In fact, poverty among cultivators is much lower. Bhalla's analysis shows that the rural non-farm sector was providing unacceptably low quality employment to increasingly large numbers of people. It is possible that the rural non-farm sector may be acting as a 'residual sector'. For example, poverty among workers in construction (which contributed 36 per cent of the additional employment) is quite high. This is also consistent with slow decline of rural poverty from 39.36 per cent in 93-94 to 36.35 per cent in 1999-00 based on employment surveys of the NSS.

6. Need for a Three-Pronged Strategy

One of the challenges of the reforms now is to improve the quality of employment and incomes in the rural non-farm sector. A three-pronged strategy is needed for enhancement in the livelihoods of the rural poor. First, the Government should have policies to improve education and skills of the workers. Second, they should have several policies to increase employment for the unskilled workers. Third, the incomes of the women have to be improved by creating opportunities in the higher productivity sectors. Most of the women are confined to agriculture; there was only 0.7 per cent increase in the share of RNFE during the reform period. For the above three strategies, pro-poor growth engines have to be identified at sub-sectoral level rather than at the level of broad sectors.

7. Case for a Pro-Poor Public Investment

Public investment in agriculture and rural non-agriculture has to be improved significantly to improve the quality of RNFE. Infrastructure development and other incentives are needed for attracting private investment. The Government has to address policy constraints on raising agricultural production, growth of small and medium business, technological progress, improved productivity of natural resources and marketing of rural products. Allowing the poor to contribute to and benefit from increased growth rates will pose particular challenges as employment in India is largely in the un-organised sector. We have programmes such as DWCRA to help the women .But most of the activities of these groups generate subsistence incomes. High income-generating activities have to be developed for women by improving their skills, technology and marketing. With 61 million tonnes of foodgrains stock, food-for-work programmes can be initiated in a big way to help poor and improve rural infrastructure.

8

Reforming Rural Financial Market

G. Raghava reddy

1. The Theme and its Approach

The evolution of a modern economy in the place of a natural economy was a long drawn out process. We have a few remnants of a natural economy in some parts of the world including our country. It is characterised by self-reliant economic units operating at the margin of subsistence and primitive technology in production. The consumption units (households) and production units(farms/firms) are almost identical. There is of course limited exchange carried on mostly with barter. The modern economy, on the other hand, is characterized by a circular flow of economic life, households engaged in consumption and supply of factor services and farms/firms preoccupied in production for the market by hiring factors of production. The costs incurred by the production units accrue to the consumption units in the form of factor rewards. The circular flow of economic activity is facilitated by the widespread use of money and credit.

* Presidential Address at the 17th Economic Association held at Guntur 7-8, February 1999. A.P.

Finance is a wider concept than money and credit. That there is a mutual interaction between economic development and financial deepening is well recognized. The empirical evidence in this regard is quite extensive in the industry and commerce in the countries of the third world and the collapse of most of the socialist economies of the second world the significance of monetary and financial management is widely recognized. The economies of the third world, with a few exceptions, are dominated by subsistence agriculture which is slowly getting transformed into commercial agriculture. Agriculture employing about two-thirds of labour force hardly contributes to less than one-third of national product. This is the fundamental factor behind the persistence of mass poverty in the rural sector of the third world. The agrarian institutions also contribute to its perpetuation rather than extinction (Pranab Bardhan 1989). The poverty curtain appears to be so strong that it cannot be lifted by piece meal efforts. Therefore, integrated rural development programmes are being launched to meet this challenge. According to Griffin(1979) there are three styles of rural development: (1) the technocratic (2) the reformist and (3) the revolutionary. With the disintegration of the USSR and the transition to a market economy in Central and Eastern Europe the scope for the revolutionary style of rural development is limited. There is a mix of technocratic and reformist styles being implemented in the sphere of rural development in the third world countries. The provision of adequate institutional credit at preferential rates of interest is one of the major planks of technocratic-cum-reformist strategy of rural development. Dale W. Adams(1986) points out that the arguments used to defend cheap agricultural credit are unsound, are based on value judgements, go counter to economic logic and are not supported by empirical evidence. Much of the confusion about interest rates would disappear if policy makers and development technicians stopped thinking of credit as an input, recognized the importance of real rates of interest and clearly understood fungibility. Sound policies cannot be built upon unsound assumptions and arguments. Financial sector reforms are being formulated and implemented with varying degrees of coverage and success in different countries of the world. Learning from experience is a continuous process for individuals, groups and institutions including the state if mistakes are to be corrected and avoided. I propose to deal with the nature and functioning of the rural financial market and examine the case for its reform. Our approach to the subject is an exercise in positive economics. However, there are a few value judgements, which properly belong to the domain of welfare economics, creeping into our analysis because the structure and performance of the rural financial market, like any other market, have consequences for the welfare of present as well as future generations of rural masses.

2. Rural Financial Market in Retrospect

A rural financial market (RFM) is a set of relationships between buyers and sellers of financial assets in the rural sector. Financial assets consists of debt claims and ownership claims. Debt claims include verbal and written promises to pay. Ownership claims give holders rights of access, use and control. The relationships between participants are based on transactions that include borrowing, lending and transfer of ownership of financial assets (Von Pisehke etal 1983). RFM consists of informal sector intermediaries, formal institutions and private borrowers and lending without intermediaries. Intermediaries generally pool funds from saving units and allocate them among borrowing units. As economic development proceeds, financial intermediation also advances in all sectors of economic activity. Besïdes providing a medium of exchange the financial system helps in the mobilization and allocation of capital as well as transformation and distribution of risk. In the colonial era the rural financial market was narrow and dominated by non-intermediating borrowers and lenders and informal sector intermediaries in India. The provision of Taccavi loans was an eye-wash and very much restricted in its frequency and coverage of beneficiaries. It was primarily a relief programme during times of economic distress caused by famines or the inclemency of the weather god (K.G. Karmarkar 1999). The agricultural cooperative credit delivery system was a failure due to the interaction of a multiplicity of institutional and non-institutional factors. Debt relief legislation was sporadically undertaken to save the indebted agriculturists from the exploitation of informal sector agencies. This legislation like most of the legal enactments was a paper tiger as many inbebted agriculturists could not take advantage of it either due to ignorance or legal expenses or both. Hence, the informal sector institutions especially the moneylenders were plundering the peasantry especially during drought and depression just like the colonial plunder of India by the British. The dawn of Independence and the advent of development planning necessitated the design of an alternative institutional farmework for the supply of suitable and adequate rural credit. Thus, in the place of the laisse faire regime a regulatory and promotional regime characterized by institutional innovation, directed lending and subsidized credit was formulated and implemented (Rangarajan 1998). These developments of the rural financial market and their use and abuse are briefly sketched and examined in what follows.

3. Institutional Innovations

The report of the All-India Rural Credit Survey (1954) is a remarkable document that set the ball rolling for the initiation and implementation of rural credit policy in India. Finding that rural credit was inadequate and unsuitable and 50 years of credit cooperatives have failed and realizing the need to replace the informal sector credit, the committee recommended an integrated scheme of rural credit. This committee also underlined the utter neglect of rural credit by the urban-oriented commercial banks and made out a case for their entry into the sphere of agricultural finance. Towards this approach it also recommended the nationalization of the Imperial Bank of India. It is now common knowledge that the State Bank of India which came into existence in 1955 in the place of the Imperial Bank of India is one of the leading commercial banks of the world with a huge network of branches and banking operations in the rural sector.

The nationalisaton of 14 commercial banks in 1969 was an act of political expediency often justified by economic rationale and social justice. The nationalization of 6 more banks in 1980 was similarly justified on the same logic. Thus, including the SBI and its 7 subsidiaries, 28 commercial banks were brought into the fold of public sector. Public sector banking has become a play ground for the politician and political intrusions have weakened the organisainal effectiveness eroding the profitability of banking posing problems for their long-run sustainability. The establishment of RRBs in 1975 was an innovation in the annals of mass banking. The RRBs were intended to be hybrid institutions absorbing the virtues of the rural cooperatives and urban-oriented commercial banks as low-cost institutions. At the end of March 1996 there were 196 RRBs with a network of 14, 497 branches. The branches of scheduled commercial banks have risen phenomenally from 5,175 in 1969 to 65,485 in 1997 and the proportion of rural branches rose from 18 per cent to 52 per cent during this period.

The cooperative credit system had also witnessed several developments mostly of a quantitative nature. There have been several exercises in reorganization and consolidation of different streams of credit under a single window system as in Andhra Pradesh. The cooperative credit system in most of the states is a three-tier system. There are about 93 thousand PACS with a membership of 966 lakhs spread over 93 per cent of rural habitations under the jurisdiction of 363 district central cooperative banks and 28 state cooperative development banks at the end of March, 1996, there were 733 primary land development banks (PLDBs) and 19 SLDBs engaged in the long-term operations. NABARD is rendering refinance and technical advice to cooperatives.

The multi-agency approach to rural credit has been evolved to incorporate demand-following and supply-leading finance. It has been in operation for a fairly long period and is evaluated from different perspectives leading to conflicting conclusions. Often it is assessed in terms of breaking into new frontiers with an outreach and access to hitherto neglected groups and regions and sectors of productive activity achieving the respective targets. The emphasis is on the needs and interests of the borrower with an utter neglect of the motivating factors underlying lending activity. This is in contrast with the emphasis laid on the supply side of the labour market. However, since the mid-eighties and especially after 1991, the perspective has changed to the supply side of the credit market. The financial sector reforms attempt to transform the credit units. In otherwords, the built-in ex-inefficiency is sought to be reduced if not altogether eliminated.

4. Directed Lending

Directed lending is an important feature of regulated rural financial system under the control of the Central bank and the government. The cooperative banking more so in the sphere of agriculture has been subjected to a regime of controls that the basic principles of cooperation are hardly found in practice in India. As mentioned earlier short-term cooperative credit is administered through a three-tier system, with PACS at the base, the CCBs at the intermediate rung and SCDBs at the apex. Cooperation is a state subject and is governed by the cooperative enactments of each state. But from the financial angle, the NABARD is the apex organization at the national level as it is the refinancing and promotional agency of cooperative credit organizations. Therefore, the cooperative credit structure resembles the four-fold caste structure of Hindu society. Both are segmented, hierarchical and pyramidical. The cooperative credit structure is interconnected through a two-way flow of funds - the larger flow of funds going downwards from higher financing agencies to lower lending agencies. The reverse is the case with the caste structure. This analogy cannot and need not be stretched further lest it should become irrelevant. The financial dependence of base level institutions deprives them of their independence with regard to allocation of credit because of the directions that accompany the downward flow of funds at all levels including the multi-lateral financial institutions at the global level. Only members of the PACS are entitled to borrow from it. But during 1994-95 hardly 18 per cent of members are borrowers. Most of the loans are short-term. The share of weaker sections comprising tenant cultivators, agricultural labourers and others was 6 per cent in accounts (borrowers) and 4 per cent in amount borrowed during 1994-95. the Farmers Service Societies (FSS) initiated in 1975 are intended to cater to the credit needs of small and marginal farmers providing integrated credit supply services and technical guidance. The Large-sized Multi-Purpose Societies (LAMPS) are intended to render credit-linked services to the people of tribal and hill areas.

The allocation of credit from commercial banks to agriculture and allied activities has shown a significant improvement since 1969. Throughout the period of pre-nationalisation (1951-1968) agriculture received a very low proportion, a little more than 2 per cent of total commercial bank credit. The introduction of the concept of priority sector lending broadly coincided with the act of nationalization of 14 banks. The priority sector, consists of agriculture, small scale industry and a few other activities. Exports are treated as a separate category. Targets of priority sector credit are fixed and revised from time to time. The target stands at 40 per cent since 1985. sub-targets were also fixed; 18 per cent for agriculture and 10 per cent for weaker sections. These targets were over fulfilled by the commercial banks as well as the cooperative banks in the initial stages. Of the total scheduled commercial banks credit priority sector proportion went up from 15 per cent in 1969 to 42 per cent in 1999. More than 80 per cent of it is direct finance.

IRDP is the most important programme of poverty alleviation in the rural sector. Since its inception 52 million families have been assisted till March 1998. A sum of Rs. 20,324 crore was mobilized from banks as credit to the beneficiary units, the target groups are Scheduled Castes/Tribes, agricultural labourers, rural artisans, marginal and small farmers. Targets in terms of coverage of beneficiaries and volume of credit disbursed were more than met in most of the years. Under IRDP, a special scheme known as DWACRA has recorded phenomenal progress both in quantitative and qualitative terms.

5. Subsidised Credit

Directed lending and subsidized credit are two sides of the same coin and therefore go hand in hand. Policy makers put forth a variety of arguments to justify subsidized credit. The rationale of these arguments – eight in number – (1) the usury argument (2) high income countries charging low rates, (3) lenders getting cheap money (4) lender viability, (5) farmer behaviour (6) income transfer mechanism, (7) high interest rates being inflationary and (8) the second best argument – is being questioned among others by Dale. W. Adams. The reality is that it is much easier for the politician to expand the supply of cheap credit than to undertake land reform, get new agricultural technology adopted, build and maintain rural roads, install new power, irrigation and drainage systems and ensure universal literacy and health care. Therefore, politicians find that intrusions into rural financial markets are irresistible. Political opponents of the regime also find it difficult to attack such efforts as they are often regarded as criticism of the activity or persons for whom credit is provided. The social and economic costs of low rates of interest are generally hidden and poorly understood that cheap credit often appears to be an exception to the rule that there is no free lunch. Those who benefit from cheap credit develop a vested interest in its perpetuation and therefore there is a much less chance for reform in the installation of flexible nominal rates of interest that result in stable and positive real rates of interest.

6. Changing Perspectives and Assumptions

The assumptions and perspectives of directed lending at concessional rates of interest by the formal institutions are in a state of flux. The Narasimham panel on banking sector reforms (1998) concluded that "the large number of unremunerative branches and directed lending as proximate causes for the high level of non-performing assets and low profitability of the banking industry". The traditional view that credit, like fertilizer, is an input in farm production is called into question. It is pointed out that a loan is not an input because its fungibility gives the borrower command over any good or service that can be purchased. In other words, it provides additional liquidity to the borrowers. It is, therefore, more appropriate to view credit as a product of financial intermediation. Additionality, substitution and diversion are the terms that define some of the problems fungibility poses for credit projects according to Von Pischke and D.W. Adams. Additionality is the situation of difference with project finance. Diversion is an extreme form of substitution and is ubiquitous in institutional credit and cannot be checked with the best of supervisory mechanisms. The modern theory and its assumptions are not difficult to understand. The difficulty lies in escaping from old theory and its assumptions as JM Keynes remarked in his General Theory (1936). The traditional theory and its assumptions are rooted in outmoded dogmas of a bygone age and sanctified by the custom and convention of a traditional society but not by economic logic relevant to a modern economy.

7. Iron Law of Interest Rate Restrictions

State regulation of rates of interest like that of wage rates is not of recent origin. The regulation of interest rates starts with ceilings and wage rates with the minimum though it is reversible in different contexts. During the colonial era interest rates charged by informal sector agencies were sought to be controlled by legal means. This tradition in addition to direct intervention in the fixation of deposit and lending rates of interest continues in one form or the other. A regime of interest rate restriction is an indispensable component of supply-leading finance. But more often than not controlled rates of interest have frequently resulted in consequences opposite to those envisaged and have repressed savings mobilization, retarded financial intermediation and thereby contributed to lower rates of economic growth. C.G.Vega has proposed an Iron law of Interest Rate Restrictions which has a remote resemblance to the Iron Law of wages of the classical school though the operating mechanisms are quite different. According to Vega's law as interest rate ceilings become more restrictive, the size of the loan granted to rationed small borrowers decreases. This results in a redistribution of loan portfolios in favour of bigger borrowers. Through these mechanisms interest rate ceilings have been an important determinant of limited access to institutional credit and high degree of concentration of loan portfolios that characterize rural financial markets. It has been estimated that on an average only 15 per cent of farmers in Asia and Latin America and hardly 5 per cent in Africa had access to institutional credit; about 20 per cent of borrowers have received 80 per cent of credit disbursed. A recent empirical investigation in Hugly district of West Bengal corroborates this tendency where the access to bank credit by farm size was as skewed as that of land and 15 per cent of top households mopped up 50 per cent of bank credit. The distribution of cooperative credit was found to be less uneven though per capita credit was positively correlated with landholdings.

Institutional credit rationing takes two forms according to Von Pischke: (1) Intensive and (2) Extensive. The former involves lending to a relatively small target group and providing its members large amounts of credit. It is a case of supply-leading finance par excellence as in the case of term loans of development banks including PLDBs. Extensive rationing is intended to provide credit access to a large number of farmers in broad target groups. It implies a wider coverage of borrowers with relatively small loans as in the case of RRBs. Either form of rationing by political criteria easily leads to poor loan discipline which includes delinquency, deceit, corruption and thereby sowing the seeds of its own financial destruction.

8. Effects of Low Rates of Interest

The low nominal rates of interest and their adverse effects on savings, borrowing and formal financial institutions are often inadequately understood. The distinction between nominal and real rates of interest is also rarely drawn. In the face of the Latin American rate of inflation low nominal rates of interest often become negative real rates of interest undermining the incentives to save and encouraging the propensity to consume pushing forward the inflationary expectations. Low and nominal rates of interest tend to benefit borrowers at the cost of savers and raising ex-inefficiency of financial institutions.

Interest rate restrictions through their effects on the distribution of credit among rationed and non-rationed borrowers of heterogeneous character aggravates the unequal distribution of wealth and income. This result is due to (1) profits received by large borrowers as a consequence of increased command over resources permitted by loans (2) transfer of income implicit in under-priced credit and (3) resource transfer implicit in partial or total default. Thus, efficiency in the allocation of resources, inducement to save and invest in financial assets, an equitable distribution of wealth and income and viability of financial institutions are adversely affected by the regime of controls over nominal rates of interest and call for deregulation and liberalisation of interest rates and directed credit operations.

9. Structural Changes and Operational Pitfalls

The relative share of institutional sources of credit of the rural households in total cash debts rose steeply from 7.1 in 1951-52 to 61.2 per cent in 1981-82. We do not have the figure for the share of institutional credit for the recent period and therefore it is presumed that the same position is valid even for the recent period. On this presumption we may safely conclude that this structural change in the rural credit delivery system has considerably reduced the stranglehold of the rural trinity namely the landlord, moneylender and the trader. All the formal institutions have contributed their mite towards this sustained expansion as a substitute and complement to informal sector credit. In this process the formal institutions have been confronted with several problems undermining their viability and very existence.

Of the 363 central cooperative banks only 171 were found to be operating with profits towards the end of March, 1996. Their overdues at Rs. 4835 crore constituted 31 per cent of the demand. Only 52 per cent of PACS had been identified as viable. Overdues of PACS at Rs. 4455 crores constituted 33 per cent of demand at the end of march 1996, during 1995-96 only 44 out of 196 RRBs had made profits. The remaining 152 RRBs have sustained losses aggregating to Rs. 468 crores. The proportion of overdues of RRBs has shown a declining trend in 1990s from 60 per cent 1992 to 39 per cent in 1996. The comparable figures for the commercial banks are 46 and 39 per cent respectively eroding their profitability. The non-performing assets of commercial banks and RRBs constituted 18 and 36 per cent of outstanding advances at the end of March 1997. The level of overdues of LDBs at 50 per cent and 31 per cent of demand in 1992 and 197 is slightly better than commercial banks. Thus, the high level of overdues which are agency-neutral constitute the cancer of the system and needs surgery.

The rapid expansion of the rural branch network has become an instrument for the transfer of savings from the rural to the non-rural sector. The share of deposits and credit of the rural branches increased disproportionately from 6.3 and 3.3 to 14.7 and 11.5 per cent respectively in 1969 and 1997. The difference in the level of deposits and credit i.e., 3.0 and 3.2 percentage points represents the net outflow of funds from the rural to the non-rural banking sector. The C-D ratio of rural braches has declined from 61.2 per cent in March 1990 to 47.3 in

March, 1996. This is yet another proof of the pumping of funds from the rural to the non-rural sector.

PACS have been able to mobilize deposits to the tune of 17 per cent of their working capital. 52 per cent of their funds are from borrowings from higher tiers of the system. This is described as onesided intervention in the financial market. Neglecting deposit mobilization, intervention solely on the lending side tends to fragment rural financial markets further. Credit channels do little to stimulate rural savings (Von Pischke). Onesided intervention goes against traditions of self-help and principles of cooperation. Although the rural branches of commercial banks and RRBs do not encounter onesided intervention, they are faced with a host of operational problems. Among others, high operating costs and non-performing assets are eroding their profitability in the context of administered rates of interest and directed lending.

Unless the cooperatives, RRBs and rural branches of commercial banks learn in terms of mobilisation of resources, lending policies and procedures and recoveries especially from the Bangladesh Grameena Bank and Bank Rakyat Indonesia there is little prospect of their sustainability and vitality in the long-run. Peer monitoring contributes a great deal towards better loan recovery at reduced cost as these experiments have demonstrated. Self-Help Groups (SHGs) have proved to be a success in India as elsewhere and banking is to be attuned to and linked with these groups as in the case of DWACRA (NABARD, 2000-2001).

10. Fragmented Markets

The rural financial market like its counterpart on the labour front is highly fragmented and segmented due to the heterogeneity of lenders, borrowers and intermediating institutions. Imperfect information and moral hazard characterize these segmented markets. These markets are also characterized by monopolistic competition if not by oligopoly and monopoly (Virmani, 1982). Take the case of the institution of money lending which is as old as money itself. The moneylenders are a heterogeneous lot, although they are broadly classified in rural India into two groups namely professional and agriculturist. They are either individual or family enterprises. Their business practices and methods differ between categories and locations. Unlike the cooperatives, they operate mainly with their own funds and charge high rates of interest. Often these rates are described as usurious and exploitative and are supposed to impose a dead-weight burden on the borrowers who are mostly drawn from the weaker sections of society. However, there is a saving grace of moneylenders credit being prompt, flexible and informal. These positive features, not-withstanding the adverse social effects, have contributed to the survival and even flourishing of this institution for centuries. Recent research in India had brought to light that moneylenders do not regularly receive returns that are higher than their opportunity costs. In other words they do not derive monopoly profits. Bouman (1989) points out that valuable services are rendered by moneylenders to borrowers at very nominal costs. These services cannot be provided by formal lenders under any circumstances. He, therefore, calls for a revaluation of the role of informal finance in the process of development as formal lenders can learn much from informal lenders about the strategies for rural financial intermediation. Instead of attempting to destroy informal intermediaries, innovative approaches that build on their strengths are long overdue. Institutional pluralism on the financial front rural or urban is the counterpart of secularism on the national front.

Interlinkage of credit market with input and output agricultural markets is a characteristic feature of backward agricultue (K. Basu 1984). It is very much evident in areas undergoing transformation of traditional agriculture as in the case of Karnataka and Andhra Pradesh. Cotton farmers suicides in these states have brought to light the interpenetration of credit with other markets. The trader class which deals with seed, fertilizer and pesticides supply short-term loans under conditions that inputs worth Rs. 1000 need to be bought at Rs. 1200 if payment is made after harvest. Apparently there is a nominal rate or no rate of interest being charged. Also the inputs sold are often adulterated leading to low productivity besides the operation of other uncontrollable risks in crop production, storage and marketing: under such circumstances, the policy stance must be focused on curbing adulteration and unfair trade practices in agricultural marketing besides credit access through the institutional credit and crop insurance.

11. Concluding Remarks

A market-friendly approach to rural credit delivery must reconcile the conflicting interests of lenders and borrowers and ensure the sustainability, viability and vitality of the formal financial institutions. Directed lending like planning by direction has proved to be a failure in ensuring efficiency of the institutional system and allocation of scarce resources and ensuring equity in their distribution. Therefore, reform of this system poses a formidable challenge for all the participants in the system including the state. But what about the non-participants in rural financial market? Their interests are to be safeguarded through fiscal measures like direct subsides and negative tax payments. There is, therefore, a strong case for enlarging the role of the market in the sphere of rural finance and curbing the role of the state. This is what is happening in India under the regime of new economic policy. But the pace is to be accelerated to reduce misallocation of scarce resources, ensure growth with equity leading to reduction in mass poverty.

REFERENCES

1. Pranab Bardhan (Ed) (1989): The Economic Theory of Agrarian Institutions, clarendon press, Oxford.

2. Keith Griffin (1979): The political Economy of Agrarian Change, Macmillan, London.

3. Dale W. Adams, (1986): Rural Financial Markets-cases; The FAO Review, Jan-Feb 15-18.

4. Von Pischke, J-D, Adams D.W, Donalds. G, (1983): Rural Financial Markets in Developing Countries Baltimore, John Hopkins University Press, London.

5. K.G. Karmarkar, (1999): Rural Credit and Self-Help Groups, Micro-finance needs and concepts in India, Sage, New Delhi.

6. J.M. Keynes, 1936, The General Theory of Employment, Interest and Money, Macmillan, London.

7. Bouman, F.J.A (1989): Small, Short and Unsecured Informal Rural Finance in India, Oxford University Press, New Delhi.

8. Rangarajan, C 1998 Indian Economy, Essays on Money and Finance, UBS Publishers, and Distributors Ltd, New Delhi.

9. Aravinda Virmani (1982): The Nature of credit Markets in Developing countries A Framework for policy Analysis World Bank, Washington, D.C.

10. Basu, K. (1984a): The Less Developed Economy: A critique of Contemprary Theory, Oxford: Basil black well.

11. NABARD (2000-2001): Annual Report, Mumbai.

9

Static and Dynamic Gains of Micro-Finance:

An Empirical Study

Dr. N. Sugayya

1. Introduction

The bourgeoning literature on bank finance and its impact on farm economy cannot be easily covered. No attempt is made here to undertake even a highly selective coverage. However, the literature may be broadly classified into two schools of thought. The first school is based on neo-classical model and naturally emphasises the role of market mechanism and decries the intervention of state in allocation and direction of credit. The World Bank's approach is guided by this line of thinking. The other school of thought derives its inspiration from market failure argument and advocates state intervention to safeguard the interests of deprived groups like small farmers with less access to credit in the organised market. India's credit planning model is based on the second school of thought and that is why in the late sixties major banks have been nationalised and several directed credit programmes have been launched. But of late, there is a rethinking on the basis of past experience and lessons drawn from all over the developing world regarding the abuse of such programmes (Von pichke ed. at, 1983). A high rate of overdues, among others, has become a stumbling block in the management of rural credit delivery system, which has been transformed beyond recognition in India under the regime of development planning (RBI, 1991). An attempt is made in this paper to examine the impact of bank finance on the farm sector with special reference to the field investigation in Chittoor district of A.P.

2. Changed Banking Scenario in Chittoor District

Chittoor district has a population of 37.35 lakhs (provisional as per 2001 census). Its sex ratio is 966 and density is 215 per sq.Km. Rural population accounts for 78.3 per cent. There are three revenue divisions, 66 mandals, 5 muncipalities, 1366 gram Panchayats. It lies on the southern most part of the State and one of the 4 districts which together comprise Rayalaseema region, one of the less developed regions of the State of Andhra Pradesh. The selection of chittoor district is dictated by considerations of familiarity and proximity. The selection of mandals and sample households was random, systematic and strafied respectively. A pretested, structured schedule was canvassed among the respondents besides meeting the concerned officials, bankers and village elders and other stakeholders.

Just as in the country, there has been a structural change in the agricultural credit delivery system in Chittoor district. The Chittoor District Co-operative Central Bank (CDCCB) with its network of 9 branches, 174 Primary Agricultural Credit Societies has vastly expanded its credit operations. The commercial banking system including Sri Venkateswara Grameena Bank, which is the Regional Rural Bank of the district has been widely expanded and the annual action plan of the district covers almost all sectors by all the banking institutions including the CDCCB. The Credit-Deposit (CD) ratios and priority sector advances and recovery situation are broadly in conformity with that of the national situation and the additionality has a visible and invisible effect on the credit market and its linkages with other markets. Our purpose is to explore some of the effects classified into static and dynamic gains accruing to our 172 samples situated at KGP, KKN and GVP in Yerravaripalem, Gangadhara Nellore and Pulicherla mandals of Madanapalli, Chittoor and Tirupati revenue divisions of Chittoor District in Andhra Pradesh, the fifth largest State of India.

3. Objectives and Hypotheses of the Study

The specific objectives of the study are:

1. to examine the impact of bank intervention on the interest rate structure;
2. to assess the static gains;
3. to evaluate dynamic gains to bank finance to the borrower households; and
4. to examine the structure of credit market in terms of its interlinkages.

Hypotheses

Based on the above objectives, the following hypotheses have been formulated and tested in the present study.

1. There is no significant change in the structure of interest rates consequent upon bank intervention.
2. The static gains are not significant and evenly distributed.
3. There is no significant variation in the impact of bank finance on income and employment generation across different size groups

4. There is no significant change in the linkages between credit and other markets due to the flow of bank credit.

4. Static Gains

The gains from bank finance to borrowers may be divided into static and dynamic gains. There are a variety of definitions and interpretations of economic statics and dynamics (JR Hicks 1937). One of the most widely used concepts of statics and dynamics is that the former is concerned with equilibrium and the latter with disequilibrium and change (Gardner Ackly 1985). The former involves a cross sectional analysis as well as the shift of the economic variables from an initial equilibrium to a new equilibrium in which case it becomes a matter of comparative statics. The latter method involves a time series analysis that traces the movement of the economic variables between one equilibrium position and another. In other words it is concerned with the path rather than the destination itself. Generally speaking an equilibrium is a situation in which each individual agent is doing as well as it can for itself, given the array of actions taken by others and given the institutional framework that defines the options of individuals and links their actions (Kreps DM 1992). The static gains of bank finance pertain to its impact on the structure of interest rates and the benefit derived by the borrowers due to low rates of interest charged by the banks. There is an element of subsidy in the borrowings from the banking system and this also confers a static benefit on the borrowers. Overdues to the banking system have become an important feature of the rural credit delivery system and borrowers benefit at the expense of banking system. In the case of dynamic gains a host of variables appear on the stage and undergo a change due to bank financing. These variables are generally restricted to assets, liabilities, employment and income generation. These are taken up

Table–1. Differences in interest rates in sample villages 1994-95

(Per Cent)

S. No		*Difference of Interest Rate between Bank and Others at*											
		KGP				*KKN*				*GVP*			
		M	*S*	*Me*	*L*	*M*	*S*	*Me*	*L*	*M*	*S*	*Me*	*L*
1.	Co-operatives	2	2	1	0	2	2	1	0	2	21	0	0
2.	Money Lenders	26	18	9	3	38	30	21	14	32	24	15	6
3.	Traders and Commission Agents	22	20	6	0	14	9	3	0	26	18	13	6
4.	Land Lords	14	9	3	0	22	12	6	0	20	16	9	3
5.	Friends and Relatives	18	12	9	3	20	16	9	3	20	16	13	6
6.	Others	26	20	13	6	26	-	9	3	26	18	13	6

Code

M = Marginal
S = Small
Me = Medium
L = Large

KGP = Kamalaiahgaripalli of Yerravaripalem Mandal, Madanapalli Division.
KKN = Kotrakona of Gangadhara Nellore Mandal Chittoor District.
GVP = Gaddamvaripalli of Pulicherla Mandal Tirupati Division.

Source: Field data

in this paper in order to focus our attention on the static and dynamic gains.

The static gains of additionality of bank credit have been considered in terms of the difference in interest rates, subsidy attached to the loan and default. A summary of these variables is presented in the ensuring sections. We present field data which give summary of the difference of interest rates charged and therefore the advantage derived by the samples in the credit market.

The difference in the rates of interest decreases as farm size increases primarily due to equity oriented farm credit planning. Therefore, the static gain is higher for marginal and small farmers than medium and large farmers. They too gain in terms larger additionality and therefore higher liquidity. Hence, we reject the first part of our second hypothesis that the static gains are insignificant.

The findings in regard to the magnitude of subsidy and default are presented in Table 2 and they are size-neutral, and lead to the rejection of the second part of the second hypothesis that the static gains are evenly distributed.

Table–2. Quantum of Subsidy and Default in Sample Villages

Village	*Category*	*Subsidy as a per cent of loan*	*Overdue to borrowings percentage*
KGP			
	Marginal	45	38
	Small	46	46
	Medium	39	70
	Large	31	54
	All	42	53

KKN			
	Marginal	42	52
	Small	50	70
	Medium	46	60
	Large	55	62
	All	46	60
GVP			
	Marginal	41	45
	Small	47	49
	Medium	41	52
	Large	44	55
	All	43	51
	Total	**44**	**55**

Source: Field data

5. The Dynamic Gains

The dynamic gains from bank credit are analysed in terms of their effect on the selected stocks and flows pertaining to our sample households. The immediate effect of borrowing is on the rise in the liability of the household. It takes sometime to get the asset formed and generate employment and income out of it. We have analysed the dynamic gains to the different categories of formers in Table 3. subsequently, we have regrouped our respondents into two categories namely those that figure under IRDP and those that are not covered i.e., excluded from the perview of IRDP.

The effect of bank credit on the selected stocks and flows of the samples is summarised in Table 3.

The effect of additionality on asset formation and liabilities is significantly different at all villages and for all categories. Credit is the asset of the lending institutions and the liability of the borrowing public and credit is a much broader category than bank credit although we have restricted our scope to bank credit in this context. The differential effect on assets and liabilities is due to the time lag involved in asset creation. The income effect is significantly higher than the employment effect and the latter is inversely related to farm size but not the farmer. Therefore, additionality has a differential effect on the dynamic gains of our samples.

Table–3. Effect of Additionality on Assets, Liabilities, Income and Employment in Sample Villages (1994-95)

(Per Cent)

Village	*Category*	*Assets*	*Liabilities*	*Income*	*Employment*
KGP					
	Marginal	18	30.2	12	12.2
	Small	21	23.9	14	10.2
	Medium	07	19.3	18	6.3
	Large	07	15.5	21	3.6
	All	12	29.7	16	8.5
KKN					
	Marginal	13	28.1	21	7.3
	Small	17	26.4	18	5.8
	Medium	22	15.8	14	5.0
	Large	26	13.0	13	2.8
	All	19	18.6	16	5.5
GVP					
	Marginal	24	21.8	17	4.6
	Small	13	17.1	19	3.6
	Medium	18	13.9	13	3.3
	Large	11	9.5	16	3.0
	All	16	16.5	16	3.6
	Total	16	22.0	16	3.8

Source: Field data

Table–4. Income and Employment Effect on Groups in Sample Villages (1994-95)

(Per Cent)

Village	Category	Group	Income		Employment	
			% variation	Gap	% variation	Gap
KGP						
	Marginal	**IRDP**	16.6	14.4	14.6	6.4
		Non- IRDP	2.2		8.2	
	Small	**IRDP**	21.0	12.8	41.0	9
		Non- IRDP	8.2		32.0	
	Medium	**IRDP**	19.6	2.7	31.0	6.9
		Non- IRDP	16.9		24.1	
	Large	**IRDP**	22.4	3.6	6.2	1.4
		Non- IRDP	19.8		3.8	
	All	**IRDP**	17.9	3.3	24.8	4.4
		Non- IRDP	14.6		20.4	
KKN						
	Marginal	**IRDP**	27.7	10.4	11.2	6.5
		Non- IRDP	17.3		4.7	
	Small	**IRDP**	23.3	10.4	8.1	4.5
		Non- IRDP	12.9		3.6	
	Medium	**IRDP**	15.2	2.7	9.7	7.0
		Non- IRDP	12.5		2.7	
	Large	**IRDP**	14.0	1.7	7.8	6.4
		Non- IRDP	12.3		1.4	
	All	**IRDP**	21.4	8.4	10.5	9.8
		Non- IRDP	13.0		1.7	

GVP					
Marginal	**IRDP**	20.8	8.8	7.6	6.6
	Non- IRDP	12.0		1.0	
Small	**IRDP**	22.7	7.5	5.5	4.1
	Non- IRDP	14.8		1.4	
Medium	**IRDP**	15.4	4.0	5.4	3.9
	Non- IRDP	11.4		1.5	
Large	**IRDP**	17.3	2.5	5.4	4.1
	Non- IRDP	14.8		1.3	
All	**IRDP**	20.4	8.9	5.4	3.8
	Non- IRDP	11.5		1.6	
Total	**IRDP**	19.7	7.2	14.4	5.9
	Non- IRDP	12.5		8.5	

Source: Field data

Table 4 shows, even though obliquely, the differential impact on income and employment on IRDP and Non-IRDP beneficiaries of our samples. It is evident that the gap in the growth of income and employment is inversely correlated with farm size in all the villages. It implies that the dynamic benefits are higher to the lower strata than the higher strata.

6. Segmentation and Interlinkage

The dichotomy, in the credit market is extensively noted in the literature (Gupta, 1995)

The credit market remains highly segmented reinforced by the concentration of land ownership and other resource endowments (K. Griffin 1979, K. Basu 1984). The effect of additionality on rates of interest and other interlinked contracts is portrayed in tables 5 and 6.

Table 5 shows that the fall in the rates of interest rates charged by the three dominant informal credit agencies is inversely correlated with farm size and therefore we reject the hypothesis namely that "there is no significant difference in the structure of interest rates consequent upon bank intervention".

Table 6 indicates that the proportion of diversion is size-neutral. The share of D, R, M and E in diversion is also size-neutral.

Table–5. Difference in Rates of Interest Charged by "Trinty"; 1994-95

(Per Cent)

Village	*Agency*	*Marginal*	*Small*	*Medium*	*Large*	*All*
KGP						
	Moneylenders	-4	-4	-3	-3	-4
	Traders and Commission Agents	-3	-2	-3	0	-3
	Landlords	0	0	0	0	0
KKN						
	Moneylenders	-6	-4	-4	-4	-5
	Traders and Commission Agents	-3	-3	0	0	-3
	Landlords	-4	-3	-3	0	-3
GVP						
	Moneylenders	-6	-4	-2	-3	-4
	Traders and Commission Agents	-4	-4	-4	0	-2
	Landlords	-4	-4	-3	-3	-2

Source: Field data

The share of marketed surplus taken by M, T and L is inversely correlated with farm size in respect of paddy and groundnut but positively related in the case of sugarcane. The share of forced sales as represented by sales at the time of harvest and upon agreed prices is inversely correlated with farm size and has tended to decline marginally compared with the situation before. Hence we partially reject the hypothesis that "credit market inter-linkages do not vary significantly due to the flow of bank credit"

Table–6. Nature and Extent of Diversion and Interlinked Contracts in Sample Villages: 1994-95

(Per Cent)

Village	*Category*	*Percentage of diversion of Bank credit*	*Share of D, R, Ms and E in diversion*	*Share of Marketed surplus by MT and L*			*Share of sales at harvest Time and agreed price to M, T and L*	
				P	*G*	*S*	*B*	*A*
KGP								
	Marginal	35	74	85	78	88	64	59
	Small	31	84	81	75	90	53	47
	Medium	34	71	76	65	91	47	38
	Large	36	83	65	58	95	14	13
	All	34	79	77	69	91	44	39
KKN								
	Marginal	36	75	86	80	85	76	72
	Small	55	73	80	76	89	62	52
	Medium	46	67	78	67	92	58	47
	Large	43	75	67	58	93	13	11
	All	45	72	78	70	90	52	45

GVP							
Marginal	46	80	83	77	87	65	59
Small	47	77	76	73	91	63	54
Medium	54	64	75	63	93	39	36
Large	43	76	64	56	94	14	12
All	48	73	74	67	91	45	40

Source: Field data

Code D = Durables of the household
R = Re-payment of past loans
Ms = Marriages and other social ceremonies
E = Education, health and other services
M = Moneylenders
T = Traders and Commission Agents
L = Landlords
P = Paddy
G = Groundnut
S = Sugarcane
B = Before
A = After

7. Policy Implications of the Study

The foregoing findings of micro-level investigation have several implications for the design and formulation of micro-finance projects in the farm sector. Despite the persistence of top-down bureaucratic process in the administration of micro finance by the commercial banks, the static and dynamic benefits are quite visible and tend to benefit the hitherto disadvantaged sections and vulnerable groups of the rural economy. The benefits accruing to those covered under IRDP are higher than those not covered by IRDP and there is a pro-poor bias built into the credit system and it needs to be strengthened, if the fight against extreme poverty is to be a success. Micro-finance as an instrument of fighting poverty has come of age and international micro-credit summits are regularly held for dissemination of knowledge and replication of successful experiments like that of Grameen Bank of Bangladesh.

REFERENCES

1. Von Pischke JD et.al (1983): Rural financial Markets in Developing Countries: Their Use and Abuse, The John Hopkins University Press LTD, London.
2. RBI, (1991) Report of the Committee on the Financial System, Bombay.
3. J.R. Hicks, (1937): Value and Capital. Oxford University Press (OUP), London.
4. Gardner Ackly, (1985): Macro Economic Theory, Prentice, Hall of India Private Limited, New York.
5. David M. Kreps, (1992): A course in Microeconomic Theory, Prentice, Hall of India Private Limited, New Delhi.
6. Suraj B. Gupta (1995): Monetary Economics Institutions Theory and Policy, S. Chand and Company Limited, New Delhi.
7. Keith Griffin, 1979: The Political Economy of Agrarian Change, Macmillan, London.
8. Kaushik Basu, (1984): The Less Developed Economy, Oxford University Press, Delhi.

10

People's Participatory Forest Management:

*The VSS**

V. Reddappa Reddy

Introduction

The Joint Forest Management (JFM) was initiated on a larger geographical canvass in India aiming at protection, rejuvenation and development of forest. The programme envisages people's partnership in forest management. This is against the earlier thrust of forest 'policing', which believed people as destructors of forest. Impact of similar people oriented forest development programmes of Bangladesh and Nepal, however, did not show any significant positive results. The Community Forest Programme of India, initiated in early 1980s with a component for people's support and participation, too had a high failure rate. Thus the pronounced problem is that, the programme stands on an untested foundation of people's participation. The dearth of literature explaining

* Published in Asia-Pacific Journal of Rural Development, December, 1999.

the impact of participation in forest management calls for detailed discussion on JFM to provide feed back on its working, understand the problems in its implementation and help in moulding the future policies. Such discussion may help in the generation of literature on emerging patterns of people participation in development, protection, sustenance and sharing of other common property resources. Discussion on this subject may also add to the literature on changing dynamics of rural leadership.

The paper is primarily based upon the experiences in participatory rural appraisal, field observations and evolution of the programme. The present paper is designed to delineate the important emerging issues and identify the areas of immediate concern. The main objectives of the paper are: (1) to trace the history and background of people's participation in forest management, (2) to examine the mechanism of JFM, (3) to review the available literature on JFM and (4) to explore the emerging issues in the adoption of JFM in India. The paper is presented in three sections. Section I deals with genesis and mechanism of JFM. The available literature has been reviewed under Section II so as to delineate the emerging issues. Section III deals the issues of immediate concern.

I

Poverty and Forests: The Controversy

Poverty and poor were considered as enemies of healthy forests. The reasons for such a stand, however, do not stand the scrutiny. In fact, richer sections are responsible for higher rate of forest degradation as compared to poor and vulnerable groups. The following discussion proves the issue without an iota of doubt.

Railways and naval ships used a significant amount of wood in their laying and construction respectively. The pulp and paper industry causes the cutting of healthy and heavy trees on a larger scale as compared to the tree used by poorer sections for household purposes. Blaming the poor for the use of wood in railways, in the making of ships and use in pulp and paper industry will not stand any rationale test.

The wood used by richer sections for their palatial buildings and big houses was much more than the wood used by poorer sections in the construction of their small and, mostly, thatched houses. The rich use mostly teak and *sal* and other fine varieties of trees; whereas poor use only substandard and minor trees in house construction. The implements and equipment necessary for cutting the forest trees on mass scale are not owned by poorer sections but by richer sections. Further, it is these richer sections alone that are capable of both legally and illegally transporting the wood to urban areas so as to become big and fat.

The poor were also blamed for cutting the trees. In fact they are only labourers cutting the trees for the use of richer sections. The poor work in forests only to earn a livelihood rather than with the intention of cutting and destroying the forests and make profits from tree cutting and selling of wood. If alternative employment and income opportunities were available, the poor would not have ventured into the forests.

The poor were also blamed for cultivating the forest fringe areas. The fact is these lands were given to poor in the process of poverty eradication and as a mechanism of reduction of inequalities in land ownership between rich and poor of rural areas. The lands handed over were given only as *D-Form pattas*. These are only marginal lands not giving any significant productivity and most of these lands are already in the hands of richer sections. In this context, it is noteworthy to point out that, the lands used by industrial houses and large private farms were also causing significant reduction of forests. But for reasons of beyond comprehension, this aspect was ignored while blaming the poor for forest destruction. Poor, especially Scheduled Tribes, were blamed for cutting the forests and practicing *jhum* (shifting) cultivation. For growing the food alone they were cutting the trees and cultivating the lands. At present such shifting cultivation is totally banned in India. Though this practice is banned no alternative sources of employment and income are shown to these sections. The temporary measures in this regard are failing the poor in their fight against poverty and hunger.

All these erroneous conceptions led to keeping the poor outside the forest management for pretty long time. Only the introduction of JFM programme during the late 1980s has helped in promoting the poor as partners of forest management.

Genesis of Joint Forest Management

Information on systematic forest management in India could be traced back to British period. The forest management has undergone a metamorphosis during that period. For a period of 120 years, i.e., between 1750 and 1870, forest management was confined to the harvest of the largest sizes of the best species viz., teak and *sal*. And natural regeneration was assumed during the period. During the next 50 years, ending with 1920, forest management comprised of merciless removal of all growth interfering with teak and *sal*. The principle followed was 'selection cum improvement and sustained yield of the desired species and sizes'. The forest management treated all other miscellaneous trees and species as weeds, on which tribal families depended for their survival; implying neglect of people. During the World War II, forests were fully exploited and forest management suffered the most.

After Independence too, forest management was battered due to unhealthy 'forest policing' practices. All along this significant history of forest management, the people were neglected and were treated as manifestating agents of forest destructors. Such commercial forest management and its objectives of clear-cutting system, sustainable timber production, forest preservation and practicing of forestry in isolation, coupled with neglect of people, has miserably failed the forests and proved detrimental to sustainability (Shah 1994: 472-4). All this mismanagement and the resultant dangers of ecological imbalance have called for reassessing the 'organic-linkage' between people and forests, and JFM sought to restore that relationship.

People's participation was not uncommon in forest management in India and in other South-Asian countries. Social Forestry Programmes of India, Community Forestry Programme of Nepal and Community Forestry Project of Bangladesh have been the major interventions that provided scope for people's participation in forest management. These programmes, however, were meant to develop forestry outside the conventional forests. At micro-level too, important examples can be traced from the recent past. A temple priest managed the *'Devara Kadus'* jungle with the help of local people in Coorg district of Karnataka (Gupta 1997: 572). The *Kumaun* forests in Uttaranchal region of India were brought under *Vana Panchayats* in 1931. The *Vana Panchayats* of the local villages were left to manage their own forests (Mishra 1997: 568). Based on Punjab Forest Commission recommendations, Cooperative Forest Societies were formed to manage and develop forests in Kangra district during 1937-38 (Sharma 1997:537). In Bihar large chunks of workable forests were transferred to people for management and protection during 1958 and 1959 (Gupta 1997: 573). The greatest watershed in people's participation in forest management, however, comes from the success story of 'Arabari' experiment in Midnapore district in West Bengal: made possible by few dynamic forest officials. The other stimuli were provided by the success stories of forest protection and management by people of Olgapur in Karimnagar district in Andhra Pradesh; and the role played by Forest Protection Committees in protecting forests in Kudada of East Singhbhum district in Bihar. The forest protection movements such as *'Chipko'* and *'Appiko'* in the Himalayan ranges have provided the final fillip for the programme (Venkati Madari 1997: 62, Roy 1997: 524 and Bina Agarwal 1997:62). By 1998, 20 States in India were implementing the JFM programme (Suresh Prabhu 1998:vii).

Joint Forest Management Explained

The JFM is a strategy that does not transfer the ownership of forests from State to local communities; but organizes forest management with people's participation in limited forest tracts. Restructuring the forms of access and handing over the instruments of 'forest-control' to the nearby villages would accomplish this (Ford Foundation 1990 and Poffenberger 1990). The programme is an intervention to evolve organized and collective thinking of local communities on the issues of forest management. All the ingredients of a sound management system i.e., scientific and professional options, social and anthropological dimensions and economic principles are synergised, for drawing maximum benefits for the community. The programme involves people in resource generation through motivation, active involvement in management and sharing of benefits from forest through institutional arrangements. It further aims at the conversion of a hostile population living in the fringes of forest areas as friends, and ultimately into forest resource managers and resource users (Bahuguna 1997:473). Based upon the above explanation the following inherent assumptions could be delineated from the JFM programme.

- Forest department is failing to manage forests;
- People would like to exclude bureaucratic control on forests;
- Community participation in the management of common property resources, especially forests, is essential;
- Forest cannot be regenerated on its own and intervention from the local community is essential;
- Local community is having better skills and stake in sustainable use of forest;
- People should have a stake in the formulation of 'Micro-Plans' that were prepared aiming at forest development and village development;
- All the sections of the society should be represented in the village bodies managing forests;
- People's participation remains half of the full representation in the absence of women;
- The community funds can raise the quality of rural life;
- The JFM can generate mutual respect between foresters and people; and
- Benefit sharing in JFM will be feasible in the long run too (Gopa Pandey 1997: 530).

Mechanisms of Joint Forest Management

Since the mechanics of JFM has no common set of rules for all, each of the States is adopting is own practices; depending on local conditions. However, the main framework has been more or less the same. Under

JFM programme, initially, forest staff will establish a working relationship with the community (or village) adjacent to degraded natural forests. People of the community are explained the concept of JFM and its working; so as to motivate the people to protect and develop the forest. The local Non Governmental Organizations (NGOs) are also activated for the purpose. Later the villagers are requested and helped to form into a Village Forest Committee (VFC). Members of the VFC consist of one member each from all the households of the village. The VFC elects a President, Secretary and Executive in a democratic manner to help the running of its day-to-day activities.

The VFC and the forest staff prepare a working document called 'Micro-Plan' jointly. Local available NGOs would also be involved in the Plan preparation. The forest department approves this Micro-Plan and requisite funds would be kept at the disposal of the VFC. Care is taken to identify the immediate needs of the forest and people, ranking priorities, available funds, etc. by conducting a Participatory Rural Appraisal (PRA). The Micro-Plan primarily covers measures that help eco-regeneration. They include soil and water conservation measures, new plantations and fire protection. The needy would be provided employment and income through activities like construction of check dams, digging of contour trenches, bush clearing, singling, pit digging, plantation, fire protection and raising of fodder undertaken in forest.

The usufructs like grass, forest fruits and singling waste and *'tendu'* leaves will be shared among the VFC members. In the long run, when forest becomes self-sustainable, the share of the VFC is expected to improve multifold. The VFC is empowered to fine and take action against the culprits of the forest. All these imply that the entire success of the VFC depends on the complete participation of all members of the community.

The community is provided with a 'Village Development Fund' as an incentive to sustain the people's interest in JFM. The villagers were to utilize this fund to meet the community's immediate requirements, such as, repairs to water source, road, school and community building. To conserve fuel wood: use of smokeless *chullas,* bio-gas plants and solar cookers would be encouraged and in some instances they were supplied at subsidized rates. The women groups and self-help groups are formed to help improve the living standards of the community.

II

Issues Already Dealt in Literature

The development practitioners, world over, are constantly championing people's participation in the implementation of development projects more and more in recent years. The loan and aid giving agencies are also advocating people's participation as a precondition for assisting the development programme (UNDP 1993 and World Bank 1991). Most of the advocates of people's participation are said to have depended, often, on the results of case studies that link between performance of specific projects and people's and people's participation (Briscoe and de Ferranti 1988, Kortan and Siy 1988 and Narayanan 1995). The available literature points out the successful implementation developmental programmes with people's participation. Some recent studies also established a link between the better performance of the programmes and people's participation, based on subjective data available on large number of projects (Isham, Narayan and Pritchet 1995.) The programmes in India have also been successful when the users are actively involved in the overall system management and the system is given greater administrative and functional autonomy (Vaidyanathan 1994: 2967).

However, such a positive relation was observed mostly in irrigation programmes and no significant research was undertaken to understand the role of people's participation in the successful implementation of other developmental programmes, especially forestry.

The practice of people's participation in forest management and protection was of recent origin and the results have not been in uniformity. While macro level studies reported a dismal failure the micro and location specific level studies reported a positive scenario, and at times, extra ordinary. The macro level studies show that, the role of people in forest management programme was very little and people's opinion and participation were mostly overruled. And many a time, absence of suitable institutional mechanisms led to the failure of programme. For example, Community Forestry Scheme of India had a high failure rate in the early 1980s in the absence of effective institutional mechanism to ensure village participation in decision making and equitable distribution of costs and benefits (Bina Agrawal 1997: 6). Likewise, through Community Forest Project, Government of Bangladesh willed and planned for the people's involvement as 'users group' in forest management, but it proved ineffective (Task Force 1987). The people's participation in forest management in Bangladesh was said to be 'low' and was confined to the role of wage labourers and hired guards (Rahman 1992).

In Nepal too, people have rarely participated in any major planning decisions for forest management and regeneration, It was reported that the VFCs meant for forest management were largely ineffective, unrepresentative and had virtually no control over the local affairs (Hobley 1991).

The results at State level are no better in India. The planning pattern of forestry development programme in West Bengal has been essentially top down. The inflexible bureaucratic regulations provided little or virtually no room for accommodating local popular demands and specific contextual peculiarities (WBFD 1989). The people's participation in forest programme in the State was mostly limited to wage labour contribution, part time employment and membership in VFCs. Even worse, majority of the Scheduled Castes and women were unaware of the programme in all its components (Arnold et al 1987). The Evaluation Team of Social Forestry Project in Bihar also reported the failure of the mechanism of people's participation in forest management. The Team further noted that, VFCs are 'less representative' of people and mostly confined to fit bureaucratic purpose (Anold et al 1990) The story in Karnataka is no better. People's participation was confined to just men and women were ignored. The Staff of forest department mostly manipulates the elections to the Executives of the VFCs either directly or indirectly. Some people are of the opinion that the JFM programme is merely a way of passing on some of the responsibilities of forest department to the villagers (Marie Correa 1996: 1383-4).

Compared to the negative face observed in macro level studies, the results at micro and case study level are positive. When the forest got under the wings of local people, they are providing a protective 'human-fence. Such an effort would automatically give relief to JFM adopted patches from stresses such as cutting, grazing and burning. These positive results are observed in many case studies conducted at VFC specific areas; but the results, however, are mostly disjointed.

Commenting on the positive side of people's participation, Hague points out that, participation helps the people to take part in deciding how nature should be treated (1985:164). The people' participation could be either self-initiated or formed through external stimuli (Roy 1997: 519). Many case studies have revealed that people are willingly participating in forest management

(Hague 1985; Malhotra and profenberger 1989; Gupta 1997; Muralidharudu, Reddy and Govindappa 1997; Satish 1997; Shah 1997; Upadhyay 1997). Regarding the motivational levels, people were rarely found wanting. It is said that in the initial years forest department had to go to the villages in Andhra Pradesh to motivate the people to form VFCs. But. now, after seeing the advantages of the programme, the JFM adjoining villagers are demanding the formation of VFCs in their villages to take up forest protection in new areas (Mukherji 1997:49).

Regarding impact, the findings are that, active participation by small farmers and landless people reversed the deforestation (Spith 1985:161) and few families who were earlier depended on selling firewood, brought from forests as a means of livelihood, have stopped its selling (Adinarayana 1997:7). People's participation helped in improving the health of the forests (Malhotra and Poffenberger 1989) and in stopping the smuggling of the forest goods (Adinarayana 1997: 6: Mukherji 1997: 47). People's participation also helped the forest department in vacating the encroached forestlands and no further·encroachment of reserve forests was allowed (Mukherji 1997: 47). Gupta estimated that the JFM has helped the forest department in freeing 28.3 per cent of the encroached forest area in Garhwa South Forest Division of Bihar (1997: 567).

It was reported that, when people are participating in developing and conserving forests exemplary results are achieved in natural regeneration and this also helped the growth of secondary forest (Muralidharudu, Reddy and Govindappa 1997: Satish 1997). The degraded forests with viable rootstocks have responded favourably to tending in the JFM adopted areas in Andhra Pradesh (Mukherji 1997: 464). The World Bank Team after completing its survey of JFM in Andhra Pradesh concluded that, wherever plantations are raised with the people's participation the survival rate was higher as compared to departmental plantations (Mukherji 1997:48).

The other findings of relevance on impact are as follows. People's participation helped in management and protection of workable forestlands and people benefited with a share in the annual coupe returns, and the 'mutual dependency' helped both forest and people (Gupta 1997: 572). People's participation helped in the better performance of JFM and relatively high returns are achieved (Shah 1997: 475). Increase in grass yield was made possible even in chronically drought-affected areas (Mukherji 1997: 48). The Programmes for forest development in a planned manner helped the generation of additional employment and income and this helped in arresting the dependency of poor on forests. Expenditure on village development activities helped in providing few facilities to the participating community. The women members of the VFCs are able to fight again alcoholism. And, JFM also helped in the formation of self-help groups (Adinarayana 1997: 8).

As could be observed from the review above, the VFC unit level case studies reported success of JFM. And, in contrast, a high rate of failure was reported when studies were conducted at macro-level. Several reasons could be cited for this variance. Important successes may have been achieved in few specific micro-units of JFM and the situations were different at every other place. A contrasting situation prevailing in two geographically adjacent areas viz., *Arabari* and *Arjuri Mouza* in Midnapore district West Bengal, shows it in detail. It was a great success in *Arabari* and a dismal failure in *Arjuri Mouza*. The success of JFM in *Arabari* was total and was considered a model for replication elsewhere. At the same time, the failure in *Arjuri Mouza* was also total. All this failure started in a year of scarcity. The protection helped the wood development in adopted areas of *Arjuri Mouza*. Due to uninterrupted growth for four years, the tree felling became economically viable (Mukherji Neela 1997:551). The subsistence needs of the individuals of *Arjuri Mouza* assumed greater importance than that of long-term community gains from the forest management. Moreover, once started the illicit felling of forest had a demonstrative effect. Which means, opportunities were not missed in using the forest growth for personal ends. It was also pointed out that, the participation succeeded initially but insecurity at some point failed it (Mukherji 1997: 551). The success was said to be due to more person oriented individual efforts. And, in many cases a viable system could not be developed and, as a result, the temporary success faded away with time (Gangophadhaya 1997:446). The studies showing positive results are mostly of case studies. Most of them are taken up either by the 'in-house' personnel of the forest department or being commissioned by it at local level. This is best reflected in the names of majority of authors and their designations. Being the case, possibility of best VFC finding the place as a 'unit of study' is away there. As such the case study results may not reflect the reality.[2]

The review also supports the contention that, people's participation in forest management was still in the process of test and cases of success are considered pilot and demonstrative and, as Khan suggests, they can at best be regarded as exceptions rather than general rule (1994: 354). The next section tries to delineate the important gaps of concern on JFM programme that are left unattended.

III

Issues of Immediate Concern

There are certain issues that are to be addressed immediately. Otherwise the JFM programme is bound to encounter difficulties at different levels of its implementation. The crucial issues are discussed below.

Productive use of loans: The international agencies like World Bank, Asian Development Bank, Overseas Development Administration and Swedish International Development Authority are involved in financing the programme. Though the plan for financing the programme was initially made to be time bound, covering limited geographical area of the country: States are expanding the extent and finances for the programme. A Joint Team from Food and Agricultural Organization (FAO) and National Bank for Agriculture and Rural Development (NABARD) visited Andhra Pradesh to study the bankable projects under JFM, and suggested few new projects (Mukherji (1997:52). Involvement of such agencies would automatically increase the number of VFCs and the amounts spent on the implementation of the programme. These amounts carry a burden of debt to be repaid. Productive use alone justifies such loans. The productive use, or otherwise, of such massive expenditure need to be properly studied in the background of weaknesses in people's participation in forest management.

Appropriate models for different situations: The external agencies involved in financing JFM are putting a condition, to provide for people's participation in JFM, while sanctioning loans/grants. While doing so, the positive relation between better performance of developmental programmes and people's participation was cited. However, the positive relation between people's participation and other developmental programmes cannot be taken as a guiding factor regarding forestry development. In the case of other developmental programmes there is an immediate gain. But in forest development programmes, it takes a pretty long gestation to materialize into any benefit of significance. Again, the VFCs formed for forestry management may not have the coherence to work as a single entity. In the preliminary stages forest management may enjoy all euphoria in the village. This may be due to new concept, new designations available to few people in VFCs, additional employment and income opportunities to poor people. But this euphoria may not last long, and in the long run, the VFCs may end up only as sleeping partners of the programme (Reddy and Reddy 1998: 17). Still more, this benefit is meant for the whole community managing forests rather than to each of the households of the community. Thus, there is very little incentive for the people to participate in the programme. It was further noticed that, when the VFCs are formed with single tribal village, the results are said to be most effective. But the results are poor when VFCs are formed with a group of villages and mixed castes (Malhotra et al 1990: 22-23). All these imply that, the inter-social, economic and political equations of a community are going to decide the rate of people's participation. As such it is of crucial importance to determine the factors that facilitate or retard people's participation in a given situation and evolve appropriate models for different situations.

Women and JFM: Women are severely affected by deforestation and change of forest tree species. Due to this reason, for any form of forest regeneration to be successful, women need to be actively involved at different stages of planning and implementation. However, this 'half' of the community seems to be completely neglected in JFM. This condition, prevalent in Karnataka, was well documented by Maritte Correa (1996). According to her, "In the majority of villages, the opinions of women are unsolicited when making JFM related decisions, but even after the decisions are made the women are not properly informed about these decisions. What is amazing is that in several places women are not only unaware of the origin of the decisions but the very existence of VFC—even when their husbands are members. Often these women have not even seen the area allotted to the VFC for plantation". It is necessary in this context to understand the factors inhibiting women participation and suggest mechanism that helps women to become equal partners in forest management.

Measuring the regeneration: the forest patches adopted under JFM are protected from tree felling, green manure collection, grazing and hunting. Such protection is bound to help improve the rate of natural rejuvenation of forests. The implementation of forest development activities like land reclamation, rain water harvesting, new plantations, fire protection are prohibiting people and cattle from entering the adopted patches are expected to help in natural rejuvenation from old stocks and the additional regeneration due to new plantations. The research must record the impact of JFM on both 'natural' and 'additional' regeneration: this could be measured by estimating the improvement in the crown density of forest. Such an assessment would help in understanding the impact of JFM in improving the greenery of forests, which, in fact, is the main aim of the programme.

Transfer of burden: The available literature focused on forest management but ignored a more delicate aspect called 'transfer of burden'. As long as forests are protected, the community must depend on alternative sources for wood, green manure and grazing. If they are to give relief to JFM areas the burden automatically is, to a larger extent, transferred to non-JFM areas. It is important to identify the areas, which alternatively bear this burden. If non-forest areas or non-JFM forest areas are taking all such burden, then it amounts to the principle of 'protect' few patches of forests and 'open' non-forest and non-JFM forest areas for destruction. This principle does no good in solving the ecological problem. As such, it is important to assess the rate of relief to JFM adopted forest patches, and the extent of burden transferred to non-JFM areas.

Opportunities for JFM displaced families: The JFM has a component to provide employment and income to the poor of the forest adjacent communities. This employment is generated by way of afforestation and measures that arrest soil degradation and improve water table. But these opportunities cannot become alternative sources of employment and income for long for all those forest dependent families. More important, the present employment generation matrix is becoming highly skewed and the process of modernization of agriculture uses labour saving devises (particularly when agriculture is in the II phase of development: Mellor 1956: 145). As a corollary, rural areas are not capable of absorbing additional labour, which were earlier dependent on those forest patches, but being displaced due to JFM protection now. A JFM village, *Darsimala*, in Anantapur district in Andhra Pradesh provided an insight in this regard. In this village 17.5 per cent of the families were dependent on forest before the village was adopted under JFM. Among these forest dependent families, only 31.6 per cent were able to find alternative sources of employment and income and the rest 68.4 per cent were in distress. For these displaced families growing forests were said to be a major attraction (Muralidharudu, Reddy and Govindappa 1997: 12). When no alternative opportunities are available do the JFM displaced families remain mute and not cut the rejuvenated forests? Or the society has any alternative mechanism to provide them with substitute opportunities? This needs to be studied.

Growth of wild animals: Forest wild animals occasionally provide an important source of 'game-meat' to rural community. A successful JFM area is bound to provide shelter to wild animals and help in their multiplication at an unhindered and speedier rate. The multiplication rate of wild animals is going to be an indicator of the impact of JFM. It is of crucial importance to find out whether the multiplication rate of wild animals has changed, and whether the arrest of hunting took place during the JFM adaptation.

Energy conservation: The impact of JFM on forest depends, to a large extent, on the adoption of measures minimizing the use of wood in food making. Due to education of motivation people may adopt energy saving devices and alternative energy sources. The JFM too supports this by way of providing smokeless *chullas*, bio-gas and solar cookers at subsidized rates. This is of crucial importance to note 'how far' people have adopted energy saving devises and impact of such adoption. Any analysis on these aspects certainly helps in understanding the factors facilitating or inhibiting the adoption of energy saving devises.

Stall-feeding practices: The JFM intends to reduce stress on forest by arresting open grazing of cattle in forest and by promoting stall-feeding practices. Well-developed agriculture offers scope to grow green fodder and sustain stall-feeding of cattle (Iyengar 1989: A-73). As agriculture is backward in India, the availability of green fodder is scarce, and consequently open gazing is practiced on a large scale. Moreover, backwardness of agriculture calls for dairy practicing as an alternative source of livelihood, and as corollary, more demand for fodder and open grazing. Under the circumstances, it is necessary to know whether community participation in JFM would stop people from using the adopted forest patches for the purpose of open grazing and improve in stall-feeding practices.

Usurping: Rural rich would hardly venture into vacuum. As long as forest has just rootstocks and saplings they do not venture into forests. But once sufficient and 'economic wood' is formed due to JFM, the same rich are bound to show more love towards forests and make efforts, and succeed too, in replacing the erstwhile partners, mostly poorer sections, of forest development. When heavy benefits start forthcoming it is difficult to keep the economic and political animal out of VFCs and forests. It was estimated that after about ten years of JFM practice, the first thinning itself may fetch a minimum of Rs. one lakh per hectare from the adopted teak areas. Bamboo forests are estimated to bring about Rs. 10,000 per hectare from the sixth year on regular basis. Yield of non-timber forest produce including grass is going to be substantially higher in the years to come (Mukherji 1997: 90-91). This good returns and escalation of market demand for timber and non-timber forest products may result in 'peoples forestry' being captured by locally powerful and dominant sections for private profit, resulting in the marginalisation of poorer sections (Haripriya Rangan 1997: 90-91). It is also difficult to avoid the political usurpers from interfering into this fertile field. When that is to happen, the poor will be forced to vacate the VFCs. This does no good to either forests or the community in general and the poor in particular. A mechanism should be developed to forestall the usurping.

Political hegemony: The present scenario of JFM leadership at community level also needs a thorough assessment. It was observed that the present VFCs are heading in the direction of political hegemony and concentration of power. Such a situation, it was feared, would not only weaken the VFCs, but also cause their disintegration (Muralidharudu, Reddy and Govindappa 1997: 12). The problems of similar nature, likely to arise in the long run, need to be studied.

Sustainability: The long term success of JFM depends on the in-built mechanism on the financial front. The finances for JFM programme are mostly coming from external agencies. Such external finances are meant only for a definite period. After the withdrawl of regular programme funds, it is estimated that a minimum of Rs. 40,000 is necessary to maintain each of the VFCs adopted forest patches (Muralidharudu and Biswas 1998). As the external financing agencies are bound to withdraw from the scene some day, it is necessary to build-up a suitable and sustainable financial system. The usufructs generated and retained by the VFCs might provide only a limited financial sustainability to the system. The gaps within this facet of self-sustainability need to be identified.

Areas for Future Research

Based on the foregoing discussion, specific issues that seem relevant for future research are: (1) Review of the level and methods of people's participation in planning, execution and management of JFM activities, identifying the factors facilitating and retarding people's participation in social, economic, political and cultural contexts; (2) Understanding the factors inhibiting women participation in JFM and suggesting measures to inculcate a better participation: (3) Assessing the impact of JFM on the relief from tree felling, grazing and green manure collection; (4) Identifying the alternative areas, which bear the burden of wood, green manure, grazing and other needs of the community when forests are protected by JFM; (5) Estimating the impact of JFM on forest rejuvenation—natural regeneration and additional regeneration—due to soil works, new plantations, silvicultural activities, etc; (6) Understanding the change in the multiplication rate of wild animals and know the rate of relief from hunting; (7) Assessing the impact on the lives of JFM displaced people—in income, employment and usufructs distribution; (8) Understanding the alternative opportunities available and level of adoption of such alternatives by JFM displaced people; (9) Identifying various sources and agencies and mechanisms that may help in the sustainability of VFCs and in their financial viability; and (10) Identifying the potential of peoples' participation in a given situation in nonforest developmental activities.

REFERENCES

1. These VFCs are called by different names in different Sates. The executive and its office bearers are also known by various designations. In few States like Andhra Pradesh, two persons (one male and one female) are chosen from each household as members of VFC.

2. This comment is not to undermine the results obtained by the authors or their integrity, but only to indicate the absence of any significant study with macro base by an outside agency. The information regarding the names and designations are available in the journals and documents from where the literature is collected.

3. The Team suggested three types of JFM projects that are bankable viz. sal regeneration, teak regeneration and bamboo plantation. The cost of the project per hectare was estimated at Rs. 27,000 per annum. Government of India projected a target of 10 million hectares of degraded forest to be protected under JFM at a rate of one million hectares annually. Based on this, annual fund requirement would be around Rs. 27,000 millions; presuming a cost estimate of Rs. 27,000 per hectare. For further information on this, see M. S. Haque, S. Kunniappan and A. M. Puri (1998), "Financial Viability and Bankability of JFM Projects in India", *The Indian Forester*, Vol 124, No.6, June.

4. For example, under irrigation projects, participants directly benefit through better irrigation and better yields of crops.

5. The non-JFM areas could be any tree growth and grazing areas in both private and public lands and non-JFM forest areas.

6. This estimate was arrived at after a detailed discussion with the Presidents, Secretaries and Executive members

of about 50 VFCs in Anantapur district in Andhra Pradesh. This amount of Rs. 40,000 is meant for replacement of casualties in plantation, repairs to checkdams and other soil works meant for soil and water conservation, watering and soil tendering for the existing plants, laying of fire-lines and to maintain the watchers for the area.

7. Adinarayan V.P. (1997):"A Success Story of Bairlooty Chenchugdem of Bairlooty Range, Atmakur Division of Kurnool District", *Vana Samrakshani*, Vol IV, No.1, July/ September.

8. Arnold J.E.M., A. Bergman and G. Djurfeldt (1987): *Forest for the Poor?* Swedish International Development Authority (SIDA), Stockholm.

9. Arnold J.E.M., R. Aslop and A. Bergman, (1990): *Evaluation of the SIDA Supported Bihar Social Forestry Project for Chotanagpur and Santhal Parganas, India,* Swedish International Development Authority (SIDA), Stockholm.

10. Bahuguna Y.K. (1997): "Joint Forest Management: Emerging Issues". *The Indian Forester,* Vol. 123, No. 6, June,

11. Bina Agrwal (1997), "Environmental Action, Gender Equity and Women Participation", *Development and Change*, Vol 28, No, 1, January.

12. Brisscoe, John and David de Ferranti, *Water for Rural Communities: Helping People to Help Themselves*, World Bank, Washington D.C.

13. Ford Foundation (1990), *Joint Management for Forests: Experiences from South Asia,* Ford Foundation New Delhi.

14. Gangophadyay P.B. (1997), "Editorial" *The Indian Forester,* Vol. 123, No. 6, June.

15. Gopa Pandey (1997), "Joint Forest Management: Perceptions of New Incumbents in Indian Forest Service", *The Indian Forester,* Vol. 123, No. 6, June.

16. Gupat H.S. (1997), "Legal Provisions for Joint Forest Management" , *The Indian Forester,* Vol. 123, No. 6, June.

17. Hague Frederic (1987), WCED Public Hearing, Oslo, 28-29 October 1985, quoted in WCED, *Our Common Future,* Oxford University Press, Delhi.

18. Haripriya Rangan (1997), "Property Vs Control: The State an Forest Management in Indian Himalyas" , *Development and Change,* Vol. 28, No. 1, January.

19. Hobley M. (1994), "From Passive to Active Participatory Forestry: Nepal", quoted by Khan Niaz Ahmed "Participation in South Asian Social Forestry: Chasing a Mirage", *Journal of Rural Development,* Vol. 13, July-September.

20. Iyenger Sudharshan (1989) "Common Property Land Resources in Gujarat: Some Findings About Their Size, Status and Use", *Economic and Political Weekly,* Vol. XXIV, No. 25, June 24.

21. Jadav and Jha (1997), "Case Study of VSS Ganeshpur", *Vana Samrakshani,* Vol. VI, No. 1, July/ September.

22. Jonathan Isham, Deepa Narayan and Lant Pritchett (1995) "Does Participation Improve Performance? Establishing Causality with Subjective Data", *The World Bank Economic Reveiw,* Vol. 9, No. 2, May.

23 Khan Niaz Ahmad (1994), "Participation in South Asian Social Forestry: Chasing a Mirage", *Journal of Rural Development,* Vol. 13, July-September.

24. Korten Francs F and Robert A Siy Jr (Ed) (1988), *Transforming Bureaucracy: The Experience of the Philippine National Irrigation Administration,* West Hartford, Conn, Kumarin Press.

25. Malhotra K. C. et al (1990), "Joint Management of Forest Lands in West Bengal: A Case Study of Jamboni Range in Midnapore District". *Technical Paper 2,* Indian Institute of Bio-Social Research and Development, Calcutta.

26. Malhotra and Poffenberger (1989), *Forest Regeneration through Community Protection,* Department of forestry, Government of West Bengal.

27. Mariette Correa (1996), "No Role for Women—Karnataka's Joint Forest Management Programme", *Economic and Political Weekly,* Vol. XXXI, No. 23, June 9.

28. Mellor John W (1956), *Economics of Agricultural Development,* Vora, Bombay.

29. Mishra Rajiv (1994), "Conserving the Kumaun Forest Through People's Participation: A Case Study", *The Indian Forester,* Vol. 120, No. 7, July.

30. Mukherji S. D. (1994), "Management Plan under the Joint Forest Management", *The Indian Forester,* Vol. 120. No. 7, July.

31. Mukharjee S.D. (1997), "Is Handing Over Forests to Local Communities a Solution to Deforestation-Experience in Andhra Pradesh (India)", *The Indian Forester,* Vol. 123, No. 6, June.

32. Mukherjee Neela (1997), "Why Joint Forest Management (JFM) Failed to Deliver? A Case Study of Arjuni Mouza, Midnapore (West Bengal, India)", *The Indian Forester,* Vol. 123, No. 6, June.

33. Muralidharudu P, V. Reddappa Reddy and K. Govindappa (1997), *People and Forest: Mutual Survival—A Case Study on the Vana Samrakshana Samithi in Anantapur District,* (mimeo), Department of Rural Development and Social Work, Sri Krishnadevaraya University, Anantapur, April.

34. Muralidharudu P, V. Reddappa Reddy and K. Govindappa (1997), *A Case Study on the Progress of Darsimala Vana Samrakshana Samithi in Anantapur District,* (mimeo), Department of Rural Development and Social Work, Sri Krishnadevaraya University Anantapur, April.

35. Muralidharudu P and Kallol Biswas (1998), "Concern for Future Sustainability of Joint Forest Management in

Anantapur", *Vana Vahini,* Department of forestry, Anantapur, December.

36. Narayanan Deepa (1995), "The Contribution of People's Participation: Evidence from 121 Rural Water Supply Projects", *ESD Occasional Paper series l,* World Bank, Environmentally Sustainable Development Department, Washington DC, processed.

37. Poffenberger (Ed) (1990), *Keepers of the Forest: Land Management Alternatives in Southeast Asia,* KUMARIN Press, Connecticut.

38. Poffenberger (Ed) (1990, *Joint Management of Forest Lands: Experiences from South Asia—A Ford Foundation Programme Statement,* Ford Foundation, New Delhi.

39. Rahman A. (1992), "Participatory Approach to Forest Management in Bangladesh: Some Major Initiatives and Lessons Leant" , paper presented for International Seminar on 'Forest Administration and Management', Michigan School of Natural Resources, Michigan.

40. Reddy V. Reddapa and D. Chenna Reddy (1998), "NGOs and People's Role in Joint Forest Management", *Kurukshetra, Vol. 46, No. 11, August.*

41. *Roy (1997), "Social Indicators towards Institutionalization of Development Programmes: A Case Study from Joint Forest Management",* The Indian Forester, Vol, 123, No. 6, June.

42. Satish (1997), In his message on the eve of release of the first issue of *Vana Samrakshani,* Vol. VI, No. 1, July-September.

43. Shah S.A. (1994), "Reinventing Tropical Forest Management in India", *The Indian Forester,* Vol. 120, NO. 7, July.

44. Sharma Jitendra (1997), "Joint Forest Management—Some Fundamentals Reviewed", *The Indian Forester,* Vol 123, No. 6, June.

45. Spith Gustove J (1987), WCED Public Hearing, Oslo, 28-29 October 1985, quoted in WCED, *Our Common Future,* Oxford University Press, Delhi.

46. Suresh P. Prabhu (1998), in his message on the eve of the release of *Micro Planning Manual for Joint Forest Management Areas,* (Edited by Bakshish Singh and V. Varalakshmi) Tata Energy Research Institute, New Delhi.

47. Task Force (1987), *Participatory Forestry in Bangladesh: Concepts, Experiences and Recommendations—A Task Force Report,* submitted to the Ministry of Agriculture, Government of Bangladesh, Dhaka.

48. UNDP (1993), *The Human Development Report 1993,* Oxford University Press, New York.

49. Upadhyay. J.K. (1997), "Village Resource Development Programme of Village Forest Committees in Bilaspur Forest Circle, Madhya Pradesh—A Case Study", *The Indian Forester,* Vol. 123, No. 6, June.

50. Vaidyanathan A (1994) "Transferring Irrigation Management of Farmers", *Economic and Political Weekly,* Vol. XXIX, No. 47, November 19,

51. Venkati Madari (1997), "Olgapur VSS—People's Initiative", *Vana samrakshani,* Vol. VI, No. 1, July-September.

52. WFED (1989), Forest Regeneration through Community Protection: The West Bengal Experience, *Proceedings of the Working Group Meeting on Forest Protection Committees,* 21—22, Forest Department, Government of West Bengal, Calcutta.

53. World Bank (1991), *World Development Report 1991,* Oxford University Press, New York.

11

Wasteland Development Through Watershed Programme:

The Case of AP

Dr.P. Krishnaiah

1. Introduction

The formation and perpetuation of wasteland represents a hidden potential for sustained agricultural development provided an appropriate strategy is evolved and implemented. It is also the surest way to attack mass poverty in semi-arid agricultural climatic zones. Watershed programme is considered to be the right mechanism to develop wasteland and tackle endemic poverty. It needs public investment, drive and social mobilisation.

With the increasing pressure of the ever growing human and cattle population, deforestation, erosion of soil, indiscriminate use of chemicals, fertilizers, pesticides and also of water, a severe threat has been caused to our Eco-system. In India, out of 329 million hectares (m.ha) of the total geographical area, nearly 50 per cent of lands are waste or degraded. While at one end, 50 per cent of lands are degraded, at the other, nearly 40 per cent of people are poor and below poverty line. With proper planning, scientific approach and efficient management, it is possible to increase the productivity of these "wasted" lands while creating huge employment opportunities for the poor. It is now firmly believed that the development of degraded lands is an important input required for reduction of poverty, since the scope for major irrigation projects is not only diminishing for want of technical feasibility but also fraught with heavy investments and environmental impediments.

Therefore, of late, development of dry lands has assumed great importance both for the central and state governments. The problem of degraded lands and their management is a complex and multi-dimensional one and requires a scientific and multidisciplinary approach. People's participation in planning, execution and maintenance of their resources in such an approach assumes significance.

The committee constituted by Planning Commission in 1987 under the chairmanship of Dr. CH. Hanumantha Rao, to go into the definition of watersheds has defined wastelands as: "degraded land which can be brought under vegetative cover with reasonable effort and which is currently underutilized, and land which is deteriorating for lack of appropriate water and soil management or on account of natural causes". The committee assessed the extent of degraded wastelands, including forestlands, to be of the order of 175 million hectares. The forest cover is hardly 10 per cent as against the requirement of nearly 30 per cent for balanced environment and per hectare forest wealth is hardly 12 cubic meters as against 90 cubic meters in countries like Canada and Australia.

2. Status of Wastelands in Andhra Pradesh

An extent of 4,881,324 hectares of the wastelands have been identified and mapped using remote sensing techniques in 19 districts of Andhra Pradesh. These constitute 19.78 % of the total geographical area. The category-wise wasteland area of 19 districts (out of 22 rural districts) in Andhra Pradesh as well as the district-wise wastelands available is shown in Tables 1 and 2. As could be seen from the data, barring some of the coastal districts which have assured irrigation facilities, many of the other districts are dependent upon rainfed irrigation. In this context watershed development assumes importance.

After gaining adequate experience in watershed treatment the government of Andhra Pradesh has given special thrust for rainwater harvesting and conservation recently. A special campaign has been launched to sensitize the people about proper water conservation and utilization under the caption Neeru-Meeru (Water and You).

3. Micro Watershed Approach

Poor management of the country's basic natural resources of land, vegetation and water has been a major cause of our impoverishment of the environment. For effective management of soil and water, the treatment must begin from ridge to valley. There cannot be an artificial division of the forest and non-forest land, as well as private and community lands, while applying various methods of treatment. Therefore, the treatment of degraded and wasteland has to be taken up in a comprehensive manner. It is to be ensured that every drop of water and every square foot of land are utilised to our best advantage.

It is necessary to co-ordinate all the programmes dealing with development of land and water on a holistic and micro-watershed approach. A micro watershed of about 500 hectares is taken as a unit for development over a period of 4 years. Such micro-watersheds are a part of a larger watershed covering a cluster of villages. The scale of investment in each micro watershed is Rs. 20 lakhs in 4 years as per the guidelines in vogue. The integrated approach for treatments includes activities like soil and moisture conservation works, water harvesting structures, social forestry, silvipasture, horticulture etc. Participatory approach through community organizations is adopted as a tool for implementation.

Table–1. Category-Wise Wasteland Area in Andhra Pradesh

Sl. No.	Category	Total	% of total Geographical area	% of total waste-lands
1.	Gullied and/or Ravinous land	68529	0.278	1.4
2.	Upland with or without scrub	1931075	7.825	39.56
3.	Water logged and marshy land	67906	0.275	1.39
4.	Land affected by Salinity/ alkalinity coastal/inland	56076	0.227	1.15
5.	Shifting Cultivation Area	1363	0.005	0.03
6.	Under utilised /Degraded notified forest land	2086912	8.457	42.75
7.	Degraded pastures/ grazing land	70929	0.287	1.46
8.	Degraded and under plantation crop	5060	0.012	0.1
9.	Sands-deserts/coastal	41542	0.168	0.85
10.	Mining /industrial waste lands	7346	0.03	0.15
11.	Barren rocky/stony waste/ Sheet rocky area	506349	2.052	10.38
12.	Steep slopping area	38237	0.155	0.78
13.	Snow covered and or/ glacial area	0	0	0
	Total	4881324	19.78%	100%

Source: Field Data

Table–2. Extent of Wastelands in the Districts of Andhra Pradesh

Sl. No.	*District*	*Area in Hectares*	*Percentage to Geographical Area*	*Total*	
				No. of Watersheds	*Area Treated (in Hec.)*
1	Adilabad	245561	15.25	453	226500
2	Khammam	174650	10.9	143	71500
3	Mahaboobnagar	249612	13.54	627	313500
4	Karimnagar	146929	12.43	35	17500
5	Ranga Reddy	146113	19.5	267	133500
6	Nalgonda	172917	12.16	379	189500
7	Warangal	149379	11.63	84	42000
8	Nizamabad	148745	18.7	25	12500
9	Medak	113760	11.95	234	117000
	Sub-Total	**1547666**		**2247**	**1123500**
10	Chittoor	587271	38.76	415	207500
11	Kurnool	387914	21.97	691	345500
12	Cuddapah	459759	29.93	284	142000
13	Ananrthapur	323345	16.9	463	231500
	Sub-Total	**1758289**		**1853**	**926500**
14	East Godavari	144975	13.41	88	44000
15	Srikakulam	110241	18.89	231	115500
16	Visakhapatnam	315138	28.24	70	35000
17	Guntur	NA	NA	NA	NA
18	Nellore	491818	37.61	188	94000
19	Prakasam	378305	21.46	472	236000
20	Vizianagaram	134892	20.63	60	30000
	Total	**3657003**		**3425**	**1712500**
	Grand- Total	**6962958**		**7525**	**3762500**

Source: Field data
NA: Not available

4. Watershed Committees

The wasteland development programmes taken up before April 1995, have performed dismally, mainly because they had been planned and implemented on a sectoral basis by part-time officials and in isolated patches without any regard for the complete micro-watershed principle and without any genuine involvement of the local people. The development process can be sustainable only when people work together as a group. The self help groups are emerging as stakeholders in the villages and the active men and women are becoming members of watershed development committees. The development activities are virtually placed in the hands of village people consisting of women self help groups and user groups, who actually plan, execute and subsequently manage the programme and maintain the assets created. NGOs are assigned an important role in guiding the watershed committees.

5. Evaluation

Andhra Pradesh is now recognized as a leader in the implementation of watershed development projects. Besides the sheer numbers, the qualitative content of the programme is also very high. The watersheds are being evaluated by using the remote sensing techniques to compare the improvement of various parameters including Normalized Differential Vegetation Index (NDVI). The NDVI is found to have gone up by 30% to 42% in watersheds after 4 years of treatment. Some of the watersheds and water harvesting structures have been evaluated by ground water department, rural development department and also the UNICEF and the positive change in water levels and significant improvement in the yields of various crops before implementation and after implementation of the watershed programme have been observed. An evaluation study carried by the Department of Rural Development in 1998 indicated an increase in water level in wells by 0.58 to 6.63 meters, additional area brought under cultivation to be 16.49 ha in Rabi and 24.77 ha in Kharif, 12 seasonal wells getting rejuvenated, 10 additional wells dug, a decrease in labour migration by 34 % and increase in daily milk production by 226.42 litres, on an average in a typical watershed (Department of Rural Development, Government of AP,1998). The coverage of the programme in the state is presented in Table-2.

While an unprecedented volume of work was turned out by watershed committees, yet there are deficiencies which need to be made up. Like other SHGs, the most conspicuous deficiency is the absence of total involvement by the user groups which is likely to retard democratic functioning of the Watershed Associations. The unbridled freedom established tends to use the funds in an unscientific manner thereby giving a go bye to larger good. The PIAs are also not adequately prepared to handle the task and the committees are also reflecting the political phenomena of the local areas with all its added evils. Fixing of responsibility on those involved in aberrations, intensified training and transparent and democratic regime would further enhance the sustainability of the strategy.

12

Long Hours, Meagre Earnings and Poverty

P. Purushotham

The Industry

Pamidi is a small rural town (population: 31,000) in the drought-prone district of Anantapur, Andhra Pradesh. Ready-made garment (RMG) industry in this town provides regular household self-employment to about 1200 workers in this district where farm employment is uncertain and non-farm employment is valuable. RMG industry has grown into a vibrant and ubiquitous household activity in the town over the last 80 years. The industry owes its genesis to half a dozen families that have migrated from Maharashtra; these families have brought along with them the tailoring skills and entrepreneurial talents. Currently, the industry is estimated to have an annual turnover of Rs. 32 million and provides household employment to over 600 families at one cluster in cleaning, sorting, cutting and stitching waste cloth into useful garments. Over 40 families are indirectly depending on this industry in related activities such as local transport and servicing the machinery and tools. The industry is active throughout the year although its peak season spans for four months between November and February. June and July are generally lean months as the demand for the ready-mades is at the low key. Over years, the entrepreneurs have evolved some product diversification in order to utilize the factors of production during their lean months by switching over to the production of school bags. These products have a one-time demand in the calendar year. The RMG industry is an ideal case of an enterprise that clearly identified its own market-segment and built its competitive strength. The industry's growth has been spontaneous and self-supported. It meets clothing needs of the poorer households at unbelievably low and competitive prices. Its product range includes girls' frocks, knickers (children's shorts and underwear), petticoats, cotton banians, children's shirts, middies, maxis, pants etc. Within each product line, about half dozen sizes are available.

Industry Operators and Their Earnings

The players in the industry can be grouped into four categories viz., (a) wholesale rag traders (six in number), (b) retailer-cum-master traders (28), (c) workers who oscillate between self-employment and wage employment, depending on their access to credit (900) and, (d) wage employed workers (200). The industry buys the raw materials i.e., waste cloth on weight basis almost at throw away price from textile mills in Bombay, Surat and Ahmedabad. The average cost of this material on arrival at Pamidi works out to Rs. 30 per kg. while it ranges from Rs. 20 to Rs. 60. The rags are sorted out, cleaned, stitch-joined, ironed and cut to required sizes and designs in the premises of the entrepreneurs and the material is handed out to job-workers on sub-contract (piece-rate) basis. Workers utilize family labour to manufacture the clothes.

In recent years, due to the growing incidence of unemployment, about 60 young men from nearby villages have started commuting into Pamidi for work in readymade garment industry. In the evenings they carry home raw-materials and designs for their family members. Usually the wages are worked out on piece-rate basis and paid on the same day or the following day. As stated earlier, the industry has built its viability on the strategy of low margin and high volumes. The following price data indicate its relative place in the readymade garment market.

Pricing of Pamidi Readymade Garments vis-à-vis Regular Brands

(Reference fabric: girls' frock, reference year 1997)

Size (shoulder) In inches	*Production cost Rs.*	*Sale price, ex-factory wholesale, Pamidi Rs.*	*Regular readymade product price (quality not comparable) Rs.*
6	5	6	30
18	12	18	60
22	15	22	90
26	18	24	110
30	20	26	140

The demand pattern is as follows:

(Reference fabric: girls' frock, reference year 1997)

Size (Shoulder) in Inches	*No. Pieces per kg.*	*Market share in per cent*
6	16	10
18	14	25
22	12	25
26	10	10
30	7	30

Demand is well-distributed in the hinterland of 250 sq.km. Over 65 per cent of the demand comes from the regional markets such as Bangalore. Tumkur, Hubli, Shimoga, Davanagiri, Bagalkote, etc. from Karnataka and about 25 per cent from the sub-regional markets in the districts of Kurnool, Cuddapah, and Chittoor of Andhra Pradesh while the local market accounts for less than 10 per cent. The entire output is marketed at village *hats or shandies* in rural areas and pavement markets in town areas. Buyers are from very low-income segments of population such as agricultural laborers and working poor.

The wage structure in the industry is as following:

(Reference fabric: girls' frock, reference year 1997)

Activity	No. of workers in the industry	Wage rate per piece Rs.	Average daily earnings of worker Rs.
(i) Cutting/stitching	275	1.60	35
(a) Workers with own sewing machines	550	200	25
(b) Workers without sewing machines	200	25	21.50
(ii) Cleaning and sorting	70	-	15
(iii) Ironing	70	-	35

In 1997, there were over 700 sewing machines and 6 machine-repairers in the town. Detailed cost analysis of the industry indicates that the industry's value addition accounted for about fifty per cent. The raw material cost works out for over 50 per cent and the wage factor 30 per cent, Interest 12 percent of the cost of production. The earnings cannot be classified into profit and remuneration for the self-employment although the entrepreneurs do have an opportunity cost in the market. These surpluses worked out to eight per cent on turnover and over 130 per cent on the equity employed.

Production Cost (Annual Production)

Element of Cost	*Rs.*	*Per cent*
Raw material	15.82	49.38
Wages		
(a) Cutting	2.81	
(b) Stitching	6.36	
(c) Other operations	0.31	
Total wages	9.48	29.59
Interest	3.86	12.04
Depreciation	0.20	0.62
Transport and other expenditure	0.22	0.69
Profits and returns to self employment	2.26	7.05
Total cost of production	32.04	100.00

Credit Scene

In 1997, about 20 entrepreneurs have invested over Rs.11 million of which Rs. 2 million has been their equity, Rs. 0.5 million bank finance and Rs. 8.5 million from the unorganized money market. The household level self-employed workers, master-traders and cloth traders are borrowing from the non-banking financial corporations

Category of borrower	*Average size of loan amount Rs.*	*Actual amount received by the borrower Rs.*	*Number of install-ments*	*Size of install-ments*	*Effective rate of interest per annum*
Household level self employed worker	3000	2700	100, daily	30	90
Master trader	10,000	9,000	5, monthly	2000	48
Rag-trader	90,000	81,000	6, monthly	15,000	41

which number over 45 and dot the entire cluster. Raising a loan from these agencies is not a difficult task. A few hours of notice is sufficient for the moneylenders to arrange the disbursement. The following typical transactions give a better view of the terms prevailing in the money market.

These lenders monitor the borrowers' finances very closely and do not hesitate to levy penal interest at the slightest delay.

Women Workers

The industry is viable and does not see even remote threat from regular brands which are sold at higher prices commensurating higher quality. Cleaning and sorting workers are unskilled women who earn the lowest wages in the industry. Nothing much can be done to improve their earnings. However, there are about 200 women workers engaged in stitching. Since they lack productive assets (sewing machines), which constitute threshold level of productive assets, they are not able to seek self-employment. Although they do work on piece rate basis, their earnings can go up by at least 15 to 20 per cent if they take up job work on sub-contract basis. This is feasible only if they possess the sewing machines for themselves so that they can synchronize family work with the job work. Workers without own sewing machines are paying a monthly rent of Rs. 50 per machine, which costs Rs. 2000.

Need for Professional Intervention

The National Institute of Rural Development, Hyderabad has been observing closely the industry for the last several years and suggested to the District Rural Development Agency (DRDA) to consider assisting some women workers under central poverty alleviation programmes such as IRDP and DWCRA. By 1996 only two women have been assisted under IRDP. Another three women were assisted with a package of development assistance under SIDBI sponsored Rural Industries Programme. All five moved towards sustainable self-employment. In 1997, 90 women workers were organized into DWCRA groups by Mandal Development Office. The manner in which these groups were formed and 'assisted' needs to be mentioned here.

There was no clarity in the group objective. All members said that they joined the group because the Mandal Development Officer wanted them to be organized into a group. They were expecting an immediate loan from the government. They were not aware that they must start saving even if it meant a very small amount. They did not meet as a group. And group discussions did not take place. Surely, the women never thought that they could form into a group which could build their inner strength and acquire organizational and collective strength.

A year-long observation of this intervention suggested that the extent and scope of coverage was so little that the women had no confidence in the intervening institution. First of all, the intervention method was so rigid and impersonal that it did not allow flexibility or participation of the women workers who could potentially gain from the intervention. It was carried out by officials who had neither understood the concept of self-help group nor believed in its efficacy. Pamidi women workers were just 200 in number among nearly 80,000 such rural poor who constituted their target group. The officials did not think of linking these self-help groups to formal financial institutions such as development banks or Rastriya Mahila Kosh who could have offered the potential of micro-credit financing. The women workers had shown no trust in the exercise; hence no progress was made in consolidating their thrift operations. In fact, they did not save any thing to meet their consumption or production requirements. To obtain work-orders on sub-contract basis, each worker required a fixed capital of about Rs. 2000 for acquiring the machine, tools and equipment and another Rs. 5000 towards working capital. Such intervention could enhance the earning by about 20 per cent. Not much of external support was required in terms of technology or markets to operationalise this intervention strategy.

The local bankers including the RRB branch did not respond to the micro-credit needs of the workers. However, they were willing to operate through an intermediate agency, possibly NGOs which of course were neither active nor had the required expertise. Nothing less than comprehensive intervention by a committed, professional institution which understood the concept of SHG and could effectively link the micro credit with complete range of micro-enterprise development services, including the supply of raw materials, could bring any positive change in the lives of these women.

The Intervention

One year of persuasion by DRDA and its Mandal Development Office in Pamidi could help in arranging micro-credit to not more than six women. This researcher shared the need for micro-credit intervention with SIDBI, NABARD and a few state level NGOs in Andhra Pradesh. Of these, BSIX, a corporate NGO working for the promotion of a livelihood among rural poor through provision of financial services and technical assistance, has responded to this need.

BASIX worked out an effective mode of intervension. Based on intensive study of credit requirements of these women, since 1998, it has provided Rs. 44 lakhs to about 500 women self-employed in the industry, the average loan to a women being Rs . 8,800. All the credit was provided to meet the working capital needs.

These loans were unsecured and carried a rate of interest of 20 per cent per annum. The women found the terms very attractive as the normal interest rates in the local money market was between 36 to 60 per cent. The recovery rate was also quite encouraging, at 99 percent. This intervention resulted in enhancing the per capita earnings by at least 15 per cent. The micro-credit operations targeted to these women were viable and professionally rewarding for the NGO.

Summary

Availability of work does not necessarily mean an escape from poverty for the self-employed if they had to rely on expensive and exploitative money market for working capital as a major portion of their earnings had to be given up to meet the debt-servicing commitments. Although the state sponsored SHG movement was making clear progress in different parts of the state, the local administration could not meet the scale and intensity of credit requirements of the self employed women in the Pamidi RMG industry. Credit, at reasonable terms, was the basic need of the industry. When that could be ensured through a professional and cost-effective intervention, the workers' real earnings could be increased by 15 per cent. The intervention also suggests that if the development inputs are properly targeted, some of viability of some of the rural micro-enterprises could be restored.

13

Employment and Earnings of Women in Urban Informal Sector

A Study of Kavali Town in Andhra Pradesh, India

J.M.J. Vinodhini

1. Introduction

The definition of urban informal sector has been the subject of debate. What is undisputed is that a large proportion of urban economic activity has not been adequately measured or described. The known but undocumented components of the urban labour force go under the label of the informal sector (also called the unorganized sector, the lower circuit, or the bazaar economy). The developing countries are striving for development through different strategies to ensure a higher rate of growth of urbanisation as well as income per capita. Due to structural imbalances, institutional rigidities, resource inadequacies and under utilization of available resources development is getting lopsided. The urban social and the economic infrastructure in the developing countries is utterly inadequate to ensure the fulfilment of basic needs of civilised life. The situation is most acute and glaring for those situated in squatter settlements or slum areas. Urban-based industrialisation introduces the polarisation and hierarchisation of men's and women's work roles (Ester Bosrup, 1970).

Traditionally women have been confined to domestic chores and self-employment at home or in family enterprise (Malavika Karlekar 1987). This is characteristic of most traditional subsistence-oriented agricultural economies. There is a distinct difference between male and female informal labour markets. The male labour market spectrum includes, at one end, unskilled marginal workers subsisting in such casual jobs as hawking and car washing and, at the other end, small-scale, family owned enterprises that are viable, efficient, and labour-intensive. The informal female labour market is organised along different lines, because women's choice of activity is determined by the norms of female seclusion (World Bank 1989). But with the advent of modernisation and industrialisation wage employment for women began to take place. In the initial stages of industrialisation and urbanisation there was a stiff resistance to women being employed for wages especially in the middle class families. In the poorer classes this resistance was weakened by economic compulsion. In the developing countries due to limited industrialisation and urbanisation women workers tend to be concentrated in the informal sector characterised by non-wage employment (Maithri Krishna Raj, 1979).

The informal sector activities are primarily those of petty traders, street hawkers, piece-workers and other groups on the streets of the towns and cities. Due to rapid urbanisation employment in the informal sector had been growing faster than the formal sector despite some obstacles and absence of government support or regulation. It thus in effect, became the employer of the last resort. The employment, earnings, entrepreneurship, organisational and legal aspects and working and living conditions of the participants in the informal sector have a significant role in the Third World metropolis. Gender discrimination and gender gap are widely prevalent in the urban informal labour market and women are the victims of exploitation and oppression (SSS, 1988).

The concept of informal sector was first used in a study in Ghana by Keith Hart (1973) and also taken up in the Report of the ILO/UNDP employment Mission to Kenya (1972). Subsequently, it gained considerable currency in literature. Jan Breman (1976) examined the utility of the concept of informal sector in a small town in western India and considered aspects relating to the origin of the concept, size of informal sector, fragmented labour market and labour force. With this background, we pass on to our empirical field of investigation. Sethuraman. Joshi and papola also sought to explain the concept in detail. Of these, Sethuraman's work is pioneering.

2. Research Site and its Location

The choice of Kavali town for our empirical investigation needs some justification. There are three municipalities in Nellore district of Andhra Pradesh. They are Nellore, Gudur, and Kavali. Kavali town has been purposively chosen because of considerations of proximity and convenience for the author, who has made Kavali town and its neighbourhood her laboratory of research at one stage or the other. Incidentally Kavali happens to be one of the medium municipal towns which is to be developed to relieve over urbanisation of large towns like Nellore. It is also typical in the sense that its economy is dominated by commercial enterprise and petty trades and occupations. Besides agriculture and allied activities there are also a considerable number of households who depend upon the tertiary sector for their livelihood. We present a brief outline of Kavali town and its socio-economic setting before we elaborate on the methodology of our study and the findings emerging from it. Kavali town is located at

14°.57' North latitude in the north-eastern part of Nellore district. It is on the GNT road (National High Way No.5) at a distance of 53 kms, north of Nellore. It is also a railhead on the Gudur – Vijayawada broad gauge section of the South Central Railway at a distance on 226 kms, north of Chennai (Formerly Madras). It is the headquarters of a Revenue Division in the district. The town was constituted into a municipality in the year 1967. The population of the town increased from 8635 in 1901 to 65110 in 1991 registering a linear growth rate of 66.35 per cent during this period from 1901 to 1991. Its present population is approximately 85 thousand (2001 census).

Non-agricultural enterprises, comprising own account enterprises and establishments, accounted for 99 per cent at Kavali town, 90 per cent in Nellore district and 91 per cent in Andhra Pradesh. The higher proportion of the enterprises for Kavali town is not surprising as urban sectors are comparatively dominated by non-agricultural activity. 65 per cent of own account establishments are concentrated in wholesale and retail trade, followed by 15 per cent in community, social and personal services and 10 per cent in manufacturing at Kavali. These proportions get slightly modified if the role played by the establishments is taken into account, but the ranking of these activities is not altered. Kavali is a commercial town mostly thriving on trade and services (78.4 per cent of establishments), having a slender manufacturing base with 10 per cent of establishments. In the case of the district and Andhra Pradesh manufacturing accounted for nearly one-thrid of the establishments. The share of wholesale and retail trade establishments was marginally higher than manufacturing, which is an index of the persistence of commercial character of a transitional agrarian economy of Nellore and Andhra Pradesh. Community, social and personal services account for 19 per cent and 18 per cent of establishments in the district and the State, compared to 22 per cent at Kavali. This is a reflection of urban-bias in the investment choices even under the regime of planned economy. That the share of Own Account Establishments (OAEs) in total establishments is higher under all major categories of activities in the non-agricultural sector, is an index of the role played by the informal sector in the economy of Kavali town, Nellore district and Andhra Pradesh (Government of Andhra Pradesh 1986).

The commercial life of Kavali town is centered in the main bazaar situated along the Grand Trunk Road with its wholesale and retail shops and commercial establishments. The retail shops operating in the town specialize in textiles, appliances and utensils, tools, fancy goods, medicines, stationery and the like. Specialised shops deal in rice, spices, oil, soap and kerosene. The larger wholesalers import manufactured products from Chennai, Mumbai and other cities or towns and distribute them to retailers in the town and all over the revenue division. Fair price shops run by private dealers under the direction and control of State government sell rationed articles some of which are earmarked only for yellow card holders of low income category. Tea and cigarette shops found at intersections and along densely populated streets of the town are known as bunks or panbeedi shops. Bunks made of wood are easily portable from place to place, depending upon business prospects. Bunks are operated by persons of different groups, caste and religions denominations by both females and males due to low investment and easy entry. Occupational exclusiveness, a significant feature of the caste system, is also losing its force in urban areas such as Kavali. Traditional roles performed in the village system continue to be performed at Kavali, but the performance of these role is no longer determined solely on the basis of caste. We notice that social segregation and occupational exclusiveness are at a stage of transition. There are definite signs of social integration and occupational mobility due to education and urbanization. Due to persistence of knowledge gaps and information problems the gap between the poor and non-poor segments of Kavali society is widening and restricting the operation of the forces of social integration and occupational mobility (World Bank, 1988-1989). Against this background we propose to outline the details of our study.

3. Sample Design of the Present Study

The types of work undertaken within the female urban informal sector is distinguished by location (outside the home or home-based): type of employment (wage earner, piece-worker, self-employed and type of industry group manufacturing, construction, services, or trade), There are two main sub-sectors within the female informal sector: 1). Home-based production either as piece-workers or self-employed: micro-entrepreneurs" and 2) Work outside the home, mostly as unskilled wage earners in manufacturing, construction, or services. In the first sub-sector women work in a segregated environment and perform market-oriented activities compatible with their domestic responsibilities. Following the approach of the World Bank study we have adopted the same classification of female workers of Kavali town and estimated their universe and taken a 5 per cent sample as shown in Table 1. It may be noted that ours is a stratified random sample of female workers. The usual procedure of listing the households and selecting the samples with the help of the table of random numbers is followed.

The female informal sector of Kavali town is quite diverse and complex and located in different nooks and corners of the town. It was rather difficult for us to prepare an exhaustive and accurate list of workers and their work. On the basis of extensive visits to the different areas and

Table–1. Sample Design and Size

Sl. No	*Categories*			*Universe*	*Sample*
1.	Home-bassed workers				
	(a)	Piece-workers		296	15
	(b)	Micro-entrepreneurs		322	16
2.	Workers outside the home				
	(a)	Wage workers			
		(i)	Agricultural labour	262	13
		(ii)	Construction workers	478	24
	(b)	Self-employed			
		(i)	Trade	338	17
		(ii)	Fruit vendors	642	32
		(iii)	Vegetable vendors	577	29
		(iv)	Flower vendors	139	07
		(v)	Fish vendors	322	16
	(c)	Services			
		(i)	Domestics	423	21
		(ii)	Sales Girls	258	13
		(iii)	Tailoring Workers	301	15
	Total			**4358**	**218**

Source: Field Data

contacts with the people engaged in these activities a list has been prepared. 5 per cent random sample was thought to be representative of the universe of our study. It is a stratified sample in the sense that the activities are categorized into two groups and 12 sub-groups. Depending upon the concentration of units in different areas, area-wise, random sample for each category was made and ultimate sampling size is arrived at 218 as shown in Table 1. Field work was conducted during 1997–98 in different areas of Kavali town by the author and two of her fellow researchers. Interviews were conducted in the mornings and afternoons usually sitting on a cot or mat in the sunshine or under some shade. Privacy and confidential conversation were difficult when people lived cheek by jowl. Our aim was to fill up the open-ended interview schedule only on the basis of responses of the women concerned. We encountered considerable problems in questions relating to age and income. No respondent appeared to be clear on either her age or her family's income. Thus we noted down approximate ages and incomes within speficied ranges. Though the schedule was in English, we translated the questions into Telugu. Filling up a schedule was not always easy, with other women, the occasional man, curious children and dogs crowding us. Data thus gathered and the insights gained during the time of field investigation form the basis of our findings.

4. Marital Status

Among the residents 55 per cent of workers are married while this proportion is higher in respect of migrants and stands at 67 per cent. Unmarried workers account for 20 per cent among the residents and 13 per cent among the migrants. The residual workers are either windows/divorced/separated. The higher proportion of married women workers among migrants is understandable because of the several constraints that are to be faced by un-married women workers in the urban setting which is generally hostile towards women. In the case of women belonging to labour households marriage is no hurdle to employment. Economic necessity and the social environment induce married women to take up work in addition to domestic responsibilities such as cooking food, up-bringing children and care of the old aged. It may be noticed that except in the case of sales girls married women are found employed in all categories. 9 per cent of un-married women workers are working as sales persons among the residents, while it is only 2 per cent among the migrants. It means that resident labour households have a better access to trading activity and the agencies operating it than migrants. Fruit vending absorbs more number of women both among residents and migrants than any other category.

5. Caste and Occupation

In the traditional Indian society especially in Hindu society there has been a four-fold caste hierarchy and caste and occupation were identified and rigidly adhered to. Partly because of British rule and mostly because of modernisation, industrialisation, education and urbanisation the caste-occupation nexus has been broken especially in the urban sector (Ramaswamy and Uma Ramaswamy 1981). However, in the rural society the traditional linkages still operate and the society and economy continue to be fragmented and segregated on the basis of caste and religion (World Bank, 1989). We incorporate the distribution of our respondents in 12 categories on the basis of religion and caste. These details are incorporated is Table 2.

We have classified our respondents into not only residents and migrants but also Hindus and non-Hindus. Among the non-Hindus, Muslims predominate and Christians constitute a minority. The Hindus are again divided into two groups for our purpose. They are the upper castes and lower castes. The Brahmins, Vysyas, Rajus, Reddys, Kammas and Balijas constitute the upper castes of Kavali town (Daniel A. Moulton 1976). All the others who are classified as backward communities and scheduled castes and tribes for administering the benefits under different programmes of the Government are put in the category of lower castes. The proportion of non-Hindus is higher (25 per cent) among the migrants than among the residents (20 per cent). Micro-entrepreneurs are mostly from the lower castes, while sales girls are from upper castes. In respect of other categories of respondents there is a fair distribution and representation of caste groups in all occupations. This implies that caste and

Table–2. Religion and Caste of the Residents and Migrants by Category

	Categories													
	(I)	*(II)*	*(III)*	*(IV)*	*(V)*	*(VI)*	*(VII)*	*(VIII)*	*(IX)*	*(X)*	*(XI)*	*(XII)*	*Total*	%
1. Residents Total	9	4	6	16	11	18	12	5	7	14	11	9	122	100
(a) Non-Hindu	1	–	–	3	3	4	3	–	1	2	4	3	24	20
(b) Hindu	8	4	6	13	8	14	9	5	6	12	7	6	98	80
(i) U. Caste	3	–	–	–	7	3	–	–	–	–	7	5	25	26
(ii) L. Caste	5	4	6	13	1	11	9	5	6	12	–	1	73	74
2. Migrants Total	6	12	7	8	6	14	17	2	9	7	2	6	96	100
(a) Non-Hindu	3	3	2	–	2	5	2	2	–	2	–	3	24	25
(b) Hindu	3	9	5	8	4	9	15	–	9	5	2	3	72	75
(i) U. Caste	–	1	–	–	3	5	1	–	–	1	2	1	14	19
(ii) L. Caste	3	8	5	8	1	4	14	–	9	4	–	2	58	81

Source: Field Data **Note:** U. Caste = Upper Caste L. Caste = Lower Caste

occupation nexus on the one hand and religious seclusion on the other are getting marginalised. In other words, we have a labour market with a diminished degree of imperfection. It may be noted that extensity and purity are the basic characteristics of a perfect market either of labour or commodities. "Extensity... refers to the total volume of goods and services available for sale and purchase. Purity refers to the market principle unhampered by non-market considerations such as for example, friendship, kinship, caste and class. The perfectly pure and extensive market is, of course, only an ideal. It does not exist even in the most industrialized and commercialized societies" (Ramaswamy and Uma Ramaswamy, 1981)

6. Age of Respondents

For the purpose of this variable that is age of respondents we have classified our samples into three age groups and re-classified the twelve categories of occupations into four categories namely (i) Home-based workers, (ii) Wage workers, (iii) Self-employed and (iv) Services. The second, third and fourth categories are employed outside the home. We present the age profile of our samples under these four categories in Table 3.

Among our samples 37 and 36 per cent fall under the category of young in the case of the residents and migrants. The middle aged account for 52 and 55 per cent among the residents and migrants. Therefore 90 per cent of our residents are in the active age group by Indian standards. Even the residual 10 per cent of the respondents are active and are mostly in fruit, vegetable, flower and fish vending which fall under the III rd category as these activities are not strenuous. Sales girls and tailoring workers are in the young age group as is required by the nature of the job. Micor-entrepreneurs who figure in the first category are predominantly in the

Table–3. Age of Sample Residents and Migrants

	Categories					
	(I)	*(II)*	*(III)*	*(IV)*	*Total*	*%*
Residents						
17-29 (Young)	4	6	12	23	45	37
30-39 (Middle)	9	15	30	10	64	52
50 and above (Old)	–	1	11	1	13	11
Total	**13**	**22**	**53**	**34**	**122**	**100**
Migrants						
17-29 (Young)	3	7	15	9	34	36
30-49 (Middle)	14	7	28	4	53	55
50 and above (Old)	1	1	5	2	9	9
Total	**18**	**15**	**48**	**15**	**96**	**100**

Source: Filed Data

Result of Chi-square test

Residents: Chi-square = 26.80
DF = 6
Critical value = 12.592
Significant at 5 per cent level

Migrants: Chi-square = 9.98
DF = 6
Critical value = 12
Not significant

middle age group. In the case of other trades there is no such age identification.

7. Reason for Migration

Mobility is the very essence of the market principle with regard to labour. 44 per cent of our respondents are migrants. There are a multiplicity of reasons for rural to urban migration. Two major theoretical approaches to the problem of rural–urban transfer are popular in the literature (M.P Todaro, 1982). The best known of all employment models relating specifically to the developing countries is that originally formulated in 1954 by Arthur Lewis and formalized in 1961 by Ranis and Fei. In the Lewis- Ranis–Fei model the under-developed countries consist of two sectors: (1) a traditional, agricultural subsistence sector characterised by zero or very low productivity "surplus" labour and (2) a high productivity modern industrial sector into which labour from the subsistence sector will be gradually transferred. Some of the assumptions and structural elements of this model are called into question. The most widely used expected income model of rural-urban migration is associated with Todaro and Harris. Despite the existence of urban unemployment, the model postulates that migration proceeds in response to urban-rural differences in expected rather than actual earnings. The model has four basic characteristics: (1) Migration is stimulated primarily by rational economic considerations of relative benefits and costs. (2) The decision to migrate depends on expected rather than actual rural-urban real wage differentials. (3) The probability of obtaining an urban job is inversely related to urban unemployment rate. (4) Migration rates in excess of urban job opportunity growth rates are not only possible but rational. Keeping in mind the postulates of the Todaro-Harris model of migration and following the analytical approach of NSSO we have constructed Table 4 and classified the resons into 9 groups. Table 4 follows.

"In search of employment", "In search of better employment" and "business contract" are grouped under the category of economic reasons and accounts for 36 per cent of migrants. There are also psychological reasons for migration which pervade the reasons sighted in table 4 starting from 4 to 9. The psychological element cannot be easily separated from the non-psychological or the real reasons for migration. We tend to accept the operation of the expected income model of Todaro-Harris type in our case. The migrants could settle into almost all the categories though not on equal footing although they predominate in vending activity which is easily accessible.

8. Sources of Migration and Duration

Where do the migrants come from? Is it from the immediate neighbourhood of Kavali town? Or from far off places outside the district? In order to answer these questions we have constructed Table 5 based on the information drawn from our field investigation. Table 5 follows.

The sources of migration shown in Table 5 are classified into 4 categories (a) within the Mandal, which is the administrative unit above the bottom unit. (b) within the district (c) within the State of Andhra Pradesh and (d) outside the State of Andhra Pradesh. As it happens most labour markets in the rural sector and urban informal sector are localized in character. Migrants are mostly from within a radius of 15 to 20 kilometers that roughly coincides with the boundaries of the revenue Mandal, we find that 54 per cent of migrants are from within the mandal and 28 per cent from within the district. Those from outside the district and the State are negligible- on account of the operation of the forces of local competition. Wage differentials across space excluding major cities and commercial agglomerations tend to diminish and do not induce migration from far off places to small towns like Kavali. We have observed that outside our sample most of the migrants are commuters from neighbouring villages like Musunuru and Sarvayapalem

Table–4. Category-wise Distribution of Migrants by Reasons

Sl. No.	Reasons	Categories													
		(I)	(II)	(III)	(IV)	(V)	(VI)	(VII)	(VIII)	(IX)	(X)	(XI)	(XII)	Total	%
1.	In search of employment	1	3	1	2	1	2	3	1	2	1	–	–	17	18
2.	In search of better employment	2	–	2	–	–	1	4	–	1	–	–	–	10	11
3.	Business contract	1	–	1	1	1	1	1	1	–	1	–	–	8	8
4.	For pursuing studies	–	1	–	1	–	–	–	–	1	–	1	2	6	6
5.	On marriage	1	4	2	1	1	3	5	–	2	–	–	–	19	20
6.	Due to migration of parents of earning member	–	–	–	–	–	1	1	–	–	1	1	4	8	8
7.	Lack of security or social adjustment	1	2	1	2	1	3	2	–	1	2	–	–	15	16
8.	Due to natural calamities	–	1	–	–	–	1	–	–	2	1	–	–	5	5
9.	Other reasons	–	1	–	1	2	2	1	–	–	1	–	–	8	8
	Total	6	12	7	8	6	14	17	2	9	7	2	6	96	100
10.	Economic reasons, 1+2+3	4	3	4	3	2	4	8	2	3	2	–	–	35	36

Source: Field Data

Table–5. Sources of Migration

	Categories												Total
	(I)	*(II)*	*(III)*	*(IV)*	*(V)*	*(VI)*	*(VII)*	*(VIII)*	*(IX)*	*(X)*	*(XI)*	*(XII)*	
(a) Within Mandal	4	5	4	3	3	6	11	1	6	5	–	4	52
(b) Within District	2	3	3	4	3	3	4	–	2	2	–	1	27
(c) Within State	–	3	–	–	–	4	2	1	–	–	2	1	14
(d) Outside State	–	1	–	1	–	1	–	–	–	–	–	–	3
Total	**6**	**12**	**7**	**8**	**6**	**14**	**17**	**2**	**9**	**7**	**2**	**6**	**96**

Source: Field Data

as in the case of most industrial workers at Coimbatore (Ramaswamys 1981).

The duration of migrants of Kavali town exceeds a period of 10 years in respect of only 3 migrants and the rest of them migrated during the past one decade. Nearly two-thrids of them have migrated during the past four to seven years. The average duration of migrants stay at Kavali works out to 4.5 years.

9. Work Participation Rate and Labour Force Participation Rate

The concept of work participation rate used in our empirical study is the same as that of the Census concept in India. We have adopted the usual principal status concept and calculated the work participation rate (WPR) of our respondents in terms of their migratory and non-migratory status and in terms of their occupational status. We start with the data set in table 6 Work participation rate of migrants is slightly higher than residents for both males and females in the case of tailoring workers. The WPR of males among migrants exceeds that of residents by 3.07 percentage points and females by 2.71 percentage points. The disparity in WPR based on sex is also marginally higher for migrants than for residents. Gender disparity in WPR is the highest in the case of agricultural labour among both residents and migrants and lowest in the case of micro-entrepreneurs among residents and vegetable vendors among migrants. The lower WPR among females is not a true indicator of the contribution made by them to the household economy because their domestic chores and responsibilities do not figure in the computation of WPR. The results of 't' test are shown under Table 6 and they are not significant for residents but significant for migrants.

Let us turn our attention to labour force participation rate (LFPR) which is a better indicator of the employment status of workers than that of WPR. The relevant statistics are computed by occupational status for both residents and migrants and incorporated in Table 7.

Table–6. Distribution of WPR by Residents and Migrants

	Categories											
	(I)	*(II)*	*(III)*	*(IV)*	*(V)*	*(VI)*	*(VII)*	*(VIII)*	*(IX)*	*(X)*	*(XI)*	*(XII)*
Residents												
Males	50	46.15	50	52.94	54.16	42.30	43.90	41.17	43.47	40.90	40	41.37
Females	45.45	45.45	43.75	51.51	52.17	38.17	41.17	37.5	42.10	38.09	36.36	38.46
Gender disparity (M-F)	4.55	0.7	6.25	1.43	1.99	3.53	2.73	3.67	1.37	2.81	3.64	2.91
Migrants												
Males	50	46.87	50	43.47	50	40.47	48.78	40	46.15	47.61	44.44	44.44
Females	40	44.82	44.44	40.90	46.66	37.5	48.71	37.5	43.47	44.44	37.5	41.17
Gender disparity (M-F)	10.00	2.05	5.56	2.57	3.34	2.97	0.07	2.5	2.68	3.17	6.94	3.27

Source: Field Data

Result of T-test

Residents
't' value : 1.1854
't' Critical value 2.0738
Not significant

Migrants
't' value : 2.53
't' Critical value 2.0738
Significant at 1 per cent level

Table–7. Distribution of LFPR by Residents and Migrants

	Categories											
	(I)	*(II)*	*(III)*	*(IV)*	*(V)*	*(VI)*	*(VII)*	*(VIII)*	*(IX)*	*(X)*	*(XI)*	*(XII)*
Residents												
Males	91.66	83.33	88.88	94.44	92.30	95.45	94.44	85.71	90	94.44	92.85	91.66
Females	90	80	85.71	94.73	91.66	94.73	85.71	83.33	87.5	87.5	91.66	90
Gender disparity (M-F)	1.66	3.33	3.17	–0.29	0.64	0.72	8.73	2.38	2.5	6.94	1.19	1.66
Migrants												
Males	83.33	93.33	90	90	87.5	94.11	95	75	91.66	90	75	87.5
Females	75.00	92.30	87.5	88.88	85.71	93.93	89.47	66.66	90	87.5	66.66	85.71
Gender disparity (M-F)	8.33	1.03	2.5	1.12	2.04	0.18	5.53	8.34	1.66	2.5	8.34	1.79

Source: Field Data

Result of 't-test

Residents 't' value : 1.6655
't' Critical value 2.0738
Not significant

Migrants 't' value : 2.53
't' Critical value 2.0738
Not Significant

The LFPR is calculated as it is done in the standard literature (The World Development Report, 1995). That is we have taken the proportion of those who are actually working among age group of workers. We notice that the LFPR is marginally higher among residents than among migrants most probably due to better access to information on job opportunities and network of contacts. Gender disparity is also marginally lower in the case of residents than among the migrants for the same reasons. LFPR is the highest both among males and females in the case of fruit vendors and lowest among male micro entrepreneurs and lowest in the case of flower vendors and sales girls. Among the females LFPR is the highest in the case of fruit vendors and lowest among sales girls. Gender disparity is the highest in the case of vegetable vendors among residents and flower vendors among migrants. It is the lowest in the case of traders among residents and fruit vendors among migrants. The result of 't' test are given under Table 6 and LFPR is not significant for residents and migrants.

10. Education Status and Earnings

The literature on the economics of education has thrown up ample evidence regarding the positive relationship between the level of education and earnings. (Psacharopoulos, and Woodhall. M, 1986 UNESCO, 1971). Labour households of the informal sector have limited access to education. The question of quality of education does not figure at all. The schools that they attend at their young age, primary or secondary are run by local self-government that is the municipality or the Panchayati Raj bodies such as the Mandal Prishad or the Zilla parishad. The standards of education in such institutions are very poor and even a person who has gone through a 10 years schooling lacks skills in reading or writing correctly. Therefore, the impact of such education on earnings tends to be minimal. We have set out the details of years of schooling of our respondents and their average earnings in Table 8.

One of the notable features of labour households in the informal sector is the high incidence of illiteracy. In our case, illiterates account for 33 per cent. This proportion is significantly lower than the national average of 49 per cent (2001 census). Therefore 67 per cent of our respondents are literate in the technical sense. Of these, 47 per cent have completed primary education. 20 per cent of them have entered the domain of secondary education but only 2 per cent have completed 10th class. The correlation between level of education and average earnings is negative though insignificant. This finding is contrary to the general tendency widely encountered in the sphere of the economics of education (Ibid). The respondents, both literate and illiterate are almost evenly distributed among different categories of occupations.

11. Experience and Earnings

Work experience is a proxy for formal education and training. Due to the socio-economic conditions of workers in the informal sector, the labour market is dominated by those with less than 10 years of schooling as we have noted in Table 8. They enter the labour market at an early age, in several cases as child labour: they get experienced in the world of work and they are hard pressed to take up different types of activities. However, with work experience they tend to move slowly and steadily into relatively higher income brackets. There is a positive and perfect relationship between work experience and average earnings (r=0.9983). The highest dispersion is found in the case of workers with two years experience and the lowest in the case of workers with twenty two years experience, the other values lie between these two extremes.

Table-8. Distribution of Education by Category of Respondents

Years of schooling	Categories (I)	(II)	(III)	(IV)	(V)	(VI)	(VII)	(VIII)	(IX)	(X)	(XI)	(XII)	Total	Per cent	Average earnings PM Rs.
0	9	5	3	11	4	13	4	1	6	9	3	4	72	33	1067
1	–	1	2	1	2	2	6	–	2	1	–	1	18	8	1250
2	–	2	–	4	1	2	2	–	3	–	–	–	14	6	1196
3	–	1	2	1	1	3	2	–	–	1	–	1	12	6	1188
4	1	2	3	1	2	9	7	–	3	6	1	2	37	17	1095
5	–	4	2	1	2	3	4	2	–	1	–	2	21	10	1119
6	2	–	–	2	–	–	1	–	1	–	–	1	7	3	864
7	–	1	–	1	–	–	–	4	–	–	–	–	6	3	667
8	1	–	1	–	4	–	3	–	1	2	4	3	19	9	921
9	1	–	–	1	1	–	–	–	–	1	3	–	7	3	875
10	1	–	–	1	–	–	–	–	–	–	2	1	5	2	892
Total	**15**	**16**	**13**	**24**	**17**	**32**	**29**	**7**	**16**	**21**	**13**	**15**	**218**	**100**	**1066**

Source: Field Data

Table–9. Workers by Experience and Earnings Per Month (Rs)

Experience (Years)	*No. of Workers*	*Lowest Earnings*	*Highest Earnings*	*Average Earnings*
2	25	300	450	363
4	22	475	650	522
6	28	650	800	713
8	32	750	975	843
10	24	1050	1250	1127
12	27	1225	1350	1282
14	15	1375	1500	1428
16	13	1550	1700	1604
18	14	1750	1950	1839
20	11	1850	2000	1914
22	7	1925	2400	2116
Total	**218**	**998**	**1176**	**1070**

Source: Field Data

12. Occupational Mobility

Immobility of labour is supposed to be one of the characteristic features of under-developed countries. Dualistic models of development as well as migration models of Tadaro-Harris type have offered useful insights into the dynamics of the labout market. We, therefore, notice not only horizontal mobility but also vertical mobility. Vertical or occupational mobility like horizontal mobility is a complex phenomenon and is determined by a multiplicity of factors governing the operation of the informal labour market (Ramaswamys 1981). We do not have the requisite data set to probe into the determinants of occupational mobility. We have data on the number of job changers and job changes which give us an approximate idea of occupational mobility of our samples. The relevant data are presented in Table 10.

Table–10. Work Experience and Job Changes of Respondents

Work Experience In years	*No. of Workers*	*Per cent*	*No. of Job Changes*			
			0	*1*	*2*	*3 and above*
1 – 6	75	34	12	37	17	9
6 – 12	83	38	23	33	21	6
12 – 18	42	20	14	18	7	3
18 and above	18	8	8	3	3	4
Total	**218**	**100**	**57**	**91**	**48**	**22**

Source: Field Data

Results of Chi-square test

Chi-square : 15.14
DF : 9
Critical value : 16.919
Not significant

It may be seen from Table 10 that 57 respondents of our sample have not undergone any change of job. 161 respondents have undergone job change and the number of job changes being 258. The average job change per worker was 1.6. We notice that those with 20 years of experience had the highest average job changes i.e, 2.33 and the lowest average job change pertains to those with 4 years of work experience. For the sample as a whole, we find a positive correlation between work experience and occupation mobility as measured by average number of job changes.

13. Sources of Household Income

By definition labour households draw a major proportion of household income by selling their labour services. But the self-employed households derive their income from their enterprise/trade. We have classified the sources of income of our sample households into four categories as shown in Table 11.

Table-11. Share of Different Sources of Aggregate Monthly Household Income of Residents and Migrants

Monthly income Sources	*No. of Residents*	*Income (Rs.)*	*Average*	*Per cent*	*No. of migrants*	*Income (Rs.)*	*Aver age*	*Per cent*
Wages	33	23727	719	35	24	24096	1004	54
Self-employment	51	41922	822	40	46	19688	428	23
Property income	22	5412	246	12	17	3468	204	11
Transfer payments	16	4272	267	13	9	2007	223	12
Total	**122**	**75333**	**2054**	**100**	**96**	**49259**	**1859**	**100**

Source: Field Data

The major source of income for the residents is through self employment and it contributes to 40 per cent of household income. The second major source is income from wages (35 per cent). The third source is from transfer payments (13 per cent) and the last source of income is from property (12 per cent). However, in the case of migrants 54 pr cent of household income is contributed by wages and transfer payments account for 12 per cent.

Self-employment income is significantly lower than their population proportion and stands at 23 per cent. Property income contributes to 11 per cent. We therefore, notice a structural variation in the composition of household income of residents and migrants. The insignificant share of property income for both residents and migrants is primarily due to their slender asset status. Transfer payments arise on account of private and public channels in order to provide social security to these vulnerable groups. Analysis of variance has been used to compare the average wages and incomes among the groups. The F value for the group of residents is 87.9940 which is significant at 1 per cent level (critical value = 2.88). In case of migrants the F value is 84.5472 which is also significant at 1 per cent level (critical value = 2.70). This shows that for both residents and migrants the wage and income difference is very significant.

14. Levels of Income

Because of the low productivity of employment and occupation of our respondents the incomes earned by them as well as their households tend to be very low and they carry on a hand to mouth existence. We incorporate the level of income by category of our residents in Table 12.

We notice from Table 12 that the vast majority of our respondents are caught up in a low income equilibrium trap. Ragnar Nurkse's vicious circle of low income, low saving or negative saving, inadequate consumption, poor nourishment and therefore poor physique characterise the daily struggle for existence. If we take Rs.1000 per month as the cut off line for poverty 59 per cent of our respondents fall into the poverty trap. The cutoff point at Rs.1000 per month and therefore 12000 per annum is justified on the basis of comparatively higher cost of living at Kavali than the national average. The incidence of poverty according to this head-count measure is higher (50 per cent) for non-home based and lower (10 per cent) home based workers. Thus we notice a significant variation in the incidence of poverty across categories of occupations of our respondents. Thus the challenge of poverty is as grave at our research site as it is in some parts of rural India and Ethiopia (The World Developed Report, 1990 Rural Poverty Report, 2001).

Table–12. Income by Category Per Month

Income (Rs.)	*Categories*				*Total*	*Percent*
	I	*II*	*III*	*IV*		
0 – 400	3	1	10	6	20	9
400 – 800	16	6	27	19	68	31
800 – 1200	2	6	22	11	41	19
1200 – 1600	7	14	22	10	53	24
1600 – 2000	3	8	16	3	30	14
2000 – 2400	–	2	4	–	6	3
Total	**31**	**37**	**101**	**49**	**218**	**100**

Source: Field Data

Results of Chi-square test

Chi-square : 24.6951

DF : 12 (last row merged for analysis)

Significant at 1 per cent level.

15. Gender Disparity in Wages and Earnings

Gender disparity in wages and earnings of workers is one of the most widely discussed and debated issues in contemporary society (UNDP, Human Development Report, 1995) as it has been for at least a 100 years past if not earlier. The social foundations and economic rationale are often questioned by feminists and social activists. A part of the explanation for disparity based on sex may be offered in terms of discriminatory policies pursued by households and governments. It may be noted that human capital theory cannot offer a satisfactory and adequate explanation for the persistence of disparity in wages and earnings of female and male workers. There are deep seated sociological, cultural and traditional foundations for the persistence of this phenomenon in the informal labour market where the ILO conventions and recommendations on labour standards and the legislative enactments on equal remuneration for men and women do not come into operation. No wonder even the minimum wages Act is more often than not flouted than observed. The department of labour remains a silent spectator rather than an instrument of implementation of labour standards and laws (GOI, Ministry of Labour Annual Reports). In Table 13 we incorporate the empirical facts on wages and earnings of our respondents and the extent of disparity.

One of the most glaring features of wages and earnings of informal sector labour households is the operation of low level equilibrium trap. In our case it is evident except in the case of construction workers. This is partly due to the skill and strain and dexterity involved in the trade. But even here considering the incidence of unemployment, higher level of wages disappears into thin air. On the contrary domestic servants earn the lowest wages without any type of unemployment: although there is an element of underemployment in their work. The same thing is true

Table–13. Average Wages and Earnings Per Day (Rs)

Sl. No.	*Category*	*Male*	*Female*	*Female wages as % of male wages*
1.	Piece workers	50	35	70
2.	Micro-entrepreneurs	70	45	64
3.	Agricultural labour	50	30	60
4.	Construction workers	85	65	76
5.	Trade persons	45	25	56
6.	Fruit vendors	40	29	73
7.	Vegetable vendors	35	20	57
8.	Flower vendors	20	10	50
9.	Fish vendors	65	40	62
10.	Domestics	–	15	–
11.	Sales persons	30	20	67
12.	Tailor workers	65	45	69

Source: Field Data

in regard to vendors with the exception of fish vendors where the price margins are wide partly due to the perishability of fish. We notice that the disparity in wages of females as a proportion of male wages is the highest in the case of sales persons and lowest in the case of construction workers. The other categories are placed between these two extremes. The difference between the wages of males and females is statistically significant with t-value = 10.4354 (paired t-test), at 1% level. The average wage for women is rupees 33 which is lower than the wage for men which is rupees 50.45.

Another dimension of gender disparity may be noticed with reference to the share of women earnings in household income on the one hand and the share of women's work in total work turned out by the household both within as well as outside the household. Wage/

earnings disparity is the root cause of the lower share of womens earnings in household income. Another related factor is that much of the contribution of women in improving the quality of life of the household remains unseen, urrecognised, overlooked, and un-accounted for, both socially and economically. In most cases, these gender based inequities remain rooted in deeply held social prejudices that prescribe the role of man as breadwinner and woman as the home maker. Such problems of perception leading to domestication of women in terms of household work are also linked with and result in other forms of deprivation at the household, community and social levels. At the household level, the persistence of the socially unjust dichotomy in the gender role generates unequal access to and control over resources and decision making power between the females and the males. The inequities are further reinforced by male-dominant social norms governing the rights and responsibilities of women and men. The correlation between Hy, Wy is only r=0.2817 which is not significant at 5 per cent level. It means women's income is not a significant element in household income.

The disparity in the proportion of earnings and work in our sample households by categories as worked out and presented in Table 14 offers abundant evidence of the inequities sited above. No wonder one of the recent workshops held by the CIRDAP felt that the position of women has deteriorated in terms of the feminisation of poverty, alienation from rights, and exclusion from participation. (CIRDAP 1998). The reason for the disparity between the share of earnings and work is deeply embedded in the social foundations and economic perceptions which were moulded by hidden or explicit bias against women. Therefore, women are disadvantaged by their class and gender.

Table–14. Share of Women's Income in Household Monthly Income

Sl. No.	*Categories*	*Average Household Income (Hy) (Rs.)*	*Average Women Labour Income (Wy) (Rs.)*	*Wy as per cent Of Hy*
1.	Piece workers	2589	984	38
2.	Micro-entrepreneurs	5988	1759	29
3.	Agricultural labour	2369	829	35
4.	Construction workers	4767	1716	36
5.	Trade persons	2168	607	28
6.	Fruit vendors	2252	563	25
7.	Vegetable vendors	2157	582	27
8.	Flower vendors	1612	484	30
9.	Fish vendors	2947	943	32
10.	Domestics	1563	406	26
11.	Sales persons	1764	547	31
12.	Tailor workers	3228	1065	33

Source: Field Data

Summing Up

The urban economies of the developing world are characterised by economic, technological and sociological dualism. The process of immeserising growth often leads to distress migration of large numbers of unskilled labour. Rural to urban migration flows further accensuate the process of urbanisation leading to several socio-economic problems. The size, structure and performance of the informal sector of the urban economy vary widely across time and space. Therefore, there is a case for updating our knowledge of the emerging trends especially in the context of the winds of economic liberalization blowing at a rapid pace. Information asymmetry and information gaps characterize product and factor markets. The urban informal labour market is no exception. On the basis of a sample of 218 women workers engaged in a wide range of economic activities in the informal sector of Kavali town, we have attempted to capture a glimpse of the impurities and imperfections of the informal labour market. Of the 218 respondents 122 are residents and 96 are migrants. The demographic characteristics of our respondents exhibit significant variation in many respects, such as marital status, caste and occupation nexus, Work Participation Rate, Labour Force Participation Rate and the like. Harris-Todaro's expected income model of migration seems to be applicable to Kavali women migrants. Migration is restricted to a narrow geographical range within the district in respect of 82 per cent of migrants. The average duration of migrants' stay is 4.5 years. Gender gaps in work experience, earnings and mobility are striking. Similarly, there is structural difference in the composition of household incomes of residents and migrants. Share of women's income in total household income ranges between a low of 25 per cent in the case of fruit vendors and a high of 38 per cent in respect of piece workers. There are deep seated sociological and cultural factors besides economic that contribute to the persistence of gender disparities in employment and earnings which need to be further explored at different locations and in different occupations for meaningful policy interventions to promote women empowerment.

REFERENCES

1. Ester Boserup (1970): "Women's Role in Economic Development "Oxford, New York.

2. Malavika Karlekar (1987): "Poverty and Women's Work: A Study of Sweeper Women in Delhi", Shakti Books, New Delhi.

3. World Bank (1989): "Women in Pakistan: An Economic and Social Strategy" Washington. D.C.

4. Maithri Krishna Raj (1979): "Women and Development Analytical Perspectives", Mimeo.

5. Suryanarayanan, S.S. (1988): Information base for the Informal Sector: The Indian Journal of Labour Economics, Vol. 41, No. 3 July-September. pp. 459-461.

6. Keith Hart (1973): Informal Income Opportunities and Urban Employment in Ghana, Journal of Modern African Studies, London.

7. Jan Breman (1976): A Dualistic Labour System: A Critique of the Informal Sector concept, EPW, November 27.

8. World Bank (1989): World Development Report-Oxford University, Press, New York.

9. E.A. Ramaswamy and Uma Ramaswamy; (1981): "Industry and Labour: An Introduction, Oxford University Press, New Delhi.

10. Ibid.

11. Daniel A. Moultan (1976): "Philosophical/Psychological foundations for Non. Formal Education Curriculum Development in India., Ph.D Dessertation, The University of Texas at Austin (Mimeo).

12. Ibid.

13. Michael P. Todaro (1982): Economics for a Developing World, Second Edition, Longman, New York.

14. Ibid.

15. World Bank (1995): The World Development Report, Oxford University Press, New York.

16. Psacharopolous. G and Woodhall. M. (1986): "Education for Development-An Analysis of investment choices", Oxford, New York.

17. World Bank (1990): The World Development Report, Oxford, New York.

18. UNDP (1995): Human Development Report, Oxford, New York.

19. Government of India: Ministry of Labour (1997-2001) Annual Reports, New Delhi.

20. CIRDAP (1998): "Increased Household Income and Rural Women in Asia; Impact on Status and Activities", Report of the Research Meeting, 27-29 July, Kaulalampur, Malaysia, Dhaka, Bangladesh.

Part—III

ROLE OF INSTITUTIONS

14

The Role of the State in Rural Poverty Reduction*

Azizur Rahman Khan

This paper considers the roles of different stakeholders-the government, the non-governmental organizations (NGOs), private business and the civil society-in the alleviation of rural poverty in developing countries. It focuses on the appropriate combination of effort by these stakeholders by evaluating the experience in some contemporary cases of rural poverty reduction.

Section I considers the principal components of a strategy for poverty reduction. Section II analyzes the roles of different stakeholders in some East Asian countries which succeeded in achieving the most dramatic alleviation of rural poverty in recent history. Section III identifies the "comparative advantage" of the state and the other stakeholders in the implementation of different components of the strategy for rural poverty reduction by

---

* The paper was written for the "Inter-American Development Bank-Indes; workshop on strategies in Rural poverty Reduction, experiences from Latin America and East Asia" in Tokyo-Shimane, Japan June, 4-8, 2001.

comparing the experience of the successful East Asian cases with the less successful contemporary experience elsewhere.

I. What Needs to be Done for the Alleviation of Rural Poverty?

Poverty is typically more widespread in rural societies than in urban societies. World Bank's estimates show that for the poverty threshold corresponding to PPP$ 1 per capita per day, 75 per cent of the world's poor were living in rural areas at the end of the twentieth century.[1] World Bank's projections suggest that, despite a rapid increase in the proportion of world's population living in urban areas, the proportion of world's poor living in rural areas will continue to be 60 per cent or more by the year 2025.[2] The reduction of rural poverty must be the dominant focus of the war on world poverty not only because a large majority of the world's poor are rural but also because most of the urban poor are migrants trying to escape rural poverty. Dealing with rural poverty is in some sense tackling the problem at its source.

While the profile of the poor varies among countries and regions, it is by now well established that an overwhelming proportion of the rural poor consist of the small holder farmers and wage laborers, both in agriculture and rudimentary non-agricultural activities, with a disproportionately high share for female-headed households, disadvantaged castes, ethnic minorities and displaced peoples. For most of these groups the only significant resource endowment consists of the capacity for human labor. In most cases this asset takes the form of the capacity for unskilled labor, with little human capital endowment. A significant proportion of poor households also suffers from inadequate labor endowment due to a combination of a few able-bodied adults, large family size and a high dependency ratio.

To overcome poverty the poor need to be able to convert their labor resources into income entitlement. This can be attained by: (a) increasing wage employment; (b) increasing real wages through a rise in labor productivity/labor demand; (c) increasing the opportunity for self-employment for the poor workers; (d) enabling the poor to improve their productivity in self employment; and (e) improving the terms of exchange for the output of their self employment. This of course needs to be supplemented by income transfers, or other forms of direct assistance, for the poor households who have an inadequate endowment of labor resources. A decline in fertility, leading to a decline in the dependency ratio, also helps overcome poverty.

The principal elements of a development strategy that promotes all the above poverty-alleviating processes may be highlighted as follows:

1. *Rapid labor-intensive growth providing the poor with productive and remunerative employment.* This involves the entire gamut of development policies which is impossible to summarize in this short paper. First, a high rate of growth needs to be assured by the adoption of comprehensive policies encompassing incentives for domestic capital accumulation and attraction of capital from abroad; policies for the effective deployment of investment resources in socially profitable activities; and the creation of appropriate institutions conducive to the pursuit of growth and efficiency. Secondly, growth must be accompanied by an appropriately high output elasticity of employment. The incentive system must promote a high labor intensity of investment. For example, it must avoid the artificial cheapening of capital which is widespread under the system of import-substituting industrialization. Economic institutions inhibiting the use of labor must be replaced by employment-friendly institutions. For example, in countries with concentrated landownership,

e.g., the Philippines and Brazil, the intensity of labor use in agriculture has been low due to the widely-observed phenomenon of the inverse relationship between farm size and labor use per hectare and the withholding by large landowners of tracts of land from cultivation for speculative purposes, resulting in the restriction of employment and output in agriculture.[3] As a consequence of these distorted policies and institutions, employment and wages have grown too slowly to permit a reduction in poverty that is commensurate with the rate of economic growth under appropriate policies and institutions. A more employment-friendly system of land control is necessary for growth to be highly poverty alleviating. Growth-induced employment expansion in agriculture and the rural economy has the most direct effect on rural poverty alleviation. But, in the long run, the welfare of the rural poor depends on the rapid employment-intensive growth of the entire economy and a gradual transfer of labor from agriculture to non-agricultural activities (and possibly, to a lesser extent, a transfer of rural labor to urban employment).

2. *Conversion of the poor into productive entrepreneurs engaged in self employment.* In rural societies of most developing countries the incidence of poverty is often far greater than average for the smallholding farmers and self-employed non-farm categories. Overcoming poverty for these groups is often a matter of a more intensive utilization of household labor by an improved access to productive assets. Redistribution of land, and/or an improved access of the poor to the use of land under favorable rental/tenancy arrangements, is a powerful method of improving the income and welfare of the poor. Other methods are the provision of credit, infrastructure and public services for non-farm microenterprise and granting access to education and training that makes the poor more productive as entrepreneurs (see below). Targeted public action is essential for the promotion of the access of the poor to these resources.

3. *Increasing the productivity of poor workers in both wage employment and self employment.* The principal policy to enhance the productivity of the poor is to endow them with greater human capital: skill, education and health. Successful targeting of public resources is necessary to offset the inadequate capacity of the poor to make private investment in the acquisition of human capital.
4. *Improving the terms of exchange for the produce of the poor.* Improved terms of trade for activities in which the poor are concentrated, both as wage workers and self-employed microentrepreneurs, helps alleviate poverty. For this, an improved access to infrastructure, market and services is essential.
5. The above measures should enable the poor households with an adequate endowment of labor to progress towards overcoming poverty. *The poor households without an adequate endowment of labor will require more direct assistance in the form of income transfer.* The ability of a developing country to mobilize resources for income transfer is limited. *Special measures will also be needed for labor-disadvantaged households*, e.g., the female-headed and female-labor-intensive households who can not compete for the usual kind of employment in the market place.

While the determinants of the decline in fertility are not easily traceable, it appears that they are closely related to increased education, better health, declining infant mortality and generally the poverty reduction policies outlined above. The process is helped by the easy access of the poor to the means of contraception.

II. The Role of the State in Rural Poverty Alleviation in Some East Asian Countries

The East Asian countries, like the Republic of Korea and Taiwan, are among the most successful contemporary cases of rural poverty alleviation. In many ways these cases are similar to the experience of Japan in an earlier period. By and large, they implemented a strategy that included at least the first four of the elements identified above.

The beginning was the implementation of highly egalitarian land reforms which drastically brought down the upper limit of landownership, substantially expropriated the large landowners and redistributed land among the landless and the smallholders. This was supplemented by a number of complementary measures to support the development of agriculture and rural economic activities: government funded research in improved technology; access to credit; improved infrastructure; and improved terms of trade for agriculture. The overall development strategy succeeded in promoting rapid economic growth which was highly employment friendly. This was brought about by a system of direct promotion of worthwhile industries; public investment in the development of the infrastructure; the creation of an incentive system that induced a high rate of saving and the direction of investment to socially-profitable industries; and sound macroeconomic policies. Labor market policies facilitated a rapid change in the composition of employment by allowing a transfer of workers from agriculture to non-agricultural occupations with a low difference in wage rates between the two sectors. This was helped by the avoidance of those direct interventions in the labor market that artificially create a large difference between urban and rural wages and prevent the transfer of labor from agriculture to secondary and tertiary activities by restrictive employment practices in the latter. As a result, non-farm employment increased rapidly, bringing about a quick reduction in the share of agriculture in total employment. Large public investment in education quickly resulted in universal literacy and a sharp increase in the efficiency of the labor force. Rapid increase in employment, accompanied by a rise in real wages at about the same rate as the rise in per capita income, was instrumental in promoting equality in the distribution of income and sharply reducing the incidence of poverty both in rural and urban areas. A quick demographic transition further helped the process.[4]

In the implementation of this strategy the state had a distinct role that often differed from the role that the state had elsewhere in the developing world. The following brief look at the role of the state in the implementation the different components of the strategy for rural development and poverty alleviation brings out the main differences between these countries and the rest of the developing world.

Land Reform

The implementation of a comprehensive land reform by transforming the very unequal distribution of landownership into a highly egalitarian peasant ownership, with universal access to land, stands out as the critical element that distinguishes the experience of these countries (and of Japan and a few other East Asian countries to be mentioned below) from that of the rest of the developing world. It provided the initial impetus for egalitarian growth of the rural economy and also created a basis for the subsequent growth of the economy by expanding the size of the market, by enhancing both the ability and the incentive of the farmers to save and invest at high rates, and by promoting a steady increase in productivity that enabled a part of the rural labor force to be released for employment in the fast-growing industries and services. The features of the East Asian land reforms and the principal determinants of their success may be summarized as follows:[5]

1. Each of these countries suffered from extreme scarcity of land which is often cited elsewhere as the reason for land reform being infeasible due to small redistributable

surplus of land. These countries recognized that unequal entitlement to such a scarce factor was especially detrimental for the promotion of equality and the alleviation of poverty because of its high factor share in an unregulated market. Thus they viewed the scarcity of land as an argument for the removal, not the perpetuation, of the inequality in its distribution. They adopted a low ceiling on landownership. The highest permissible ownership unit was less than 2.5 times the average land per household.

2. Redistribution was greatly eased by the "windfall" state ownership gained over as much as 20 per cent of total cultivable land that had been abandoned by the former Japanese owners. This created a very strong basis for an initial redistribution of land before resorting to compulsory land acquisition from private landlords. Another "windfall" that eased the resource burden of financing land reform was the state ownership of the industrial enterprises, left behind by the former Japanese owners, whose stocks paid for 30 per cent of the compensation paid the landlords in Taiwan. In Korea also this was used to mop up the compensation payment received by the landlords.

3. In spite of these two extraordinary bonuses, together amounting to a very high proportion of the value of total redistribution, land reforms in these countries were not market driven. There was a substantial element of confiscation in so far as the landlords were given only 2.5 times the value of annual output of land in Taiwan and between 1.5 and 1.8 times the value of output in Korea. Reliable information on the market price of land is not available - and land prices had already been brought down in Taiwan by the successful reform of the system of land rent - but it is a fair guess that confiscation represented at least two-thirds of the land value that the landlords would have received if reforms were entirely market driven.

4. The implementation of such a confiscatory redistribution of land required a great deal of political will the want of which is often cited as the principal obstacle to land reforms elsewhere. In each of the cases under review, the impetus for land reforms came from a government that was autonomous of the vested interests including the landlords. Taiwan was ruled by the occupying Guomindang which had neither any association with nor any commitment to the landed aristocracy. Furthermore they had just learned the lesson from their defeat by the communists on the mainland that it was very important to create broad-based support among the population by redistributive measures like land reforms. In Korea the reform was spearheaded by the U.S. Army Military Government in Korea (USAMGIK) which was completely autonomous of the landed aristocracy. The threat from the north was probably an additional impetus on the part of the Korean government that started exercising authority in 1948. These special circumstances explain why there was no shortage of political will to implement reforms that hurt the landlords.
5. In both cases tenancy reforms were implemented as a prelude to land redistribution. The result of tenancy reforms was very different in the two countries. In Taiwan these reforms were apparently successful. They led to a reduction in land rent and land value which helped the acquisition of land at low prices. In Korea these reforms were not successful. They led to perverse outcomes detrimental to the tenants. The difference appears to have been due to the presence of grassroots organization in Taiwan and their absence in Korea.
6. Successful implementation of measures that involved administrative acquisition and allocation of assets below market prices, avoiding overt corruption and bribery, was possible because of extensive rural organization that the government was able to lean upon. In Korea, the lack of organization during the phase of tenancy reform under the auspices of the USAMGIK, which had very limited

jurisdiction over the rural society, was remedied by the creation of an extensive network of tripartite land committees.

7. In the case of Korea there is clear documentation that a special feature of the pre-reform rural society - namely, the highly egalitarian distribution of operational holdings of land - greatly helped the implementation of land redistribution. The process essentially represented a transfer of land title from the (predominantly non-cultivating) landlords to the actual (tenant) farm operators. There is some reason to believe that this was also the case in Taiwan and Japan. In all the East Asian cases of redistribution the process was relatively free of social turmoil. Actual farmers were not displaced. The management of land and farms was continued to be carried out by experienced farmers whose incentives were boosted by the acquisition of ownership. This East Asian feature of land rented out to tenants in equal parcels is absent in pre-reform agrarian societies elsewhere, e.g., South Asia. A full explanation of this phenomenon must be sought in the social, political and economic history of the region. It however seems likely that agro-climatic factors played an important part in this. Even rainfall and extreme land scarcity resulted in a relative unimportance of animal labor in East Asian agriculture. This made households without an endowment of draught animals eligible for tenancy thereby resulting in a highly egalitarian distribution of tenanted land. This peculiar feature of East Asian agriculture appears to have been yet another special factor smoothing the process of land reform.

China and Vietnam also expropriated the landlords after a revolutionary overthrow of the feudal agrarian system. Initially land was redistributed among the farm households to create a system of egalitarian peasant farming. This was, however, quickly abolished in favor of the collectivization of agriculture. After decades of unsuccessful struggle to create an efficient agriculture under collective institutions, these countries reinstated egalitarian distribution of land among individual households to recreate the system of peasant farming. The final outcome of the Chinese and Vietnamese experience appears to be remarkably similar to the Taiwanese and Korean experience in so far as both the paths ended up creating an egalitarian private peasant agriculture. In Taiwan and Korea the financial cost of land transfer was kept manageable by a combination of the windfall of land and assets left by their former Japanese owners and the imposition of a severely-depressed, confiscatory price on the landlords. In the Chinese and Vietnamese case the financial cost of land transfer was eliminated by the outright expropriation of the landlords. The political will for such radical "turning over" was provided by the occupying army in the former case and the revolutionary overthrow of feudalism in the latter.

The big difference between the two models is that China and Vietnam interrupted their initial land reform by a long detour along the collectivist path before returning to individual peasant farming. In retrospect it is clear that this detour was wasteful. By all indications these countries would have avoided long periods of slow growth and persistence of poverty and periodic plunge into disasters by staying with their initial land reforms and complementing the development of egalitarian peasant farming by appropriate systems of incentives and access to services and inputs. Experience has also proved wrong the fear expressed by the socialist visionaries like Mao that post-reform private agriculture would lead to polarization and low productivity.

It, however, needs to be recognized that peasant farming could not succeed within the overall framework of central planning that these countries adopted. Irrational prices, bureaucratic control over distribution of inputs and services and arbitrary procurement policies that characterized economic planning in these countries were incompatible with the development of individual farming based of egalitarian peasant ownership. The rejection of land reform in favor of collective agriculture was not an incoherent action. By the same token, individual peasant farming could be the successful vehicle for development only if these countries were able to design a market friendly and decentralized economy.

The return to egalitarian peasant farming in China saw a period of extremely rapid reduction in rural poverty. The rate of reduction in rural poverty slowed down in the second half of the 1980s when the complementary policies for rural development - e.g., improved terms of trade for agriculture, a high rate of investment in agriculture and public investment in rural education - were weakened or reversed.[6] In Vietnam the complementary policies are yet to be fully put in place although the benefits of land reform have already been clearly reflected in the performance of the rural economy.[7]

Complementary Policies to Enhance the Productivity and Income of the Rural Poor

In the successful East Asian cases, land reform was supplemented by additional measures for the improvement of the productivity of the poor and improved terms of exchange for the product of the labor of the poor. To make the most of the access to land, it is necessary to have access to complementary factors: credit, technology and inputs. The role of the state in the successful East Asian countries is illustrated by the experience of Taiwan in these areas for which documentation is readily available.[8] Prior to land reform, farmers' association and credit co-operatives in Taiwan were dominated by landlords and non-farmers with the primary purpose of providing extension service and procuring rice. In 1952, the government restructured them by consolidating them into multipurpose farmers' associations restricted to serving the needs of the farmers and ensuring the control of the farmers over them. Their activities were expanded to include accepting savings deposits, advancing credit, and providing facilities for purchasing inputs and marketing, storing and processing agricultural output. While the government was instrumental in shaping the institutional structure, it avoided involvement in the operation of these associations which were autonomous cooperatives controlled by the farmers.

The government also provided resources to agricultural research agencies. The emphasis was on the biological-chemical technology, which is employment augmenting, and not on mechanical technology, which tends to replace labor.

Agricultural price policy was used both as a method of modestly taxing agriculture, which had to contribute to the nation's capital formation because of its overwhelming size at the time, and to encourage a shift in cropping pattern away from rice and in favor of higher-valued crops, e.g., sugarcane, corn, mushrooms and asparagus. The government had widespread interventions in the market in the form of land tax in kind, rice-fertilizer barter system, and guaranteed prices to induce a shift in cropping pattern in the direction of more intensive use of land and increased days of employment per worker.

Two other components of the strategy that contributed to the improvement in the welfare of the rural poor are their increased endowment of human capital and improved access to infrastructure. In both these areas the state made very substantial investment. The state was instrumental in providing universal primary education, ensuring adult literacy and creating a basic health care system very early in the development process. It also made large-scale investment in the development of infrastructure: transportation and power supply.

Policies were broadly similar in Korea and in China in the early years of reform following the return to egalitarian peasant farming.

Broader Development Policies for Rapid Labor-Intensive Growth

The objective of improving the welfare of the rural poor cannot be pursued in isolation of the development of the urban and non-agricultural sectors. A coordinated development of the entire economy is a precondition for the development of the rural economy and the elimination of rural poverty. Successful poverty-reducing growth is characterized by a rapid transfer of labor from agriculture to non-agricultural activities. Thus a development strategy leading to a rapid overall economic growth is an essential element in the strategy of alleviating rural poverty.

The experience of Korea and Taiwan in fostering such a strategy is by now very well documented.[9] While adhering to a strategy that promoted growth and avoided gross distortions in the allocation of resources (e.g., discrimination against exports in favor of import replacement and against labor-intensive techniques in favor of capital-intensive techniques), the state by no means opted for *laissez faire.* Economic growth was not the passive outcome of the forces of free market and the global economy. It was nurtured by the entrepreneurial umbrella of the state which made sensible interventions in identifying socially-profitable industries and setting up detailed mechanisms for directing resources to those industries. Furthermore, it made large-scale investment in the development of the infrastructure and education and health services.

Among those functions that the state often performed elsewhere in the developing countries, there are certain things that the state in these East Asian countries did not do. The most important among these was the avoidance of ownership of productive enterprises in agriculture and industries which was left to the private sector. By and large the state also avoided direct involvement in the marketing and delivery of products and services. While elsewhere in the developing world inputs for agriculture were often directly distributed and controlled by the state, in East Asia these were left to private business and cooperatives operating in a market environment. As noted above, direct interventions to regulate wage rates and conditions of employment were also avoided.

The extent of redistributive measures, e.g., income transfer directed to the poor, was generally de-emphasized. While rapid growth in employment and real wages reduced the need for this instrument, it has been argued that the governments of these countries did not make a timely transition towards the institution of a system of social protection even after they attained a relatively high level of development. As a consequence, the argument goes on, these countries did not have a system of protection for those who were temporarily driven into poverty by the crisis that hit them in 1997.

III. Lessons About the Appropriate Roles for the State and the Other Stakeholders in Rural Poverty Alleviation

Contemporary debate on development policy centers around opposing views on the kind of role that is attributed to the East Asian state in the preceding section. There is a view, often advocated by the major international development agencies, that there are substantial costs associated with the kind of activist role that the state had in East Asia. This final section considers this case in the context of each of the major components of the strategy of rural poverty alleviation identified above.

First, consider the role of the state in making numerous interventions with the forces of the market and global free trade in *promoting* specific activities as a part of the strategy for rapid labor-intensive growth. There is a view, increasingly dominant in the age of globalization, that this can and usually does result in inefficient resource use. The argument is as follows: the state is liable to make mistakes in identifying socially-profitable activities; the cost of such mistakes can be very large; it is far better to allow the forces of free market and global trade to determine the pattern of allocation of resources and economic development. The argument is often expanded to suggest that investment in much of infrastructure - power, communication and transport - should be left to the private investor, responding to market forces, and education and health services should be based on cost recovery. It is not far from truth to describe this as the development doctrine that dominates the consensus among the Bretton Woods institutions and their most powerful member. Poverty reduction is visualized as the process of rapid expansion of employment in response to growth fostered by free market and free trade.

The evidence of history and contemporary development experience does not provide much support for this doctrine. In the age of rapid globalization over the last two decades, all the developing regions of the world outside Asia have failed to prevent a decline in growth despite vast reform of their incentive systems to promote free trade and free market. While the past system of distorted incentives were dismantled, they were not replaced by an alternative system of incentives for growth. In Asia economic growth, measured by the rate of increase in per capita GDP, accelerated during the period of globalization. In South Asia this was due to a very modest increase in the rate of growth of GDP and a significant reduction in the rate of population growth. In China and South-East

Asia (until 1997) the acceleration in the growth rate of GDP was sharper. Two facts need to be noted about all these Asian countries. First, in these countries the state had not abdicated in the manner suggested by the critics of the East Asian strategy. Secondly, the accelerated growth in these countries was very different from the East Asian experience discussed above in so far as economic growth has been highly disequalizing in the age of globalization. In all these cases growth became highly employment hostile in the age of globalization, thereby seriously weakening its impact on poverty reduction.[10]

In the words of Dani Rodrik "Global integration has become, for all practical purposes, a substitute for a development strategy":[11]

> This trend is bad news for the world's poor... By focusing on international integration, governments in poor nations divert human resources, administrative capabilities, and political capital away from more urgent development priorities such as education, public health, industrial capacity, and social cohesion. This emphasis also undermines nascent democratic institutions by removing the choice of development strategy from public debate.
>
> World markets are a source of technology and capital; it would be silly for the developing world not to exploit these opportunities. But globalization is not a shortcut to development. Successful economic growth strategies have always required a judicious blend of imported practices with domestic institutional innovations. Policymakers need to forge a domestic growth strategy by relying on domestic investors and domestic institutions. The costliest downside of the integrationist faith is that it crowds out serious thinking and efforts along such lines.

Development policy must combine market-friendly reforms for integration with the global economy with the systematic *promotion* of socially-profitable economic activities through public provision of infrastructure, services and targeted, time-bound support of more direct kind. Mere removal of the past inefficient system of incentives for import-substituting industrialization, in the hope that the rest would be done by the forces operating in the global economy, is nothing more or less than an act of abdication which characterizes too many of the developing countries today.

The next important issue relates to state-sponsored land reform and other programs of providing the poor with access to non-land assets. The World Bank and other development agencies have been arguing that these "confiscatory and confrontational" reforms should be replaced by "market-friendly" methods of redistributing land by inducing large landowners to sell land to the poor whose ability to purchase is augmented by the provision of credit. Such programs are being tried out in Brazil under the auspices of the World Bank. So far there is scant evidence of success of such policies in providing access to land to large groups of poor. The poor rarely posses the power and resources required to gain access to such valuable a resource as land through market transactions; the targeting of the poor to receive large volumes of substantially subsidized credit, that are necessary for such transactions, will face overwhelming problems of leakage in the direction of the non-poor. There is no reason to believe that market intermediation will result in a substantial improvement of the access of the poor to land. If the government does not have the necessary political will or independence to impose redistribution on the powerful social groups, then the answer must be sought in helping government acquire such will and independence. International development agencies have a remarkable record of pushing down the throats of the governments in developing countries loads of unpopular reforms which have at times led to their downfall. Might there be a case for the inclusion of redistribution in favor of the poor in the conditionality of policy lending with strong incentives and possible bribes for the powerful social groups?

If confiscatory and confrontational methods are ruled out, the alternative is market-driven, non-confrontational redistribution: acquisition of land from the large landowners by paying them the market price and its sale to tenants and the landless. What are the prospects of bringing about an egalitarian redistribution by this method?

The implications for reform of this kind could be illustrated for Bangladesh, an extremely land-scarce country for which the necessary information is available.[12] The top decile (i.e., rural households representing the largest 10 per cent of per capita landowners) own 47.2 per cent of land and the ninth highest decile of owners own 20.6 per cent. The bottom half of the population ranked in terms of per capita landownership had 5.7 per cent of land. Suppose 25 per cent of total land is acquired from the top decile for distribution among the bottom half of the landowners. This would still leave the top two deciles with 43 per cent of land. The overall distribution would still not be as equal as in the East Asian cases.

Even this modest redistribution by the East Asian standard would require the acquisition of approximately 2.125 million hectares of land which would be valued at $25.5 billion ($ 12,000 being the approximate average market price). Annual net output value per hectare is approximately $ 700. A reasonable set of terms of transfer to the recipients of land might be a third of the net value paid over a period of 15 years. Typical land rent being approximately 50% of net value, these terms would constitute a modest redistribution to the asset-poor households. The East Asian beneficiaries of land reform paid a much smaller price as a proportion of output. Less generous terms than these would hardly qualify as significant redistribution.

Such a scheme would require a per hectare subsidy of $ 8,500 or a total cost of redistribution of just over $ 18 billion. This does not take into account the cost of administering the program and assumes that the landlords would forego the interest on the deferred payment made by the peasants. Even so, this is 40 per cent of GDP, 4.5 times the annual government revenue and approximately 9 times the annual gross capital inflow. It is inconceivable that domestic or international resources could be mobilized to implement such a redistribution over a reasonable time horizon. The principal obstacle is the high ratio of land price to annual value of net output of land, 17 as compared to 1.5 to 2.5 during land reforms in Korea and Taiwan. These countries had the additional advantage of the windfall of public ownership of about 20 per cent of total land and a vast amount of non-land assets left behind by the former colonial power to ease the process of redistribution.

Lack of financial resources is not the only obstacle to egalitarian land reform. Few of the contemporary developing countries have the administrative capability to effect a transfer involving large subsidies without large-scale corruption and misappropriation of benefits. How did the East Asians do it? Was it the pressure of military occupation? The force or the threat of revolution? The absence of large-scale vested interest in the case of second land reforms in China and Vietnam? Or has the administrative ability in the developing countries eroded over time as the dominance of the market, without a countervailing system of public monitoring, has strengthened the incentive on the part of the bureaucracy to grab the scarcity premium?

Even for programs like micro-credit for the poor, the involvement of the government is absolutely essential, a fact that is amply demonstrated by the much vaunted *Grameen Bank* in Bangladesh. It cannot operate on market principle. Despite charging the poor recipients an interest rate that is more than twice the rate of interest at which large private entrepreneurs borrow from the formal banking institutions, *Grameen Bank* operations needed substantial public subsidy and foreign assistance through government intermediation. Despite this support and an efficient organization of the program that has drawn international acclaim, the targeting of the poor by the program in Bangladesh became distinctly weaker after initial years.[13] This is almost certainly due to the weak access of the poor to land and physical assets the endowment of which is often a determinant of the efficient use of credit.

The leading role of the state in endowing the poor with human capital is also indispensable only if the externalities of investment in these activities are so huge that the market can never be trusted as a mechanism to allow the poor to acquire enough of these assets. Inequality in private expenditure on education and health is so enormous in the developing countries that, without an offsetting distribution of public expenditure in favor of the poor, it is impossible to bestow them with the minimum endowment that is consistent with overcoming poverty.[14]

The East Asian experience demonstrates that in most of these areas the state can perform best in cooperation with the other stakeholders, the NGOs, the civil society and the private sector. In many cases a partnership between the state and the other stakeholders can result in an efficient combination of the ability of the state to deal with large-scale externalities and the efficiency of the other stakeholders in carrying out market transactions and organizing community effort. The comparison of the experience of Taiwan with that of Korea shows that the existence of grassroots organizations in the former enabled the government to successfully implement the tenancy reform that preceded the land reform while the absence of grassroots organizations led to a failure of similar tenancy reforms in Korea. These countries made extensive use of these organizations in the distribution of credit, extension services and inputs.

The East Asian example clearly demonstrates that the state should stay out of activities that involve pure commercial transactions. These include the delivery of inputs, credit and services. In much of the developing world, the state ventured into these areas as an entrepreneur. This is illustrated by the experience of the South Asian countries which resorted to direct government control of prices, distribution and delivery of inputs like fertilizer and irrigation water. In these systems, often with substantial subsidies, the poor always lose out to those who have wealth and power. The danger of governmental failure is greatest in these areas. Market is the best method of distributing these inputs and services while the vulnerability of the poor is dealt with by directly redistributive policies.

Riverside, May 7, 2001

REFERENCES

1. Amsden, Alice, *Asia's Next Giant: South Korea and Late Industrialization*, New York: Oxford University Press, 1989.

2. Ghai, Dharam, A. R. Khan, Eddy Lee and Samir Radwan (eds.), *Agrarian Systems and Rural Development*, London: Macmillan, 1979.

3. Griffin, Keith (ed.), *Economic Reform in Vietnam*, London: Macmillan, 1998.

4. Griffin, Keith, A. R. Khan and Amy Ickowitz, *Poverty and Distribution of Land*, Department of Economics, University of California Riverside, 2000 (Working Paper).

5. IFAD (International Fund for Agricultural Development), *Rural Poverty Report 2001: The Challenge of Ending Rural Poverty*, Oxford University Press, New York, 2001.

6. Khan, A. R. and M. Muqtada, *Employment Expansion and Macroeconomic Stability Under Increasing Globalization*, London: Macmillan, 1997.

7. Khan, A. R. and B. Sen, "Inequality and Its Sources in Bangladesh: 1991/92 to 1995/96", *Bangladesh Development Studies,* Spring 2001.

8. Khan, A. R. and Carl Riskin, *Inequality and Poverty in China in the Age of Globalization*, Oxford and New York: Oxford University Press, 2001.

9. Kuo, Shirley W. Y., Gustav Ranis and John C. H. Fei, *Rapid Growth with Improved Distribution in the Republic of China, 1952-79*, Boulder, Colorado: Westview Press, 1981.

10. Rahman, Rushidan Islam, *Poverty Alleviation and Empowerment through Microfinance: Two Decades of Experience in Bangladesh*, Dhaka: Bangladesh Institute of Development Studies, 2000.

11. Thiesenheusen, William C. and Jolyne Melmed-Sanjak, "Brazil's Agrarian Structure: Changes from 1970 through 1980, *World Development*, Vol. 18, No. 3, pp. 393-415, 1990.

12. UNDP, *Globalization with a Human Face, Background Papers, Vol.II,* New York, 1999.

13. Wade, Robert, *Governing the Market: Economic Theory and the Role of the Government in East Asian Industrialization*, Princeton, N.J.: Princeton University Press, 1990.

14. World Bank, *The East Asian Miracle*, Oxford and New York: Oxford University Press, 1993.

NOTES

1. IFAD, 2001, Chapter 2.

2. IFAD, 2001, Chapter 2.

3. There is a large literature on the subject. A recent empirical study documenting the phenomenon for Brazil is William C. Thiesenhusen and Jolyne Melmed-Sanjak, 1990. The paper reports that employment per hectare was 9.78 person months for farms 1-10 hectares in size and only 0.7 person months for farms 50-200 hectares and 0.02 hectares for farms 10,000 hectares and above.

4. For an account of the story see Eddy Lee, "Egalitarian Peasant Farming and Rural Development: The Case of South Korea", in Ghai et al., 1979; Kuo et al., 1981; and Dipak Mazumdar and Priya Basu, "Macroeconomic Policies, Growth and Employment: The East and South-East Asian Experience", in Khan and Muqtada, 1997.

5. For a fuller account of land reforms in the Republic of Korea and Taiwan see, Griffin, K, A. R. Khan and A. Ickowitz, 2000.

6. See Khan and Riskin, 2001.

7. See A. R. Khan, "Vietnam's Rural Economy: Performance and Prospects" in Griffin, 1998.

8. See Kuo et al., 1981.

9. Classic case studies are Amsden, 1989, Wade, 1990 and World Bank, 1993.

10. For China the evidence is compiled in Khan and Riskin, 2001. For South Asia the evidence is shown in A. R. Khan, "Globalization and Human Development in South Asia" in UNDP, 1999.

11. Dani Rodrik, "Trading in Illusion", *Foreign Policy*, March/April 2001.

12. All the distributional data are from the 1995/96 Household Expenditure Survey. Data on land value, obtained from discussions with concerned experts, was supplied by Dr. Quazi Shahabuddin, Research Director of the Bangladesh Institute of Development Studies. Value of annual net output per hectare was obtained by dividing the value added by all crop production by the net cultivated area in 1997/98.

13. See Rushidan Islam Rahman, 2000.

14. The compounding of the inequality in private expenditure between *rural* and *urban* areas, *men* and *women* and the *poor* and the *non-poor* amounts to an enormous overall disparity. This is illustrated by the ratio of per capita private expenditure on education in Bangladesh for the *richest decile* of the *urban male* to the per capita private expenditure on education for the *poorest decile* of the *rural female* of 101! See Khan and Sen, 2001.

15

Role of Credit and Non-credit Co-operatives in Rural Development

Dr. B. Ramachandra Reddy,
Dr. P. Kothandarami Reddy

1. Evolution of Co-operatives

Co-operation is considered to be the golden mean between the two competing systems of capitalism and socialism. Its philosophy is based on the principle of "each for all and all for each". It, therefore, reconciles the conflicting areas of unbridled individualism and freedom of enterprise of capitalism and subordination of the individual to that of the society under socialism. co-operation is based on the equality of individuals, fraternity among the members of society and thereby the maximisation of social welfare. It is rooted in utilitarianism of the West and 'Sarvodaya' of the East. It is truly a democracy in action if it is based on these foundations.

Germany is the birth place of co-operative movement in the world. It was during the middle of 19th century, when famine, poverty, exploitation and indebtedness were prevalent in Germany, the co-operative movement took its birth to rehabilitate poor farmers and labourers from miserable conditions (S.S. Talmaki, 1931). Mr. F.W. Raiffeisen and Herr Franz Schulze started making experiments with various methods of relief, under co-operative fold. The movement gradually spread to Europe and countries such as Great Britain, Denmark, Sweden, France and Italy successfully organised the co-operatives in different sectors to improve living conditions of their members. In course of time, Canada, Israel, Russia, China and Japan also joined the Co-operative Movement (C.R. Ray, 1976). The idea of starting Co-operative Societies in India for combating rural indebtedness and supplying rural credit at a cheaper rate of interest was first initiated by Fredrick Nicholson, a Madras civilian during 1895. The movement got accelerated with the passing of Co-operative Societies Act of 1904. Its main object was to combat indebtedness and provide credit to rural community at large (B.S. Mathur, 1999)

2. The Structure of Co-operative Banking System in India

Co-operative Institutions occupy an important position in the financial system of the economy in terms of their reach, volume of operations and the purpose they serve. Rural co-operative banks play a pivotal role in the rural credit delivery system with credit co-operation forming almost 70 per cent of the rural credit outlets. Rural co-operative banks account for around 30 per cent of rural deposits and 44 per cent of the outstanding loans and advances of the banking system for agriculture and rural development (Mithani and Gordon, 2000). About 55 per cent of the short term production loans for the agriculture sector come from co-operative credit institutions. The following chart provides in a nut shell an idea of the co-operative banking system in India.

CO-OPERATIVE BANKING SYSTEM IN INDIA

↓

State Co-operative Banks (APEX)

↓

Central Co-operative Banks (DISTRICT)

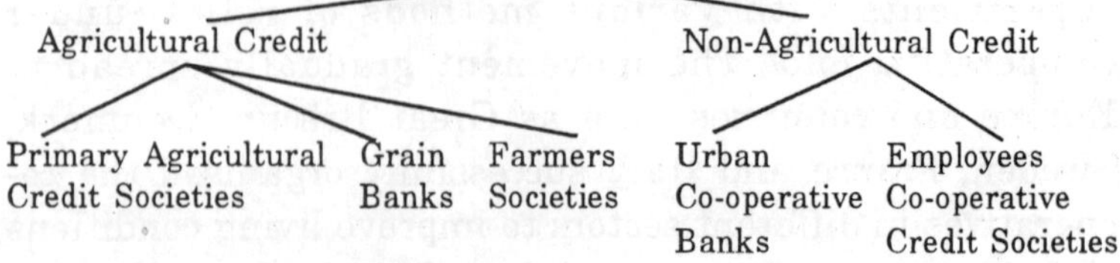

3. Co-operatives and Rural Development

Rural development in India is recognised as a sine qua non for faster economic development and welfare of the rural poor. Rural development is not confined to the development of rural areas but also the development of the rural poor into self-reliant and self-sustaining modern communities. Rural development is, therefore, the development of rural areas in such a way that each component of rural life changes in a desired direction and in sympathy with the other components. Besides, rural development also encompasses structural changes in the socio-economic situation in the rural areas in order that human welfare, which is the primary goal of all development, is secured at the earliest. Rural development, thus should embrace all the objectives of enrichment and betterment of the overall quality of rural life through appropriate development of manpower resources, infrastructural facilities and provision of minimum needs and livelihood (B.L. Mathur, 2000).

Co-operation has been accepted as an important medium for regeneration of the country's socio-economic life. In fact, co-operation in India has been recognised as a part of the pattern of Indian socialism, especially interpreted in terms of rural society. Co-operation, thus, has a very significant role to play in any programme of social and economic development of an underdeveloped country like India. India can rightly claim to have the world's largest network of co-operatives. Thus co-operatives play an important role in promoting rural development. The present paper attempts to examine the performance of co-operatives in rural development and identify their weaknesses with a view to offering suggestions for strengthening the co-operatives as an agency for promoting rural development on a sustainable basis. The performance of co-operatives in relation to rural development can be examined in terms of the contribution of the co-operative's organisation to the development of rural infrastructural facilities like roads and electricity, supply of credit for expansion and strengthening the production activities in rural areas in order to raise rural incomes, organising the marketing and processing activities for the rural producers to enhance their incomes. The following paragraphs give some indication of the performance of co-operatives in respect of different areas:

4. Progress of Co-operative Credit Societies

There are nearly 92 thousand Primary Agricultural Credit Societies (PACs) out of 350 thousand co-operatives of all kinds in the country, covering practically all the villages. The total individual membership of these PACs as on 31st March 2000 is nearly 10 crore farmers, with an average membership of 1083 per PACS. About 41.3 per cent of the total members are borrowers. About 52 per cent of the PACS are viable, about 23 per cent are potentially viable and the rest, 25 per cent are dormant. The total share capital is Rs.147405 crore, which comes to Rs. 1602 per society and the government contribution being nearly 17 per cent. The deposits of the PACs in the country stood at Rs. 6526 crore as on 31st March 2000 representing a growth of 15% over the previous year. The short–term loans advanced by PACs stood at Rs.175.31 crores in 1999-2000 i.e. nearly 30 per cent of the requirements for agricultural finance in the country. There are 367 DCCBs and 29 SCBs functioning with 823 and 12407 branches respectively purveying rural credit. The deposits of SCBs and DCCBs in the country stood at Rs. 29535 crore and Rs. 53634 crore as on 31st March 2000 representing an increase of 14.5% and 17.6% respectively over the previous year. Total loans advanced by SCBs and DCCBs increased from Rs. 30162 crore and Rs. 40252 crore during 1998-99 to Rs. 35156 crore and Rs. 46247crore respectively during 1999-2000, registering an increase of 16.6% and 14.9% respectively. The NPAs constituted 10.73% (SCBs) and 17.5% (DCCBs) of their total loans and advances outstanding as on 31-3-200 (wwwNABARD.org.in).

The number of State Co-operative Agricultural and Rural Development Banks (SACARDBs) at present is 8 under unitary structure and 11 under federal structure, while in Andhra Pradesh integrated structure (single window) is in operation. The number of Primary Co-operative Agriculture and Rural Development Banks (PCARDBs) is 755. The loans outstanding as on 31st March 2000 stood at Rs. 11578 crore (SCARDBs) and Rs. 7602 crore (PCARDBs) registering a growth of 10.9 and 11.5% over the previous year. The loans issued by SCARDBs as also by PCARDBs during 1990-2000 increased by 3% and 7% respectively. The NPAs constituted 18.66% (SCARDBs) and 19.98% (PCARDBs) of their total loans and advances outstanding as on 31st March 2000 (RBI Report 2000-01). Though the share of co-operative banks in total institutional credit has declined but still these banks occupy a pivotal position in the supply of rural credit. As at the end of March 2000 these co-operatives constituted 40 per cent of the total direct agricultural finance of all institutional agencies.

Weaknesses

It is a pity that despite the overwhelming importance of co-operatives in rural development, their performance could not come up to the expectation. This is due to the fact that co-operatives suffer from certain serious weaknesses, some of which are mentioned below:

(i) Resource Constraints

The Central and the State co-operative credit societies could not attract as much deposits from the general public as was anticipated. They are generally dependent on government sources to support their activities. A large number of PACs are weak and non-viable. These societies are not in a position to cater effectively to the needs of their members. As many as 43-45 per cent of PACs are incurring losses. The Review Committee concluded "The PACs are seen today not strong to discharge their responsibilities". Further, the allocation in Five Year Plans for co-operative development has been gradually declining if calculated in terms of percentage of total allocation for various programmes.

(ii) Problem of Overdues

The problem of mounting overdues in co-operatives is a matter of serious concern to the policy makers. The mounting overdues disrupt over time the flow of credit to the farmers from the co-operatives and adversely affect the capacity of lending institutions to provide adequate and timely credit to agriculture, and thus hampers the pace of economic development. Agricultural Credit Review Committee opined that the problem of overdues, "has led to the choking of credit lines and denial of financial assistance to agricultural members of affiliated banks. It may be noted that better classes of farmers are responsible for a large proportion of overdues. This is a matter requiring serious attention of all those interested in the progress of co-operative movement. The overdues have increased from Rs. 2842 crores in 1991-92 to Rs. 4876 crores in 1999-2000 which constituted more than 22 per cent of the total overdues. Further more than 69 per cent of the total overdues are 'old' for over 3 years and only 31 per cent 'current for less than 3 years'. The problem of overdues has been aggravated because of shortsighted political interventions.

In case of long-term co-operative credit structure the main problems are: (1) viability of PCARDs/branches of SCARDBs, (ii) legal constraints to take-up lending for non-land based activities, (iii) mounting overdues, and (iv) lack of functional coordination with the short-term credit wing. The viability problem of PCARDBs arises because the average margin available to SCARDBAs is only about 3.6 per cent and loses about 0.65 per cent to 1 per cent at the PCARDBs in their lending.

The overdues problem of CARBs has become more serious over the years even when their loans result in the creation of productive assets, and should normally generate adequate incremental income to repay the loans. Though the Agricultural Credit Review Committee considers "the phenomenon of high overdues... more puzzling", the major damaging factor relates to external political environment which is not conducive to recovery, absence of fear of legal action leading to willful default.

(iii) Dependence on External Finance

Dependence on external sources of finance is another serious defect of the co-operatives. The ratio of deposits to working capital is less than 6 per cent in many states. The credit societies depend largely for their working capital on central financing agencies and these agencies in turn, depend on the NABARD and the State Governments. Thus horizontal deposit system was neglected, while vertical funds coming from CCBs, SCs and NABARD become more important. This compels central financing agencies to charge high rates of interest from members. So long as the primary societies continue to lend funds mostly deposited by non-members or borrowed from other sources, they remain only quasi co-operative in nature.

(iv) Unproductive loans:

Large loans have very often been given for unproductive purposes to members who may have concealed their old debts. Such loans could not be repaid punctually and consequently, the overdues were accumulated. The management has often been reluctant to take necessary stringent action against the defaulters (B.L. Mathur, 2000).

5. Progress of Non-credit Co-operative Societies

(a) Agricultural Marketing

Unorganized marketing of agricultural produce, forced sales and low prices received by the producer farmers have been important factors contributing to the backwardness of the rural areas. The co-operative marketing started with the formation of Co-operative Marketing Society in 1913 to undertake the supply of essential inputs and to arrange for the sale of members produce. However, co-operative marketing to a systematic basis started in India after the year 1956. The value of agricultural produce marketed by all co-operatives during 1955-56 was only about Rs.53 crore. The Second Five Year Plan accorded considerable importance on the development of co-operative marketing. By the end of 1960-61, there were 24 apex marketing societies, 171 central marketing societies and 3108 primary marketing societies which handled agricultural produce worth Rs. 174 crore. This amount reported by the Committee on Co-operative Marketing (1966), represented only a negligible fraction of the total marketed surplus of agricultural produce. By and large, co-operative marketing did not make any progress in the country during the Second Five Year Plan period. An important step in this regard to the development of co-operative marketing during this period was the establishment of the National Co-operative Development Corporation and Warehousing Board in 1956 for planning and promoting programmes for the production, processing, marketing, storage, import and export of agricultural produce through co-operatives. During the plan period the National Agricultural Co-operative Marketing Federation (NAFED) was also set up to coordinate the activities of apex state co-operative marketing societies and also to promote inter-state trade. A new department of co-operation was also created at the centre in order to pay special attention to the co-operative movement in the country.

Arrangements were also made for providing financial assistance by the State to the marketing co-operatives by way of contribution to their share capital, loans and subsidies for the construction of godowns, grading units and cold storages in the co-operative sector and subsidies for managerial costs. During the IX plan period 452 additional primary co-operative marketing societies were organised, thus bringing the total number of state partnered societies to 2231 in addition to 900 marketing societies that were organised outside the plan programme. There were also 1600 district level marketing societies, 19 apex state marketing societies, 3 state level commodity federations and one national level federation.

(b) Marketing Society

During the Fourth Five Year Plan, emphasis was laid on the strengthening of the existing marketing societies at the primary level and grading, pooling and other improved techniques were introduced. The National Development Corporation of India established in 1962 initiated the various schemes such as establishment of technical cells in apex marketing societies, creation of a pool of key personnel for marketing co-operatives, formation of price stabilization fund in marketing societies to safeguard them against losses and financing for share capital etc. The agricultural produce handled by the marketing co-operatives far exceeded the plan target of Rs. 900 crore. However, the inter-state disparities still existed and regional imbalances are very much visible despite best efforts to strengthen the co-operative marketing structure. The main emphasis in the Fifth plan was to consolidate marketing, provide technical guidance and assistance for improving operational efficiency of co-operatives and to develop the co-operative marketing in the co-operatively underdeveloped areas to reduce the regional imbalances.

The Ninth Plan document points out that, during the last two decades, marketing co-operatives attained significant growth in business operations and also diversified the activities manifold, yet their total share in the market still continues to be small, nor has their share kept pace with the rapidly growing output and volume of agricultural produce. Towards the end of the Plan, the co-operative marketing structure consisted of about 4000 co-operative marketing societies covering all important markets in the country with 3622 primary marketing societies, 29 states federations and one national federation namely NAFED.

The marketing of agricultural produce through co-operatives has registered substantial growth from Rs. 171 crore in 1960-61 to about Rs. 11560 crore in 1999-2000.

However, the development of marketing co-operatives has not been even in regard to organisation, turnover, profitability and importance. Marketing of sugarcane, cotton and oilseeds account for a predominant share in the total turnover of all the marketing co-operatives in the country. The activities of marketing co-operatives include commercial purchase, procurement operations, price support operation, market intervention, purchase under pooling system and pledge business. Sugarcane, cotton and oilseeds co-operatives apart from providing remunerative prices to the farmers, are also instrumental in the area development in the form of construction of link roads and setting up educational institutions. Inspite of the progress achieved by the co-operatives in marketing of agricultural produce their share in the marketing of agricultural produce is small. The performance of marketing co-operatives has not been up to expectations. Thirty two per cent of them are reported to be undertaking no marketing activity at all. Another 30 per cent are dormant. The rest are doing marginally well. Thus in view of the increasing agricultural production and marketable surplus, the marketing co-operatives have to accelerate their activities to serve the farmers and be instrumental in the initiating, strengthening and widening the process of rural development.

(c) Processing

Processing of agricultural raw materials by the co-operatives owned and operated by the farmers have made significant contribution. The co-operative processing can improve the life and economy of the farmers and the rural areas. The main areas of the processing where co-operatives have successfully entered are sugar, paddy and spinning. The perceptible achievement of co-operative processing can be seen in the sphere of sugar and cotton yarn production. The record of co-operative sugar factories is unique. During 1999-2000 crushing season, 201 co-operative sugar factories in operation produced about 74 lakh tonnes of sugar, accounting for 59 per cent of the national sugar production as against less than 15 lakh tonnes about two decades ago. Nearly 24.22 lakh cane growers are members of the 201 co-operative sugar factories and 80 per cent of them are small and marginal farmers. These processing co-operatives have not only promoted the interest of the cane growers particularly marginal and small farmers but also benefited the farmers of the region through the development of wide range of services to the rural community in their areas including education, irrigation, medical facilities and construction of link roads etc. and also helped in the development of subsidiary industries. Like sugar factories in the co-operative sector, the co-operatives spinning mills have also been organised by cotton growers and also by the ultimate users, mainly the weavers. The 111 cooperative spinning mills as on 31st March 2000 with 36.13 lakh spindlage accounted for nearly 24 per cent of the spinning mills' total spindlage of the country. The value of this yarn production through co-operative spinning mills was estimated at Rs. 613.42 crore during the year 1999-2000. However, some of the cotton mills and sugar factories are faced with a huge stock of accumulated losses. They are likely to be privatised.

Co-operatives have played a successful role in the development of dairy and milk processing and marketing. Development of dairy co-operatives have not only brought glut of milk in India but also has generated subsidiary sources of income to the small and marginal farmers and landless workers. The Amul pattern has drawn international attention and interest. A three-tier organisational structure has developed and the production base comprises primary village level co-operatives of milk producers. The key functional units consisting of district level cluster unions of such village societies and at apex level a state level federation of cluster unions. It is a vertically integrated structure. The structure embraces production, procurement, processing and marketing of milk. Ultimately, commercial integration would take place at the national level. The Government of India has set up a National Dairy Development Board (NDDB) to develop co-operative dairy all over the country. It has also developed a network of milk supply under 'Operation Flood'. There were 70914 dairy co-operatives with a total individual membership of 7.84 million milk producers in 1999-2000. There were 192 district milk unions and 27 state level federations. These co-operatives have established a processing capacity of 16.3 million litres of milk a day and powder production capacity of 732 tonnes a day. Just like the dairy co-operatives, housing co-operatives have also recorded a significant progress in recent years.

(d) Fertilizers Co-operatives

Co-operatives have brought improved technology nearer to the farmers. They have provided improved agricultural inputs like fertilizers, seeds, insecticides and also agricultural implements to their members. To provide technical support to economy in the rural areas, large co-operative organisations like Indian Farmer's Fertilizers Co-operative Ltd., (IFFCO) and Krishak Bhatiya Co-operative Ltd. (KRIBHCO) have adopted villages for their all-round development. Co-operatives now account 36 per cent of the total quantity of fertilizers distributed. The agricultural inputs distributed through co-operative marketing societies in terms of value increased from Rs. 357 crore in 1960-61 to Rs. 17139 crore in 1999-2000 an increase of about 48 times during the same period.

(e) Electricity Supply

The role of co-operatives in the electricity supply began with the establishment of Rural Electrification Corporation (REC) in 1969. There are 38 Rural Electricity Co-operatives (RE Coops) functioning in 11 states, viz., Madhya Pradesh, Andhra Pradesh (9), Bihar, Jammu and Kashmir, Karnataka, Maharashtra, Orissa, Rajasthan and Uttar Pradesh one each, West Bengal (2) and Tamil Nadu (3). By the end of March 2000, the 38 RE coops electrified

4286 villages, 2686 hamlets and intensified 4512 electrified villages. These co-operatives have energised about 0.4 million additional pumpsets, 1810 small industries and provided household connections to 0.9 million houses. RE Coops have been considered in India as an integral part of the overall development leading to increased agricultural production and stimulating overall economic growth of the area.

(f) Natural Resource Management

The main natural resources are land, water, forests and fisheries. In India the role of co-operatives in the natural resources management is of recent origin. Such co-operatives include marine fisheries, inland fisheries, lift irrigation, canal irrigation, tube well irrigation, tank management, tree growing, forest, salt production etc. There are many success stories of farmers managing irrigation in India, e.g., canal irrigation societies working in the Ukai Kakrapar project command area in Gujarat, Co-operative lift irrigation societies in many states. There is a network of fisheries co-operatives in India with a vertical structure up to the national level (8374 primaries, 81 district federations, 15 state federations and National Federation of Fishermens Co-operatives).

(g) Consumer Goods in Rural Areas

The village co-operatives have not made much progress in supplying consumption loans to the farmers. This is due to lack of funds with the primaries. Another aspect is to supply essential commodities, particularly to the weaker sections. The Government of India has launched a nation wide Public Distribution Programme (PDS), which is being implemented by the state governments. Of the total number of fair price shops allotted in the rural areas, the share of co-operatives is 26 per cent. The co-operative fair price shops supply all the items identified under the PDS.

In a few states, only co-operatives have been assigned the task. Co-operatives, however are not enthusiastic to undertake fair price shops under the PDS, because they do not find it an economically viable activity.

From the foregoing discussion it is clear that the co-operatives have made substantial contribution in improving the productivity level of rural economy particularly agriculture, creating employment opportunities through various subsidiary occupations, supplementing the efforts of government for poverty alleviation, increasing the income of producers and protecting consumers through co-operative markets. Co-operatives have also contributed towards creating infrastructure–a basic framework for rural development.

Problems

The following are the persistent problems faced by the credit and non-credit co-operative societies:

(i) Lack of Spontaneity

The co-operative movement in India did not spring from the people themselves. The movement was not voluntary, and the people did not come forward to organise societies to satisfy their needs. On the other hand the movement took the form of a government department. The villagers among whom the credit societies were started generally thought of the societies as government lending agencies.

(ii) Too much emphasis on credit

The co-operative movement failed in linking credit, marketing and processing. As a result, the co-operative societies provided loans to the farmers but did not help the latter in any other way. In certain areas different societies were started for different purposes. The failure to provide credit, marketing, processing, better farming etc., to the farmers was one of the basic factors responsible for the weaknesses of the movement.

(iii) Defective Management and Leadership

Except in case of large co-operative enterprises like IFFCO, KRIBHCO, co-operative sugar factories and certain apex level institutions, managerial efficiency of co-operatives, by and large, remains unsatisfactory. The failure and liquidation of many societies in rural areas was directly due to the defective management and leadership. The large farmers, who do not feel committed to the success of the co-operative movement, dominate the village economy nor take genuine interest in promoting the welfare of the farmer- members. Besides, the work of the societies suffered from nepotism, favouritism and partiality. In general, the management is weak and inefficient.

(iv)Lack of inter-Cooperative Relationship

Co-operation is a system and every constituent unit of the system has to act in close collaboration with other units. There has been lack of inter-co-operative relationship both vertically and horizontally. In such a situation, it becomes very difficult for the co-operative sector to project its unified strength in the economy especially in the context of globalisation.

(v) Absence of Thrift

Thrift is the backbone of the co-operative movement and, in reality, co-operation and thrift go hand in hand. But unfortunately our people do not appreciate the value of thrift. Extravagance nullifies many advantages of co-operation (E.D. Setty, 2000).

(vi)Political Influence

Political pressure on officials to recommend and grant the claims of undeserving persons handicaps mainly genuine and worthwhile cases. A man who has no political influence stoops to corrupt officials and gets things done quickly. The individual who has neither this nor the other suffers, however, worthy may be his cause.

Political interference and administrative high handedness go a long way to slacken to progress of co-operatives. Besides, the growth of vested interests, ineffective federal structure, narrow base, and excessive reliance on government aid are some of the factors that inhibit the development of co-operatives in our country. These coupled with the division of responsibility among several departments for the administration of co-operatives results in the lack of co-ordination and expert guidance.

(vii) Governments Influence

In recent years, there has been increasing tendency of interference from the government by way of imposition of restrictions leading to supersession of boards, delaying of elections, appointment of person-in-charge, etc. The situation has been further aggravated by the use of these powers by political parties in power for extra co-operative considerations.

The origin and growth of the co-operative movement in India has not been of a spontaneous character. The government have exercised practically all powers on the movement, though it pursued a policy of non-intervention (artificially). The major financial assistance and influence continues to remain a major setback to the popularity of the movement among the people. They correctly feel that the co-operative movement is still being looked after, from cradle to grave, by the Registrars and their staff. They cover almost completely the whole field of activities of co-operative societies. Added to it, the inordinate delay in the disposal of applications, is a common phenomenon.

6. Jagadish Capoor Committee Suggestions

The central government constituted a Task Force in April 1999 under the Chairmanship of Shri Jagdish Capoor, Dy. Governor, RBI to study the functioning of rural co-operative credit institutions and to suggest a package of measures for their strengthening. A summary of the recommendations contained in the report to the Central Government on July 24, 2000 is provided below (www.NABARD.org.in). Major Recommendations of the Jagadish Capoor Committee are:

- Need for strengthening the resource base of co-operative banks, especially the capital.
- Need for reducing Government control over co-operatives, giving them maximum autonomy and making them 'member driven'.
- Adoption of Model Co-operative Societies Act or dovetail the essential features of the Model Act.
- Preparation of specific action plans to remove the overlapping of controls and endow functional autonomy and operational freedom to co-operatives.
- Co-operative Banks to work like professional organizations on sound managerial systems.
- Diversification of business products as the prime need at all levels in the co-operative credit institutions.
- Co-operative Banks to initiate necessary steps for ensuring viability.
- Need to initiate measures for the rehabilitation of potentially viable co-operative banks.
- Setting up of a Co-operative Rehabilitation and Development Fund at NABARD

- Setting up of a Mutual Assistance Fund at the State level.
- Government support to co-operative banks in their recovery efforts.
- Branch licensing of DCCBs to be brought under the provisions of the BR Act, 1949.
- Need for bringing transparency and disclosure norms in respect of co-operative banks.

7. CONCLUSION

Co-operation is considered to be the golden mean between capitalism and socialism. It is based on lofty principles of equality, fraternity and freedom. Despite several odds, co-operative movement has registered a significant progress in several parts of the world. In India, during the past 100 years co-operatives have emerged and shown different degrees of progress. Credit co-operatives have been the oldest in India and are faced with a multiplicity of operational problems at all levels. Their financial performance is poor and their survival in some cases is a problem. The non-credit co-operatives are either getting marginalised or privatised due to accumulated losses. However, there are also several success stories especially in the sphere of housing and dairying. Reorganisation and better management of co-operatives on the lines of the Capoor Committee recommendations will improve the situation. The preservation and strengthening of co-operative institutions is one of crucial challenges as well as opportunities for sustained rural development.

REFERENCES

1. B.L. Mathur (2000), Rural Development and Co-operation, RBSA Publications, Jaipur.
2. B.S. Mathur (1999), Co-operation in India, Sahitya Bhavan, Agra.

3. C.B. Memoria and R.D. Saxena (1999), Co-operation in India, Kitab Mahal, Allahabad.

4. M. Mithani and E. Gordon (2000), Banking, Theory and Practice Himalaya Publishing House, Mumbai.

5. C.R. Ray (1976), Co-operation at Home and Abroad, P.S. King and Sons, London.

6. Dr. E.D. Setty (2000), Rural Development: Problems and Prospects, Inter-India Publications, New Delhi.

7. Dr.P.K. Srivastava (2000), Banking Theory and Practice, Himalaya Publishing House, Mumbai.

8. GOI, Fifth Five Year Plan, 1975-80

9. GOI, Fourth Five Year Plan, 1966-71.

10. GOI, Ninth Five Year Plan, 1997-2002.

11. GOI, Second Five Year Plan, 1956-61.

12. RBI, Report of the Agricultural Credit Review Committee, 1989.

13. RBI, Report on Trend and Progress of Banking in India, 2000-01.

14. S.S. Talmaki (1931), Co-operatives in India and Abroad, Basel Mission Press, Bangalore.

www.nabard.org.in

16

Commercial Banks and Rural Credit

V. Muniramaiah

1. Introduction

One of the chronic problems of Indian agriculture has been the lack of proper and adequate supply of credit to foster its growth. During colonial period despite the legislation for the protection of tenants, large scale transfers of land had taken place from the agriculturists to the moneylenders. The co-operative credit system was designed to provide farm credit at favourable terms but it could not take deep roots. Co-operative credit institutions have become agencies of political control. They have lost their original character of people-oriented, democratically operated institutions for promoting common welfare. The All India Rural Credit Survey, 1954 pointed out that co-operative agricultural credit was in quantitative terms little more than three per cent of the borrowings of the cultivators – what reaches the medium and small cultivators from the co-operative institutions was a mere fraction of the little that co-operatives provide (ARCS,1954). The survey showed that, in 1951-52, the private credit agencies taken together (excluding commercial banks) supplied 93 per cent of the total amount borrowed by cultivators; that of the total borrowing by cultivators, roughly 50 per cent was for family expenditure, 28 per cent for capital expenditure on farm, and 10 per cent for current farm expenditure; that relatively larger proportions of the borrowings of big and large cultivators were from institutional agencies and that the dependence of the medium and small cultivators on private agencies was much greater in that order. The non-agricultural sector of the rural economy has also suffered due to stagnant technology, sagging markets and lack of credit support. In this paper, we use the words 'agricultural' and 'rural' interchangeably for convenience, though there is a vast difference between them.

Development of institutional credit for agriculture has been one of the important planks of agricultural development strategy. Initially, this was prompted by the concern mainly for the cultivator who was being exploited by the moneylender in terms of high rates of interest, obligation to sell his produce at disadvantageous prices and, in some cases, eventual foreclosure of mortgages on his holding. With the commencement of national economic planning, however, there has been a distinct shift in emphasis with the accent on the role of credit as a positive aid to intensified agricultural production. The new agricultural strategy has lent added urgency to the need for a supporting framework of rural banking and credit. Growing high-yielding varieties of foodgrains on a large scale will entail the greatly increased consumption of fertilizer, pesticide and improved seed which, unlike traditional inputs, have to be acquired outside the farm. The resulting demand for production credit is thus not only quantitatively larger than ever before but also qualitatively different. Along side this will also grow the requirements of credit to finance the marketing of increasing quantities of inputs and farm machinery and the processing, storage, transportation and sale of a rapidly expanding volume of agricultural produce. With agriculture becoming increasingly modernized, commercialized and profitable and with a spurt in rural economic activity generally and the acceleration of monetization, the need will continue to grow for extensive institutional machinery capable of providing the necessary credit and banking facilities and also of mobilizing savings out of rising rural incomes (Darmy P N, 1970).

2. Supply of Credit and its Agencies

Rural credit in India, like most other less developed countries is supplied by a plurality of agencies generally classified into organized/formal/institutional and unorganized/informal/non-institutional sectors/markets. The size of the informal sector is generally larger than the formal sector. The cost and availability of credit in the unorganized market is being influenced by the State by different types of intervention which tend to improve the link between the two credit markets.

In the context of development planning state intervention in the credit market is justified on grounds of market failure, external economies and considerations of equity both social and regional. In India there are three types of state interventions into the rural credit market– one promotional, two regulatory and three both promotional and regulatory. The establishment of NABARD and National Co-operative Development Corporation (NCDC) is an instance of promoting new organizations of development banking. The regulatory role consists of the set of controls, subsidies, allocations, directions on the banking system framed and directed by the Reserve Bank and Government. The nationalization of commercial banks and the different schemes of reorganization of co-operative credit delivery system are instances of both the promotional and regulatory role of the State.

Formal rural credit institutions in India date back to the early 20th century when credit co-operatives were first set up in certain 'provinces' as the Indian states were then known. Since then the co-operative movement, especially in the sphere of credit, had spread to all parts of India and had taken deep roots. From time to time, high level commissions/committees were set up either by the RBI or the Government of India to examine the problems of rural finance and recommend measures for strengthening co-operative rural credit system, keeping in view the nature and dimension of credit requirements. The present 'multi-agency' system in India is the result of these efforts spread over several decades. It consists of the two wings of the co-operative structure (the short-term and the long-term credit): the commercial banks with their branch network and the RRBs with their branch network. At the national level, there is the National Bank for Agriculture and Rural Development (NABARD).

3. Role of Informal Agencies

The rates of interest charged by the constituents of the informal sector are generally higher than the formal sector. A number of institutional factors are responsible, besides the market factors, for high rates of interest in unorganized credit markets. The size of the loan is usually small and thus the fixed handling charges are relatively high. Defaults also tend to be larger in unorganized credit markets. These higher defaults are due not so much to a lower standard of morality and unwillingness to repay debts as to the fluctuations in prices and incomes derived from agricultural products, which reduce the ability of the agriculturists to repay debts at inopportune times. Inflation is another contributory factor especially in many Latin American Countries. A general statement, however, is that interest rates in the unorganized money markets of underdeveloped countries are high because the economy is underdeveloped and the money market unorganized.

The high rates of interest prevailing in unorganized money market have been a heavy burden on agriculturists. Annual interest payments have been fairly large in relation to the net income of the farmers, thus reducing his ability to make improvements on the land (John W. Meller 1968). Hence the need for intervention in and regulation of credit transactions in the unorganized money market in the context of development planning.

In India at the base of credit structure, moneylenders and indigenous bankers are the overwhelming source of finance for cultivators.

The traders and commission agents generally advance short-term clean loans to the producer-sellers. They advance small amount normally for one season and recover them when the sales are effected. Majority of the farmers who borrow from them make voluntary arrangements to sell their produce through them. In lieu of the interest, some traders and commission agents charge a marginally higher commission from producer–sellers who had obtained credit from them; and those producer-sellers who do not dispose off their produce through them are charged higher interest rates (A S Kahlon and Karam Singh 1984).

4. Commercial Banks

Till 1967 financing agriculture was considered to be the sole responsibility of the co-operative credit for agriculture and allied activities, on account of increasing emphasis laid on higher agricultural production as also the technological break through achieved by Indian farmers, the resources of the co-operative sector were found to be inadequate. Against this background, commercial banks were, as a matter of national policy, called upon for the first time in 1967 to provide finance to this sector. Their role in this direction expanded significantly after the nationalization of the 14 major scheduled commercial banks in 1969. Since then commercial banks have been financing agricultural activities and development on an increasing scale year by year and their financial involvement in this sector is growing. The entry of commercial banks into rural finance has initiated new trends by encouraging the planning process at the grass roots level and imparted a significant development orientation to deployment of funds in the rural areas. The Reserve Bank has been an active catalyst in directing the flow of bank credit to this priority sector (RBI 1984).

5. Declining Rural Branch Network and C-D Ratio

Gunnar Myrdal (1958) remarked that "studies in many countries have shown how the banking system, if not regulated to act differently, tends to become an instrument for siphoning off the savings from the poorer regions to the richer and more progressive ones where returns on capital are high and secure". This is the phenomenon of demand following finance which operates nationally as well as globally. The purpose of public intervention in the operations of the banking system is to safeguard the interests of not only poorer regions but also the economically weaker segments of society whose access to banking facilities is constrained by a multiplicity of factors both economic and non-economic. In India despite large-scale nationalization of banking in 1969, the urban-bias in commercial banking is hardly reduced. Table 1 offers some details in this regard.

The major component of the banking policy before economic reforms had been the spread of branch network into rural areas. One of the avowed objectives of bank nationalisation in 1969 was to transform the urban bias in commercial banking and make it a supply leading phenomenon. As a consequence of this rural-oriented

Table–1. Share of Rural Branches in Deposits and Credit of SCBs

(Rs) Crore

End of Year	*No. of Offices*	*As % of Total*	*Deposits*	*As % of Total*	*Credit*	*As % of Total*	*C-D Ratio*	
							RBs	*MBs*
1969*	1443	17.6	306	6.3	115	3.3	37.6	98.2
1978*	12534	45.2	2664	10.1	1530	8.4	57.4	87.9
1984*	25541	52.9	9603	13.4	6589	13.5	68.6	84.6
1987*	30585	56.2	17527	14.7	11127	15.3	63.5	71.3
1991	35216	58.1	33163	15.1	19688	14.7	59.4	71.4
1997	33008	52.0	72511	14.7	32372	11.5	44.6	75.7
1988	32890	51.2	86484	14.6	36697	11.2	42.4	74.9
1999	32856	50.5	102602	14.6	41193	10.6	40.1	76.9
2000	32719	49.9	120447	14.7	47396	10.1	39.4	82.2
2001	32533	49.4	139427	14.7	56017	10.1	40.2	84.3

* December and for other years March.

SCBs: Scheduled commercial Banks

RBs: Rural Branches

MBs: Metropolitan Branches

Source: Economic and political weekly vol.XXXVII No.5, February 2-8, 2002 P.P. 489-490.

banking development policy, we find that the number of rural branches as well as their proportion had gone up significantly in the first two decades of bank nationalization. In 1969 the proportion of rural branches was hardly 18 per cent and the figure went up to 58 per cent by 1991. The year 1991 is a significant landmark in the recent economic policy framework as it witnessed the beginning of new economic policy with greater accent on liberalization in all spheres of economic activity including banking. As a result we find that rural–oriented banking development has been given up in the post-reform period. As is evident from Table 1, we notice that the proportion of rural branches had declined to 49 per cent by March-2001. Even in absolute terms there has been a significant reduction in the number of rural branches by 2683 between 1991 and 2001. Such Institutional vacuum is sure to hurt the process providing institutional credit to the rural sector in particular and in underdeveloped regions in general. Even the new policy of expanding micro-credit facilities through bank-linked Self-Help-Groups (SHGs) will face a serious hurdle, if the rural branch network is not expanded (EPW RF-2002).

It is also noticed from Table-1 that rural deposits as a proportion of total deposits have been rising from a meagre figure of 6.3 per cent in 1969 to 15.1 per cent in 1991. However, in the Post-reform era, they have stagnated around 15 per cent, the proportion of credit disbursed by the rural branches though rising slowly over time since 1969 has tended to decline in the Post-reform period. C-D ratio is a rough measure of the flow of rural savings and credit to and from the banking system. The C-D ratio was 37.6 per cent in 1969 and has gradually risen to 68.6 per cent in 1984. This is the highest level attained during the entire period from 1969 to 2001. In the Post-reform period there has been a steady decline in the C-D ratio and touched 39.4 per cent in 2000 and slightly moved to 40.2 per cent in 2001. The dwindling of C-D ratio of rural branches from over 64 per cent to around 40 per cent has been the most disquieting aspect of banking development of the past decade. This is all the more disquieting when viewed against the RBI prescription of a minimum of 60 per cent C-D ratio that rural branches are required to achieve (EPWRF-2002). However, the C-D ratio of Metro-politan branches was 98.2 per cent in 1969. Although it has fluctuated around that figure during the first decade of nationalization, there has been a gradual decline in the C-D ratio of Metropolitan branches which touched 71.4 per cent in 1991. Hovering around that level with marginal variations it has tended to rise and reached 84.3 per cent in March 2001. These trends in C-D ratio of Metropolitan branches provide enough evidence of demand following nature of banking development due to the pulls and pressures of the Metropolitan credit market.

6. Flow of Bank Credit to Agriculture

On account of agriculture-credit friendly banking policies pursued by the Reserve Bank and subsequently NABARD and Government of India, there has been a significant increase in the flow of bank credit to agriculture in quantitative terms in the post-nationalisation era. Table 2 provides some particulars in this regard.

It may be noticed from Table 2 that the share of agriculture in total bank credit, both direct and indirect, which stood at 10.7 per cent in 1975 reached a peak of 15.9 per cent in March 1990. Subsequently, it has been steadily declining and touched a low of 9.9 per cent by March-2000. This has been inspite of the Reserve Bank's prescription of the share of agriculture at 18 per cent which remains unfulfilled. The reduction in sectoral credit allocation to agriculture and allied activities including small-scale industry explains the decline in the proportion of priority sector advances in total non-food credit from 40 per cent in March 1990 to 34.7 per cent in March 1995 and to 35.9 per cent in March 2001 (EPWRF 2002).

Table–2. Flow Bank Credit from SCBs to Agriculture and Industry

(Rs.) Crore

Year	*Amount outstanding to Agriculture*	*Amount outstanding to Industry*	*Amount outstanding to TTM*
1975 *	1071(10.7)	5777(57.7)	3167(31.6)
1980 *	3722(15.7)	11555(48.8)	8397(35.5)
1990	16626(15.9)	50486(48.7)	36840(35.3)
1995	24948(11.8)	96211(45.6)	89780(42.5)
1999	40889(10.7)	18797(49.1)	153589(40.2)
2000	45638(9.9)	213779(46.5)	200664(43.6)

* End of December and others relate to March.
SCBS: Scheduled Commercial Banks.
Figures in parentheses indicate respective percentages to total.
TTM: Transport, Trade and Miscelleneous
Source: EPW, Vol.XXXVI No.5, Feb-8-2002, P. 493.

We notice that the share of bank credit to industry has been getting reduced in the 1980s and stood at 47 per cent by the turn of the century. The tertiary sector has been getting a share of credit ranging from 32 per cent in 1975 and 44 per cent in 2000. Agriculture provides livelihood to nearly 2/3rds of the work-force but receives hardly 10 per cent of bank credit. The non-Agricultural sector therefore gets 90 per cent of bank credit though it provides employment to hardly 1/3rd of the work-force in India. No wonder the low-productivity associated with agriculture which is over burdened with population gets neglected in the credit market. The situation is likely to worsen in the years to come due to the policy of deregulation and liberalisaion of banking industry. In other words, in the post-reform era, the process of supply leading banking is getting replaced by demand following banking which has serious implications for achieving equity and social justice in the new millennium.

7. Arguments Against Directed Bank Lending

A variety of arguments are advanced against directed bank lending to priority sector in particular and regulation of interest rates and other allocations of bank credit. A few arguments are listed here under.

(a) Directed lending undermines the health of lending institutions.

The earlier banking and financial sector policy was predicated on the strong assumption of the need for supply-based, subsidy-linked and target-oriented approach to banking development. It was further supplemented by the mandated involvement of banks and some financial institutions in government sponsored programmes like IRDP and other poverty-alleviation schemes. The mainstream literature is generally skeptical about the sustainability of that supply-led strategy of financial sector development; it is generally believed that the infirmities created in the operations of banks were more severe than the achievements made (EPW, 2002).

(b) Adverse selection and Moral Hazard

A major problem of credit markets and more important that of directed credit programmes is the '*information asymmetry*' and the large agency costs associated with monitoring directed credit programmes. One of the solutions suggested in the literature to reduce '*information asymmetry*' and large agency costs associated with directed credit programme is to utilize the role of Peer Groups, Non-Governmental Organisations, Self-Help Groups in credit market. A notable success story in this regard is the case of Bangladesh Grameen Bank (BGB), which has been lending largely to small groups of women to finance small-scale self-employment activities. BGB has been very successful in effectively tackling the problems of adverse selection, moral hazard, and lack of collateral. As of January, 1996 in the case of BGB, the repayment rate was 98 per cent despite the interest rate on loans being 20 per cent. The bank's organisation of borrowers into groups means that the group acts effectively as a form of social collateral substituting for the traditional physical collateral. Thus the inherent problem of '*asymmetry information*' characterizing the directed credit programmes especially in the case of small borrowers, is effectively tackled by the peer monitoring mechanism so crucial for the success of BGB, however, in some cases, peer pressure mechanism may not work effectively, especially if the group is not homogenous and the risk-profile of the group members is not similar (RBI 1996-97).

(c) Erosion of Repayment Ethics

There is a general consensus that the strategies followed have helped to build a broad based institutional infrastructure for the delivery and deployment of credit. However, the emphasis throughout has been on achieving certain quantitative targets. As a consequence, inadequate attention was paid to the qualitative aspects of lending resulting in loan defaults and erosion of repayment ethics, to a greater or lesser extent, by all categories of borrowers. The end result was a disturbing growth in overdues, which not only hampered the recycling of scarce resources of banks, but also affected profitability and viability of financial institutions (Y.S.P. Thorat, 2000).

8. Share of Commercial Banks in Institutional Credit Flow

The flow of institutional credit for agriculture and allied activities which was Rs 31,956 crore in 1997-98 is estimated to have increased to Rs 53,504 crore in

2000-01. the total credit flow from all agencies is projected to reach a level of Rs 66,771 crore by 2001-02 (Table 3).

The total credit flow to agriculture during the period 1997-2002 is likely to be of the order of Rs 2,33,703 crore which is close to the IX plan projection of Rs 2,29,750 crore. The share of total credit flow from commercial banks to agriculture rose from 50 per cent in 1997-98 to 52 per cent in 2000-2001. It is expected to retain its share at 52 per cent during 2001-2002. The share of Co-operative Credit Institutions, in credit support for agriculture declined from 44 per cent in 1997-198 to 41 per cent in 2000-2001. The share of RRBs has stayed around 6-7 per cent.

9. Kisan Credit Card Scheme

The complexity and composite operations undertaken by the farmers have led to evolving Kisan Credit Card Scheme for the farmers to meet the total credit requirements in a comprehensive way. As this is a revolving credit facility without much documentation, the scheme is becoming popular among the farmers and branches also find it very easy to operate.

The Kisan Credit Card Scheme requires lot of publicity to bring required awareness among the farmers so that all farmers in the service area villages are covered under the scheme. Besides reducing the transaction cost, the scheme emphasizes on timely and adequate credit which will directly help in improving the production levels and productivity (RJ Kamath, 2000).

The Kisan Credit Card Scheme, introduced in 1998-99, is an innovative mechanism for facilitating access to short-term credit to farmers. The scheme has gained popularity and its implementation has been taken up by 27 Commercial banks, 373 District Central Co-operative Banks/State Co-operative Banks (Two tier structure) and

Table–3. Flow of Institutional Credit to Agriculture

Institutions	*1997-98*	*1998-99*	*1999-00#*	*2000-01$*	*2001-02@*
Co-operative Banks	**14,085**	**15,957**	**18,429**	**21,909**	**27,080**
Short-term	10,895	12,571	14,648	17,700	21,542
Medium/Long-term	3,190	3,386	3,781	4,209	5,538
Regional Rural Banks	**2,040**	**2,460**	**3,329**	**3,807**	**4,956**
Short-term	1,396	1,710	2,517	2,778	3,415
Medium/Long-term	644	750	812	1,029	1,541
Commercial Banks	**15,831**	**18,443**	**22,854**	**27,788**	**34,735**
Short-term	8,349	9,622	11,697	14,222	17,778
Medium/Long-term	7,482	8,821	11,157	13,566	16,957
Total	**31,956**	**36,860**	**44,612**	**53,504**	**66,771**
Per cent increase	21	15	21	20	25

 # Provisional **$ Estimated** **@ Projections**

Source: GOI, Economic Survey 2001-2002, P. 200

196 Regional Rural Banks throughout the country. As on November 30, 2001, 20.4 million Kisan Credit Cards involving credit sanctions of Rs 43,392 crore had been issued. Co-operative Banks accounted for 66 per cent of Kisan Credit Cards followed by Commercial Banks (27 per cent) and RRBs (7 per cent) (Economic Survey 2001-2002).

10. Micro-Finance Innovation

With a view to improving the recovery of loans from the poor as well as to reduce the transaction costs and to improve the capability of the poor through the social intermediation, a system of micro-finance delivery mechanism has been tried in different parts of the world. Under the system, borrowers get united in a group to deal with their activities including savings and borrowings. These groups are commonly known as Self-Help Groups (SHGs). The importance of SHGs is well recognized long back. However, in India the first formal attempt in this direction was initiated in 1992 with the launching of SHG Bank Linkage Programme under the aegis of the NABARD. The programme is yet to gain significant momentum at least in terms of quantum of amount issued. The cumulative number of SHGs involved in SHG Bank Linked Programme aggregating 114775 as at end of March 2000 covering an estimated number of 1.9 million very poor families in 24 states and union territories. More than 85 per cent of SHGs formed were exclusively of women members. As many as 718 NGOs were involved in SHGs bank-linked programme. In all, 266 banks representing commercial banks, co-operative banks and regional rural banks participated in the programme. Bank loans amounted to Rs. 1.9 billion (C L Ddadhich, 2000).

11. Summing Up

Historically, commercial banks have remained cut off from the domain of rural credit. Their location and outlook were such that they were urban-oriented almost everywhere. With the advent of development planning and the emergence of green revolution the demand for agricultural and rural credit accelerated and the non-commercial banking institutions could not meet it. The credit from informal sector was not only inadequate but costly and even exploitative. Hence, a strong case was made for the entry of commercial banks in the field of rural credit. The nationalization of 14 banks 1969 gave a major thrust in this direction. Consequently there was a rapid expansion of rural branches of commercial banks. Banking operations in terms of deposit mobilisaion and deployment of credit also picked up. However the C-D ratio of rural branches has always lagged behind the national average, let alone that of the methopolitan branches. As a result, the rural savings were pumped out of the rural sector into the urban commercial sector. The share of agricultural credit in the post-reform era has dwindled. In the name of banking reform the priority sector share is reduced and this is likely to have adverse cansequences for meeting the credit needs in agriculture but also for fostering microfinance innovations through the mechanism of SHG-bank linkages.

REFERENCES

1. R.B.I, 1954 The general Report of the All India Rural Credit Survey Committee (ARCS) Bombay, p. 8.
2. Darmy, P.N. 1970. Institutionallisation of Agricultural Credit–Indian experience, Banking and Development, RBI Bombay, p. 123.
3. John W. Meller et al. 1968. Developing Rural India, Plan and Practice, Corn Well University Press, Ithaca, p. 60.
4. AS.Kahlan and Karam Singh 1984, Managing Agricultural Finance Theory and Practice, Allied, New Delhi, p. 54.

5. Gunnar Myrdal 1958, Economic Theory and Under-Developed Regions Vora and Company, Bombay, p. 40.

6. Economic and Political Weekly Research Foundation 2002, Special Statistics-31, Money Banking and Finance, February 2, p. 483.

7. Ibid, p. 484.

8. Ibid, p. 483.

9. Reserve Bank of India, 1996-97, Report on Trend and Progress of Banking in India (July-June) Mumbai, p. 51.

10. Y.S.P. Thorat, 2000 Towards a Stronger and Sustainable Rural Finance in Banking in the New Millennium, Oriental Bank of Commerce New Delhi, p. 170.

11. R J Kamath, 2000, Strengthening Self-Help Groups in the New Millennium, Oriental Bank of Commerce New Delhi, p. 168.

12. Government of India 2001-2002, Economic Survey, New Delhi, p. 200.

13. C L Dadhich 2000, New Savings Linked Loan Products in Rural Finance in the New Millennium, Oriental Bank of Commerce New Delhi, p. 179.

17

Growth and Development of Self-Help Groups

Dr. P. Krishnaiah

1. Philosophy of Self-Help Approach

The Self-Help Group (SHG) strategy of development is based on the philolophy of peoples' participation in the design and execution of all schemes and activities that are meant for them. The SHGs are not only considered to be catalysts of resource mobilization, watchdogs of proper utilization but also agents of social and cultural transformation and advancement leading to an accelerated social uplift. The strategy is gender sensitive, politically inclusive, socially empowering, emotionally integrating, economically vibrant and psychologically gratifying for the vast masses who live in the clutches of penury and indignity. No wonder, there has been a phenomenal growth of SHGs in India due to the people centered pro-poor accent in the approach. Since the government has been playing the role of a friend, philosopher and guide and has been investing its vast human and financial resources for this agenda, a time has come to take a closer look at the strengths, weaknesses, opportunities and threats, if any, in the processes involved and the outcomes recorded by the different SHGs. It would help in appreciating the problems and perspectives and search for improvements, modifications and corrections.

2. Social Mobilization and Participation of Poor

The Independent South Asia Commission for Poverty Alleviation (ISACPA, 1992) argued that the centerpiece of a policy framework for poverty alleviation has to be the mobilization of the poor in order to enable them to participate directly and effectively in the decisions that affect their lives and prospects. Excessive dependence on the State for every lead in development has curtailed initiatives of the people. Obsessive pre-occupation with capital accumulation as the driving force of economic progress has resulted in neglecting the capacity of the poor themselves. Consequently, the Commission favours a strategy that "mainstreams the process of social mobilization as an essential ingredient of the growth of civil society; encourages the growth of grassroots organizations and government and private service agencies; and without compromising the dependence of these grassroots organizations, attempts to establish a symbiotic relationship between these organizations and local government institutions".

Experience after experience has proved that organizing the poor into self-governing communities works, in relation to the myriad of their felt needs. A participatory model of micro-credit initiatives implemented by NABARD in Maharashtra Rural Credit Programme(MRCP) and worldwide success story of Self Employed Women's Association (SEWA) in Gujarat and Kerala Science Movement (KSM) are a few illustrations in this direction. The significance of people's participation and community empowerment has begun to pervade the consciousness of different players in the development field—States, donors, and representatives of civil society like NGOs and CBOs.

The broad dimensions of social mobilization are becoming increasingly known in South Asia. The main objective of social mobilisation is to induce the poor to create participation of all members from varied socio-cultural backgrounds, irrespective of income, caste, gender or other discriminating characteristics. The social mobilisation effort for poverty alleviation must be based on entry points that are the key to poverty alleviation, redressal of the problems and obstacles identified by the poor themselves–food security, literacy and primary education, health, shelter, credit, productive infrastructure and employment.

3. Emergence of SHGs as an Effective Strategy

Ninety per cent of SHGs are women; they have proven to be the better savers, borrowers and investors. Most of them are from the lowest castes and disadvantaged groups. The SHGs mobilize their own savings, transform them into loans to members and plough their earnings from interest income back into equity. On that basis, SHGs and banks enter into commercial relations of mutual benefit, with low bank and client transaction costs and negligible risks. In the absence of interest rate restrictions and with repayment rates greater than 99 per cent, SHG banking is highly profitable–a message that has convinced hesitant bank managers in increasing numbers. SHGs are now forming local networks with their own cooperative financial institutions. The programme has turned into a social movement, with high growth rates in recent years. Fuelled by competence and enthusiasm at all stakeholder levels, it expands rapidly throughout India, including marginal and tribal areas. It is probably the world's largest and most successful microfinance programme for the rural poor–outstanding for its emphasis on to reach 100 million of India's rural poor with savings and credit by 2008 (NABARD 2000-2001).

The group approach is becoming more and more acceptable as evidenced by the recognition accorded by the Government of India in the on-going income generating programmes. The SHGs have become the focal point of the development schemes under the unified poverty alleviation programme "Swarnajayanti Gram Swarozgar Yojana"(SGSY) launched in April 1999 by the Government of India. NABARD's commitment to empower at least 100 million rural poor through SHGs by the year 2008 would further increase the emphasis on group approach among the rural poor, especially women (Ibid). Further, reduction in transaction cost while lending to the rural poor through SHGs when compared to the normal lending and increased recovery performance reinforce the group concept in rural credit delivery through formal institutions (Puhazhendhi et al 1999). Hence, there is a greater potential for the group approach in future while conceptualizing and implementing any programme for the rural poor, especially women. Through SHGs women are empowered to act against social evils and address social backwardness and overcome gender discrimination, inequality and exploitation.

4. Characteristics of SHGs

SHGs exhibit certain distinct characteristics. They are participative in character and embody cooperative principles of collective endeavour for individual and community development by overcoming the deeply entrenched social bottlenecks and economic hurdles. Often non-governmental organiations (NGOs) figure in their promotion and initial sustenance. Bureaucracy is often replaced by them as promotional agencies. Decentralization and bottom-up approach become the hallmark of governance. Subsidies and dependency syndromes are often replaced by repayment ethics and collective self-reliance mechanisms. Their impact seems to be all pervasive; they are emerging as instruments of cultural change and fostering norms of small family and healthy environment. It is appropriate to have an idea of the characteristics and functions of SHGs in general.

Self-Help Groups (SHGs) are also known as Membership Based Organisations (MBOs). They encompass different spheres of human activity. Their characteristics vis-à-vis those of the State, market and households are summarized in Table 1.

The State depends upon the rule of law and regulations backed by coercion, the market relies on commercial pressure. MBOs or SHGs are bound together by self-interest, local affiliation and solidarity and the private households essentially by social norms and values as indicated in Table 1.

SHGs are not an altogether recent phenomenon. Group formations such as friendship societies, community based groups such as tribes in India, cooperatives in the West and the East may be cited as examples of SHGs. However, there are some fine distinctions between the type of SHGs cited above and the ones that have emerged in the rural and urban settings of the developing world. There is an organizational, democratic, activity-based formation of groups among the poor who were hitherto neglected or bypassed by the market and the State. The DWCRA in India is a case in point. The Grameen Bank of Bangladesh and Self-Employed Women Association (SEWA) of India are often quoted as examples of the poor women of Bangladesh and India respectively empowering themselves through thrift and micro-credit. The size and composition of membership, sources and styles of leadership, organisational and managerial patterns, thrift and

Table–1. Characteristics of Organisations Providing Social Security

	State	*Market*	*Member based Organisations*	*Private households*
Instruments	Social Insurance, Social Assistance transfers provident funds	Insurance policy or contract	Mutual arrangements voluntary work	Gift Exchanges State Contingents Loans Remittances Transfers Crop insurance
Mode of operation	Top-down	Individualistic	Mainly bottom-up	Bottom-up
Incentives	Rule of law, Regulations	Maximisation of profit And/or utility, Price signals and quantity adjustment	Balanced reciprocity, self-interest, volunatarism, solidarity	Social norms and values altruistic behaviour, charity, self interest
Sanctions	Exclusion of people from programmes, withdrawal of programmes	Level of premimum limit supply of insurance	Social pressure, exclusion from the organization	Social pressure, inherent family contract

Source: Jutting (1999)

consumption levels, adjustments, decision-making areas and processes within and outside the SHGs show different degrees of divergence. Further, their involvement and participation in social and community development programmes of the State adoption and spread of capacity building by the State and NGOs and environmental protection activities,assertion of civil liberties and human rights widely vary across SHGs (CIRDAP, 2000). Their cohesiveness and operational efficiency are determined by the objective and subjective factors both endogenous and exogenous. The SHGs represent the emergence of a new paradigm in the era of poverty reduction. The poor are empowered to transform themselves and their life styles through economic betterment and social security derived from the functioning of SHGs in different spheres of human endeavour.

5. Membership Structure and Performance

Membership of SHGs is often decided by the members themselves. Often homogeneity based either on social status (caste status) or economic status (occupational status) is the guiding factor. This is justified in the Indian rural context because of the unequal social and economic relations that dominate the scene. Puhazhendhi and Jayaraman (1999) have collected primary data from 25 randomly selected Credit Management Groups (CMGs) which were selected from two different project areas, viz., Chitradurga district in Karnataka and Periyar district in Tamil Nadu. For the purpose of quantifying the factors that influence women participation in different stages of group development, the groups were post stratified based on the age of groups in 2-4 years and above 4 years of functioning were categorized as stabilizing and stabilized groups respectively. The extent of women's participation in various activities of the group was assessed through comparing with data available with NGO, along with the primary data collected from the members of the selected groups. They have been used to quantify the impact of group formation on women participation and employment generation.

In terms of occupational pattern of the members, agricultural labourers constituted 70 per cent of the membership of the groups followed by non-farm activities (15 per cent). Rural artisans constituted 9 per cent of the group members while 6 per cent of them were marginal farmers cultivating mainly under rainfed conditions. A change in the composition of occupational pattern was observed in accordance with the age of the groups. The dependence of members on wage earning was reduced by 25 per cent between new and stabilized groups.

The enterprise combination of women revealed that as a result of group formation, women were able to diversify their activities through undertaking non-farm and animal husbandry activities. Members taking up more than one activity increased from about 30 per cent during pre-group formation to about 53 per cent during post-group formation situation. As a result, the average annual net income of the members was doubled. The positive impact of employment generation on the group members, who had undertaken income–generating activities, was observed in 43 per cent of the group members. The additional employment generated through the informal group lending worked out to 172 person-days per member.

The estimated employment elasticity worked out to 0.31 during the initial period of group formation, which had increased to 0.72 during the later stage of group formation. Such a positive response in employment reaching closer to the optimum level explains the multiplier effect of the project in terms of employment generation. The impact of women's participation on social front was assessed mainly in terms of improvement in literacy level, housing facilities and level of food security which showed a marked improvement in the post-group formation period.

The accumulated savings of the members who decide to leave the group are returned. Similarly for inclusion of new member the group might insist that the member should deposit the backlog of savings of earlier months so that the savings position of the group is not adversely affected.

6. Types of SHGs

The SHGs organized in A.P can be broadly classified into the following three categories.

1. SHGs having a direct bearing on income generation.
2. SHGs focusing on natural resources management and development and
3. SHGs effecting reduction in human poverty

The nature of SHGs, the type of participants, their role, aims and objectives and the outcomes are summarized in Table 2.

Table–2. Types of SHGs

A. SHGs Focusing on Income Poverty

Type of SHG.	*Target Group*	*Aims and Objectives Participants*	*Outcomes*
Women SHGs	Women	Thrift and Credit	Micro credit for income generation and consumption
CMEY	Youth	Thrift and Credit	Self employment through Micro enterprises

B. SHGs Focusing on Natural Resources Management and Development

WUAs	Farmers	Participation in irrigation management and maintenance of irrigation sources	Increase in agricultural production and productivity
Watershed Committee	Farmers in the watershed villages	Soil and moisture conservation, prevention of erosion, dry land agriculture management and increase in agricultural productivity	Soil and moisture conservation, prevention of erosion, dry land agriculture management, increase in productivity, ground water recharge and employment generation
VSS	Members @ 1 male and female from each family	Protection of the forest, regeneration of degraded forest, soil and moisture conservation and fodder development	Increase in forest cover, harvesting minor forest produce, employment generation, ground water recharge and sustainable ecosystem

C. SHGs Focusing on Human Poverty

Mothers' Committee	Mothers of 0-6 age children and pregnant mothers	Pre-school education, supplemental health, nutrition to pregnant and lactating mothers and children in the age of 0-6 years	Improved child care and health, better adoption to the schooling
School Education Committees	Parents of school going children	Primary and secondary education, non-formal and functional literacy	Accountability of teachers, better enrollment, less dropout, improved rate of girl child education
Health Advisory Committees	Elected representatives of peoples in the local bodies	Health management, population control and sanitation	Improved health awareness, small family norm, immunization, healthy society

Source: Official Reports, Government of A.P.

7. Bank Linkage Scheme of NABARD

The core problem of rural finance is the high transaction costs of a large number of small but frequent borrowers for consumption/production needs. Transaction costs for IRDP loans have been assessed at 24.6 per cent. Transaction costs of operating a savings account with a bank was high as 10 per cent of the savings (assuming one transaction per month). (DEAR Study, 1997). To develop a supplementary credit delivery system to reach the poor in a cost-effective and sustainable manner, NABARD introduced a pilot project for linking up SHGs in 1992 (NABARD 1997).

The broad principles followed under the Linkage Scheme were:

- Savings first, no credit without savings
- Savings as partial collateral
- Bank loans to the SHG for on-lending to members
- Credit decisions for on-lending to SHG members
- Interest rates and other terms and conditions for loans to members to be decided by the group
- Joint liability as a substitute for physical collateral
- Ratio between savings and credit contingent upon credit worthiness and could increase over a period due to good repayment record, if needed.
- Small loans to begin with and different credit cycles clearly defined (Karmakar 1999)

We present a picture of SHGs credit linkage with the banks in Table 3 which follows:

During the year 2000-01, 1.18 lakh SHGs were credit linked as against 0.82 lakh SHGs linked during 1999-

Table–3. SHG Credit Linkage-Cumulative Progress 1992-93 to 2000-01 (April-March)

(Rs.Crore)

Year	*No. of SHGs linked**	*Bank Loan*	*Refinance*
1992-93	255	0.29	0.27
1993-94	620	0.65	0.46
1994-95	2,122	2.44	2.13
1995-96	4,757	6.06	5.66
1996-97	8,598	11.84	10.65
1997-98	14,317	23.76	21.39
1998-99	32,995	57.07	52.09
1999-00	94,645	192.98	150.13
2000-01	2,13,213	480.87	400.74

Source: NABARD Annual Report, 2001-02.

2000. The achievement during the year also exceeded the target of linking one lakh SHGs with banks, set in the Union Budget 2000-2001. Cumulatively, about 2.13 lakh SHGs have been credit linked till 31 March 2001. The banks disbursed loans aggregating Rs.287.88 crore to SHGs during 2000-01, which were more than crore. Banks claimed refinance of Rs. 250.62 crore from the National Bank during the year as against Rs.98.04 crore last year, registering an increase of 156 per cent. Cumulatively, till 31 March 2001, loans of Rs.480.87 crore have been disbursed by banks to 2.13 lakh SHGs with refinance support of Rs.400.74 crore from the National Bank.

8. Regional Spread

Despite good progress in other regions, the southern region continued to lead the other regions in the performance under SHG-bank linkage programme. It's share in the total achievement increased from 67% during

1999-00 to 73% during 2000-01. There was a decrease in the share of central region from 13% to 9%. The eastern and western regions also slipped marginally by 1% and 2% respectively, whereas the northern region showed a marginal rise of 1% as compared with the previous year. The SHG bank linkage programme has not registered any headway in the north eastern region, which still accounts for less than 1 per cent of the programme. In order to address the deficiencies arising from poor banking network and resultant credit flow, NABARD has been encouraging different NGOs in the region to undertake formation, nurturing and financial intermediation roles in the north eastern region. Special State specific initiatives for reaching the very poor in the region are being taken (NABARD 2000-2001).

9. Different Models of Linkage

Model 1: SHGs formed and financed by banks

Under this model, banks themselves act as Self Help Promoting Institutions i.e., forming and nurturing the groups, opening their savings accounts and providing them bank loans. As at March 2001, 13% of the total number of SHGs financed were from this category. After introduction of the 'Low Cost Module' of assistance from NABARD and making it applicable in all States during the ensuing year, it is expected that many more branches of RRBs would be involved in promotion and financing of SHGs in the coming years.

Model II: SHGs formed by NGOs and formal agencies, but directly financed by banks

This appears to be the most popular model amongst bankers. Under this model NGOs and formal agencies in the field of microFinance act as facilitators. They propagate the message, organize groups, train them in thrift and credit management and nurture them over a period. Banks, in due course, link these groups by directly providing loans to them. Major share of SHGs linked as at March 2001 (76%) is under this model as compared to 70% as at March 2000, this increase is in tune with the increase in partner NGOs and other SHPIs during the year.

Model III: SHGs financed by banks using NGOS as financial intermediaries

In this model, NGOs take on the dual role of facilitators and financial intermediaries. They help in formation of SHGs, nurturing them, training them in thrift and credit management. Eventually, the NGOs approach banks for bulk loan assistance for on lending to these SHGs. The share of cumulative number of SHGs linked under this model is relatively small i.e., 11%. However, in the years to come, a need may arise for the SHGs as also for lending institutions to look for viable sub structures for financial intermediation. This could eventually develop into an effective method to control transaction costs through economies of scale (Ibid).

10. Role of NGOs and SHPIs

The major factor behind the satisfactory growth of SHGs is the role of NGOs and SHPIs. It is the Development Manager in the case of Oriental Bank Grameen Project (OBGP). These SHGs have not cropped up overnight. Whatever gain the SHG members have got or the benefits banks have received is because of hard work of field workers (FWs) who are generally women. These FWs require 5-6 visits to the village in a span of 3-4 months to form a group. Subsequent groups in the same village however take much less time for formation, if he earlier groups were successful. The FWs face lot of problems from different quarters while promoting these groups. The first problem while entering the village is the resistance they generally face. The second problem is related to work hazard which include (i) inadequacy of training; (ii) attracting unhealthy attention from the male world; (iii) need to work late into the night; and (iv) travelling through isolated areas in infrastructurally backward places. The NGOs which can support their FWs under these hazards can succeed in linking their SHGs to banks.

All these however are not free. The costs include: (i) salary of field workers, (ii) travel cost of FWs from one village to another, (iii) training cost for FWs and other staff members and SHG members, and (iv) monitoring, controlling and supervision. For the village level framework, only the first item is most important; training cost is required for the long-term growth; travel cost is important for the operation in a cluster of villages; and supervision costs become significant when operational area is spread over more than one block, or more than one district. For operation in one district, the district level monitoring is enough. Another tier of supervision is required if the SHG network covers a large number of districts or States.

Based on the data available from Mahila Arthik Vikas Mahamandal (MAVIM), a parastatal organization and the most important SHPI in Maharashra Rural Credit Project (MRCP), the average cost per SHG per annum in the first year ranges between Rs. 620 to Rs. 3,513 depending upon the items included in the cost calculated (Dasgupta et al., 2001). The cost however declines over time as the SHG members themselves take up some of the responsibilities. In the fifth year the above cost on the basis of current price ranges between Rs.555 and Rs. 2,868. This decline depends on the strategy of concentrating on a fewer villages at first, stabilizing a large number of groups there and then moving on to other villages.

Summing Up

The Self-Help group approach to development is based on essentially the social mobilization model that is being advocated by the different multilateral agencies. The failure of top-down bureaucratic approaches to rural development has necessitated the emergence of people-based and participatory oriented strategy of development in recent years. The characteristics of SHGs are quite distinct from those of the institutions of the State and the market. Although they are not altogether new, they imbibe certain characteristics of group cohesiveness, solidarity and social commitment to improve their lot by their own efforts. There has been a rapid growth in the number and variety of SHGs in India especially in the southern region. The contributory factors are many and need to the explored and researched. The linkage of SHGs with banking institutions is proceeding at a fast rate. This linkage brings about a sort of convergence in the operation of the SHGs and the banks thereby reducing transactions cost and bridging the gap between the financial institutions and people's organizations. There are costs involved in the promotion of SHGs as they do not emerge on their own. But compared to the benefits, the cost of promotion of SHGs will pale into insignificance. The social benefits of SHGs far outweigh the private and social costs of SHGs. Hence, the case for their further expansion.

REFERENCES

1. NABARD, NABARD and MicroFinance 2000-2001, Mumbai.
2. Puhazhendhi V. and Jayaraman B. 1999 Increasing Women's partcipation and Employment generation among Rural Poor: An Approach through Informal Groups, Indian Journal of Agricultural Economics Vo. 54 No. 3.
3. CIRDAP, 2000, Fighting Poverty with Microfinance: Report of the Seminar on Sustainable local community

Development and the Role of Microcredit in Rural Development 22-26 March 1999, Bangkok, Thailand, Dhaka.

4. NABARD 1997 News Review, DEAR Study Report on SHG, quoted in Karmakar.
5. K.G. Karmakar, 1999, Rural credit and Self-Help Groups, Sage, New Delhi
6. NABARD, 2000-2001, NABARD and Micro Finance, Mumbai.
7. Ibid.
8. Dasgupta R., N B Shete, K.D. Rao and D P Khankhoje (2001) Maharashtra Rural Credit Project, ongoing Evaluation IX, NIBM Pune, Unpublished Report.

18

Micro Finance for Self Help-Groups

Dr. D. Nagayya

1. Evolution of the Programme

While there has been a massive expansion in the formal credit delivery network in the last three decades, there is perceptible gap in financing the genuine needs of the poor, especially in remote rural areas. The high transaction costs in providing small loans, perceived high risk and low credit worthiness of poor borrowers act as deterrents. Moreover, the need is more towards meeting the working capital requirements rather than acquisition of fixed assets. Under such circumstances an informal arrangement for credit supply to the poor through the forum of Self Help groups (SHGs) is fast emerging as a promising tool for promoting income generating enterprises. International and national experience has proved that availability of supplementary financial services through operationally flexible Non-Governmental Organisations (NGOs) could do much to improve the income of rural poor families.

The poor may organize themselves, into small groups of up to 20 persons, known as Self Help Groups (SHGs) to inculcate the habit of thrift and credit operations among themselves. SHGs may be organised in clusters of blocks/ districts either by reputed voluntary agencies (VAs), NGOs and/or at the initiative of branch managers of commercial, cooperative and regional rural banks (RRBs). Reserve Bank of India advised commercial banks to actively participate in this linkage programme. The scheme has been subsequently extended to RRBs and cooperative banks. National Bank for Agriculture and Rural Development (NABARD) initiated the pilot project for linking SHGs with the formal banking system in February 1992. NABARD provides 100 per cent refinance to banks on their on-lending to SHGs/VAs/NGOs. A wide variety of support services is also extended by NABARD to all agencies involved in the promotion of SHGs.

Rashtriya Mahila Kosh (RMK), sponsored by Government of India (Department of Women and Child Development) was set up in 1993 with the objective of assisting women below poverty line in undertaking income generating activities through provision of package of financial and other services, and encourage promotion of women SHGs. Its head office is in New Delhi. The main function of RMK is to provide credit for facilitating production and economic activities, along with some support for training for skill upgradation. NGOs, women credit cooperatives, and Women Development Corporations operating on sound lines with at least three years experience can avail of short and long term loans from RMK.

Rashtriya Gramin Vikas Nidhi (RGVN), established in 1990 with headquarters at Guwahati(Assam), as a non-profit society, is an organizational innovation in support of social action, Its sponsors are IFCI, IDBI and NABARD. RGVN aims to improve the quality of life of the poor or otherwise underprivileged rural and urban people through social action. It focuses action on groups which are disadvantageously placed in society, but have the potential for pursuing socially and economically productive activities. Micro Credit Programme, also known as credit and savings programme (CSP) was launched by RGVN in may 1995, as a two-year action research programme. Encouraged by its results, the programme has been extended. NABARD and SIDBI are providing support to this programme. RGVN extends financial and techno-managerial support to NGOs with a view to empowering them to implement income generating activities for the poor. NGOS in turn mobilize collective strength of the poor in making them self reliant. More than a just being a credit programme, this intervention is targeted at bringing about intrinsic attitudinal changes within the communities in the effective use of credit and thrift in livelihood strengthening.

2. SIDBI's Efforts and SIDBI Foundation for Micro Credit

Small Industries Development Bank of India (SIDBI) introduced the micro credit scheme (MCS) in 1994. The performance of the pilot scale operations has been quite encouraging. Assistance extended under this programme through 125 pilot accredited NGOS covering over 123,000 women members, yielded satisfactory results. This has encouraged SIDBI to meet the challenge by taking pro-active steps to enhance the flow of institutional funds to this sector. Keeping in view the tremendous potential of reaching out to millions of rural entrepreneurs, a further impetus in development of micro credit is essential at this stage. With that objective, SIDBI launched a Rs.100 crore SIDBI Foundation for Micro Credit (SFMC) in November 1998. The SIDBI Foundation would make use of multi-channel credit dispensation routes to extend micro credit to poor people. The SIDBI Foundation would also focus on encouraging micro fiancé product innovations besides endeavouring to simplify the procedures in availment of assistance .

The renewed approach focuses on identifying major (nodal) micro finance institutions (MFIs) as long-term partners and providing credit support for their micro credit initiatives. These MFIs, which, inter alia, include NGOs and community-based organizations (CBOs), would be selected on the basis of their credibility, track record, professional expertise, management practices and organizational capabilities/growth potential, etc. Assistance to these MFIs would be based on capacity assessment rating, business planning and resource forecasts exercise, appraisals and field visits, etc.

SIDBI Foundation would simultaneously help these MFIs by way of need-based loans and grants to strengthen their management capabilities. It will endeavour to promote and develop these agencies into strong financial intermediates who would act as major players in the informal credit segments, especially for reaching out to smaller NGOs and MFIs and for building their capabilities through management support inputs, training in credit delivery and usage. Focus will be on providing the best practices and introduction of innovative features that would contribute to the financial viability of micro credit programmes which would, in turn, ensure appropriate financial services to the poor.

With a thrust on institutional development, SIDBI Foundation will also strive to create a coherent policy framework for accelerating the micro credit movement in the country. Another direction in which a pioneering effort is made is capacity assessment rating of NGOs/ MFIs. A specialized rating agency, which was assigned the task of rating 20 MFIS, has since completed the task of rating in respect of seven institutions. SIDBI Foundation will, thus, endeavour to promote an entirely new channel conducive to the needs and psychology of the poor borrowers. SIDBI bagged Asian Banking Awards 1999 for 'Micro Credit Scheme; in the Development Finance Product/ Programme

Category for its unique features. The award was instituted among others, by Asian Banking Association and the Association of Development Financing Institutions in Asia and the Pacific.

Group approach has been extensively adopted in promoting income generating enterprises among the poor and weaker sections, in particular, with women as one significant group under the overall financial support and guidance from NABARD and SIDBI; NGOs are being linked with commercial banks for making available credit to NGOs through commercial banks or even directly. In many states and districts, SHGs are being formed with the support of NGOs which are linked to commercial banks, NABARD and SIDBI. Under rural development programmes including DWCRA (Development for Women and Children in Rural Areas), the impact of support given to SHGs has been quite visible. From April 1999, six rural development programmes including DWCRA have been integrated and the present nomenclature of the programme is Swarnjayanti Gram Swarozgar Yojana(SGSY), which focuses on cluster approach for groups of poor. Women continue to be given special attention.

Focus in the recent periods is on organizing marketing efforts, and for technology upgradation and diversification of activities for groups associated with this programme. SHGs can contribute towards improving the quality of lending by offering loans in a prompt and simple manner, ensuring need-based loans, and keeping the loan size within repaying capacity of the borrowers. Undoubtedly, SHGs have the advantage of intimate knowledge about their members as compared to the bank staff.

Under the United Nations Development Programme (UNDP)-supported Trade Related Entrepreneurship Assistance and Development Programme (TREAD) which started in 1996, SIDBI has been a major partner in implementing the programme. Under the programme, it is envisaged that an integrated package of assistance would be provided to micro finance intermediaries wherein Government of India will provide grant for capacity building of intermediaries and end users of credit, while the loan requirement for undertaking income generation activities will be supported by SIDBI. SIDBI has also entered into a MoU with Government of India recently to place the TREAD Programme on a permanent footing.

3. Task Force on Micro Finance –Major Recommendations

In order to examine and address various critical issues for a healthy and orderly growth of the micro finance sector in the country, and to evolve supportive policy and regulatory framework, a high powered Task Force has been set up by NABARD. The Task Force with the Managing Director, National Bank, as chairman, has members drawn from various Micro Finance Institutions (MFIs), banks, NGOs, RBI, SIDBI and GOI. The Task Force report was submitted by NABARD to RBI in October 1999

Major recommendations of the **Task Force on Supportive Policy and Regulatory Framework for Micro Finance** can be divided into four broad heads:

(i) Mainstreaming of MFIs and other MF structures;

(ii) Regulation and supervision of MFIs

(iii) Organisational aspects relating to MFIs, and

(iv) Capacity Building of MFIs, banks, SHGs, etc

Continuation of the SHG-Bank Linkage Programme to cover at least one-third of the rural poor population by the year 2008 through one million SHGs, as envisaged by NABARD, is a logical extension to the budget announcements of GOI for linkage of 200,000 SHGs by the year 2002-03. SHG-Bank Linkage will be a major way of banking with the poor in the coming years. Many of the NGOs will transform themselves into MFIs,and will not only facilitate micro financing, but will also themselves do the necessary financial intermediation. Similarly, many federations of SHGs will take on financial intermediation, and act as MFIs.

The Task Force has advocated a National Policy for MF for building the capacities of the poor in the management of sustainable self-employment activities besides providing them other financial services like savings, consumption credit, housing and insurance. The National Policy for MF, envisioned by the Task Force, seeks to achieve the following mission in the medium term.

"Five years hence, we are looking for a process change leading to empowerment of 75 lakh poor households, and more particularly of the women from these households, through strong and viable people's structures like SHGs and MFIs which draw strength and support from the banking system with the message that banking with the poor is profitable business opportunity for both the poor and the banks".

There is a strong case for formal recognition of MF, just like institutional credit, as a strategic tool for poverty alleviation and rural development. The National Policy should emphasise on encouraging initiatives and participation of different types of institutions in MF, bringing the micro finance activities, irrespective of the type of institutions involved, within the regulation and supervision by competent authorities, creating policy environment for closer linkages of the MF sector with the formal banking channels, and making available equity, start-up capital and capacity building funds for the existing and prospective institutions engaged in MF. The recommendations of the Task Force are intended to address the above components.

Gradually, the MFIs would be required to recover the costs of providing support services for MF like training for livelihood activities, input supply, marketing support, etc. As regards social sector interventions like health care, literacy, environmental upgradation, etc., the Task Force emphasises the need for coordination among participating institutions, and bringing MF as an add on function. Further, the focus on poor women will have to be continued as hitherto in all MF programme activities.

4. NABARD's Involvement and Future Strategy

The programme of linking SHGs with banks, which was launched by the National Bank during 1992-93 had already covered almost 2.5 lakh poor households by march 1998, and needed greater attention. A separate department called Micro Credit Innovations Department (MCID) was, therefore, set up in the Head Office of the National Bank at Mumbai in June 1998 with Micro Credit Innovations Cell (MCICs) at all the regional offices of the National Bank to meet the emerging challenges. The major functions of MICD relate to formulation of policies, coordination with government and government agencies, RBI and other national level Micro Finance Practitioners, overseeing the state level operations, monitoring the progress of SHG-Bank Linkage Programme, innovating and supporting alternative credit delivery mechanisms, promoting and facilitating banks to act as self-help promoting institutions (SHPIs), documentation and dissemination, and coordinating with external agencies. To give further boost to this programme, NABARD has set up a Micro Finance Development Fund (MFDF) with a start up contribution of Rs 100 Crore from RBI, NABARD, banks and others. This fund will provide start up funds to microfinance institutions and infrastructure support for training and systems management, and data building. Special emphasis will be placed for promotion of micro enterprises in rural areas set up by vulnerable sections, including women, scheduled castes, scheduled tribes and other backward classes.

The National Bank continues to provide 100 per cent refinance to banks at an interest rate of 6.5 per cent per annum. Other support measures provided include facilitating training of bank officials and field staff of NGOs, capacity building support on selective bodies to NGOs, SHGs, Federations of NGOs/ SHGs and other related institutions through financial assistance, faculty support, etc. Refinance disbursement by the National Bank at Rs.30.67 crore under the programme during 1998-99 registered growth of nearly 200 per cent over disbursement of Rs.10.74 crore during 1997-98. SHGs linked were 18,678 in 1988-99 compared to 5,719 in previous year. Cumulative picture of the progress of the Bank-SHG Linked Programme at the end of the March 1999, reached a level of 32,995SHGs covered with bank loan of Rs.57.07 crore, and refinance from National Bank of Rs.52.06 crore. In all, 202 banks (38 commercial banks, 129 RRBs and 35 cooperative banks) are participating in the programme covering 24 states and Union Territories. As many as 550 NGOs are participating in the programme. Women SHGs constituted about 84 per cent of the total groups linked. On the whole, the programme benefited 5.60 lakh rural poor families in 280 districts. The Southern region continues to dominate in the linkage programme with a share of 65 per cent, followed by Western (11%), Eastern (11%), Central (10%), and Northern regions (3%). Andhra Pradesh, Karnataka and Tamil Nadu states have taken the lead in promoting SHGs, and in establishing Bank-SHG Linkage. The bank linkage is generally established after the successful functioning of individual groups for about six months to a year. The concept of SHGs has not been as successful in the North East and some of the Eastern states. Area-specific programmes need to be formulated to meet the varying socio-cultural practices.

In addition to providing refinance to banks, the National Bank has been supporting various partner institutions for capacity building through grants and Revolving Fund Assistance (RFA). During 1998-99, RFA of Rs 85.5 Lakh was sanctioned to six agencies for diverse experiments such as replication of grameen model, upscaling savings and credit programme, financing SHGs in difficult areas, rehabilitation of tribal farmers through SHGs, financing SHGs for group activities, and experimenting on efficacy of federation of SHGs. As at end-March 1999, aggregate RFA/Croups Fund support aggregating Rs.13.72 crore was sanctioned under bulk lending scheme to 21 NGOs/VAs. Federations of SHGs are emerging structures in MF sector with multiple objectives of providing support services to member-SHGs channelising social sector interventions, resource balancing, and mobilization and strengthening the process of empowerment of the poor. NGOs promoting SHGs also perceive such federations not only as a cost effective delivery mechanism for extending financial services by the banking system but also as a component of their own withdrawal strategy.

After successful experimentation in Cauvery Grameena Bank, Mysore (Karnataka), in association with an experienced NGO, namely, MYRADA, more and more RRBs are involving themselves as SHPIs. Some government agencies like Zilla Panchayat have also taken initiatives to promote SHGs; and such efforts are supported by the National Bank through assistance in organising training programmes for the staff.

Not withstanding 100 per cent refinance from National Bank, commercial banks perceive this activity as unprofitable. Hence, only regional rural banks and cooperative banks take up such financing. RBI has been prevailing upon commercial banks to formulate their respective policies on micro credit and promotion of SHGs. National Bank has been organising SHG workshops involving bankers and development personnel to accelerate the process of SHG-Bank Linkage. RBI has issued a circular to commercial banks to reckon micro credit extended directly to individual borrowers or through intermediaries as part of their priority sector lending. The circular also states that micro credit should form an integral part of the bank's, corporate credit plan, and should be received at the highest level on a quarterly basis.

The National Bank proposes to link 50,000 SHGs with banks during 1999-2000. This is about one and half times of the cumulative linkage so far. Half of this target is likely to be realised in Andhra Pradesh alone. During 2000-2001, it is planned that NABARD and SIDBI will cover an additional one lakh SHGs. For the purpose, special trust is proposed to be given for training, capacity building and sensitisation of personnel from banks, NGOs and government agencies. The strategy designed by the National bank has region-specific thrusts, involving training and sensitisation of over 30,000 personnel from these organisaions.

5. Perspectives in the Light of the Experience of SHGs in Andhra Pradesh

Several development agencies have promoted and inspired formation of diverse kinds of thrift and credit groups in Andhra Pradesh to channelise the various poverty alleviation and social development programmes. These groups vary widely in terms of their membership, size, decision making process, methods of group action, etc. Majority of the NGOs in Andhra Pradesh, as in other states, are basically involved in the provision of social services to their target beneficiaries, and their attitudinal orientation, methodology adopted, and systems and procedures are so designed that require social mobilization on a large scale. With their diversification in economic sphere especially in thrift and credit activities, their resourcefulness needs to be harnessed and synthesised with SHG-Bank Linkage programme. There is need to design a comprehensive training strategy for personnel of NGOs in various aspects of managing SHGs to secure proper focus.

Similarly, the district administration is promoting thrift and credit under DWCRA programme and the present SGSY (Swarnjayanti Gram Swarozgar Yojana). UNDP project for institutional development as grass roots for poverty alleviation is being implemented in the three districts of Anathapur, Maabubnagar and Kurnool, which envisages use of thrift and credit groups promoted under the project as a conduit for channelising their health, nutrition, education and other development programmes under the approach referred to as community-based convergent services. World Bank project on District Poverty Initiatives (DPIP) is being implemented in the six districts of Adilabad, Anathapur,Chittoor, Mahabubnagar, Srikakulam and Vijazanagaram. The project basically aims at improving capacities if community-based micro credit systems and their synthesis with other local common interest groups. An attempt is being made to synthesise these patterns with the SHG concept of NABARD and assimilate then under SHG-Bank Linkage programme. However, the induced formation of groups needs to be cautiously pursued without undermining the autonomy of groups- a critical element in the effective functioning of the SHGs. Nevertheless, the groups so formed do provide the opportunity to financing banks to expand their exposure to SHGs.

There is also imperative need to enlarge the coverage of SHGs in the advances portfolio of banks as part of their corporate strategy, to recognise perceived benefits of SHG financing in terms of reduced default risk and transaction costs. In the meanwhile, the banks need to devise suitable policy guidelines for appraisal, monitoring and supervision of SHG advances together with necessary documentation. Further efforts are needed to internalise these guidelines and build confidence on their operating personnel before their strategy gets going. Professionalisation of personnel of NGOs to cope up with the task is one step, and changing the mindset of bankers to promote SHGs and support them either directly or through SHPIs/NGOs/VAs is another major step. This is a gradual process. Andhra Pradesh has established a good record of performance of integration of different programmes and involvement of banks. Orchestration of credit and non-credit programmes such as counseling, supply of raw materials, organising marketing efforts and bringing in technology input is being pursued vigorously.

REFERENCES

1. National Bank for Agriculture and Rural Development (NABARD) (1999a), *Banking with the Poor: Financing Self Help Groups*, Hyderabad.
2. _______(1999b), *Report of the Task Force on Supportive Policy and Regulatory Framework for Micro Finance–Summary and Recommendations*, Mumbai.
3. Small Industries Development Bank of India (SIDBI) (1999), *SIDBI Report on Small Scale Industries Sector 1999*, Lucknow.

19

Role of Voluntary Agencies in RD

Dr. I. Satya Sundaram

Rural Development is a vast field. As such, a multi-dimensional approach is needed for the upliftment of the rural poor. Funds alone cannot bring about prosperity in rural India. An unfavourable power structure is also responsible for worsening poverty in rural areas.

The voluntary agencies (VAs) have entered the rural field in a big way. Their number may be around two lakh.Their utility has been recognized by the government. In fact, they are treated as partners in progress. The failure of government sponsored schemes has further enhanced the role and image of the VAs.

A major cause for the failure of rural schemes is that the poor suffer from what is called the dependency syndrome. Our government had given the impression that rural development means extending subsidies to the poor. Naturally, the beneficiaries are interested more in subsidies and other incentives like concessional credit, not in hard work.

Failure of Rural Schemes

Crores of rupees have been spent on schemes meant

for the rural poor. The expenditure on centrally sponsored schemes, numbering 210, in 2000-01 is a whopping Rs. 31,000 crore. But, the high incidence of leakages cannot be ignored.

What is surprising is that even the limited funds made available for rural schemes are underutilised.

Take the case of Rural Infrastructure development Fund (RIDF) which has been in operation since 1995. Over the years, a total amount of Rs.18,000 crore has accumulated in this fund through allocations in the central budget, but actual utilisation by the states has been coming down over years. Of the total Rs.18,000 crore accumulated under the RIDF, total loans disbursed amounted to Rs.6296 crore only by 2000 AD. Also, three states -Uttar Pradesh, Andhra Pradesh and Maharashtra- account for 38 per cent of the total disbursements. So far no state has been able to fully utilise the sanctioned funds.

The employment generation programmes suffered from many deficiencies. They concentrate on one or two activities like road construction without taking into account the needs of the region. Most of the assets created are not durable. The maintenance of assets is poor. Thus the benefits are of short-term nature and seasonal[2].

Most employment generation programmes are implemented without proper plan. Funds are spent towards the close of the financial year. Funds are also wasted by inflating muster rolls. Also, contractors are employed by some Gram Panchayats for execution of some works[3]. There is no coordination among agencies involved in the implementation of employment schemes.

The asset distribution programmes like IRDP too suffered from many drawbacks. The selection of ineligible beneficiaries is one problem. Other problems include: lack of infrastructural facilities,absence of technical guidance to beneficiaries; lack of coordination between the bank and block officials and under-financing of projects which subsequently resulted in poor return.

Some of the assets provided failed to generate any income. The quantum of investment available per beneficiary family proved to be inadequate. In some cases, the subsidy amount was not adjusted immediately after providing assets to the beneficiaries.

Also, most programmes failed to emerge as area specific[4]. Hence, complementary linkages are missing as IRDP is not based on decentralised micro level planning[5].

Merits of Voluntary Agencies

The strength of VAs lies in their capacity to understand the local needs, problems and resources; their capacity to involve local people and secure their cooperation and participation; and their desire to experiment with new programmes, strategies and approaches for rural development without incurring large expenditures[6].

Some prefer action groups (AGs) to VAs. The AGs have deepened and broadened the basis of democracy in the country. They have strengthened the resource base for the poor through various development schemes[7].

The merit of VAs lies in their proximity to the people and their sensitivity to the needs of the community. They can give the personal touch to the services they offer. They are capable of bringing people together and motivate them to participate in the development process.

The VAs are most appropriate to activate and informally oversee the delivery system and to make it effective at the village level to respond to the felt-needs of the village poor[8].

Broadly, the VAs are engaged in the issues related to women and child development, environment protection, social uplift of the underprivileged classes, rural development, health and medical aid programmes,rural infrastructure development, organising people for self-develoment,self-reliance and self-sufficiency etc.,[9]

Too much priority is being given to empowerment of women. The VAs are best suited to undertake this task. The VAs are generally small, flexible and cost effective and they work on behalf of weaker sections. They recognise that when people set their own goals, develop their own approaches and take their own decisions, human creativity and local problem-solving skills are released and the resulting development is likely to be self-sustaining.[10]

Empowerment can be measured by the ability of the collective to alter conditions. The VAs have the potential to be significant vehicles of empowerment because of their ability to reach the grassroots.[11]

Only democratic institutions can serve the rural poor effectively. In the case of VA, the distance between leaders and members is minimal. The stress is more on action based forums than on representative bodies.Thus, planning and implementation become proximate.[12]

The VAs have conducted experiments and also provided new leadership at the grassroot level . They are not handicapped by unnecessary rules and regulations. They are in a position to evolve low cost delivery systems.

Voluntary action is said to be essential in areas where awareness and conscious participation of the people is critical for success. They are also best suited to organise the weaker sections.

Limitations of Voluntary Agencies

The major deficiencies of the voluntary sector are summarised thus: most of them are centred round on an individual or a small group of leaders; many of them have turned out to be short-lived, and their activities have been effective only in certain pockets of the vast rural hinterland. Their growing dependence on governmental and foreign funds is a matter of concern. Above all, they have failed to build a united front of the various oppressed strata and to give an alternative direction to the dominant political economy of development in the country.[13]

Some negative factors of VAs are:[14]

- there is no accountability of the activities of these agencies.
- there is hardly any transparency and internal democracy in the organisation; and
- many of them are not financially self-reliant.

Most VAs face leadership crisis because they are started by one person or a few individuals. They control the organisation. They are neither appointed nor elected. The activities in such organisations centre round a key person and his/her chosen team, and naturally the organisation collapses when the leaders depart or lose interest in it.[15] Also, voluntary workers are being fast replaced by paid-workers.

A large number of VAs solely depend on foreign funds. Misutilisation and misappropriation of money are heard quite frequently. Some are said to be maintaining links with foreign donor agencies to finance programmes outside their avowed objectives. Some are accused of indulging in destablising activities posing a threat to the unity of the country. Some are reported to be serving a particular community and nurturing sectarian ideals causing harm to the social fabric of the society.[16]

It is feared that VAs are increasingly bureaucratised, undermining their performance. There are organisations which have huge funds at their disposal. They run programmes professionally with paid personnel and a small percentage of volunteers. Work done without expecting anything in return which is hallmark of voluntarism is disappearing.[17]

Lack of professionalism is a major problem facing the VAs. This creates problems in the preparation of project reports. While some agencies have developed professionalism, others do not try to acquire professional help. Hence, they are not in a position to properly assess the development potential of the local and regional resources.[18]

The weakness of these organisations is that there is no worthwhile forum, local or regional, for exchange of experience. There is no unified action for the delivery of services and for solving problems.[19]

Thus, the VAs, though theoretically sound, have exhibited many weaknesses in their actual operation.

Strengthening Voluntary Action

It needs to be noted that VAs by themselves cannot bring about rural development. They must seek people's support and government help. Voluntary action cannot be a substitute for the government's role in the rural sphere. However,VAs and government agencies should avoid duplication of works, leading to wastage of resources. Of course, there should be rapport among VAs themselves.

New schemes and programmes suitable to local conditions will have to be planned and evolved. The VAs will have to be given initiative in formulating and projecting such new schemes.[20]

The VAs must concentrate on income generating projects not only in the interests of the beneficiaries, but even for strengthening their own resource base.

The VAs and government departments should be treated as partners in progress. That is necessary to realise optimum returns from investments made in the rural field. However, the VAs should not become unpaid extension agencies of the state apparatus.[21]

The limited funds available for rural development ought to be utilised productively, and the benefits should not be of short-term nature. As the objective is growth with social justice, social action deserves every encouragement.

REFERENCES

1. *The Hindu,* September 18, 2000.
2. Programme Evaluation Organisation, Planning Commission, November 1980: Evaluation of Food For Work Programme. Final report. Government of India, New Delhi.
3. Annual Report of the Ministry of Rural Development 1993-94.
4. Annual Report of Department of Rural development 1987-88 Government of India, New Delhi. 1988.
5. I. Satya Sundaram (1987): *Rural Development:* A text Book for University and College students. Himalaya Publishing House, Mumbai. p. 287.
6. K.K. Mukherjee: 'Voluntary Oraganisations in Rural Development', *Voluntary Action,* July-August 1979. Section II. p. 3.
7. Mangesh Kulkarni: 'The Political Discourse of Voluntarism in India', *New Quest,* January-February, 1998. p. 25.
8. D.Bandyopadhyay: 'Voluntary Organisations and Panchayats', *Mainstream,* March 29, 1997. p. 12.
9. Pankaj Naithani: 'NGOs and Rural Development', *Kurukshetra,* September 2001. p. 36.

10. Suman Jain: 'Empowerment of Women through NGOs the SEWA Bank Experience' in Kamta Prasad (Ed.2000): NGOs and Socio Economic *Development Opportunities.* Deep and Deep Publications Pvt Ltd. New Delhi. p. 113.

11. Ibid. p. 113.

12. I. Satya Sundaram (1986): *Voluntary Agencies and Rural Development.* B.R. Publishing corporation, New Delhi. p. 164.

13. Mangesh Kulkarni: op.cit. p. 32.

14. D. Bandyopadhyay: 'Voluntary Agencies as Agents of Transformation', *Mainstream,* October 23, 1999. p. 23.

15. R. Sooryamoorthy: 'Have NGOs lost the Spirit of Voluntarism?' *The Hindu,* October 27, 1998.

16. R. Sooryamoorthy: 'NGOs: Need for a code of Ethics', *The Hindu,* January 19, 1999.

17. Shakuntla Balaraman and Visa Ravindran: 'Changing Face of Voluntarism' *The Hindu,* November 29, 1998 (Magazine Section).

18. Planning Commission, Government of India,1978. Report of the Working Group on Block Level Planning. p. 10.

19. Gopal Krushna Sahu: 'Voluntary Organisations for Rural Development', *Kurukshetra,* June 2000. pp.20-21.

20. I. Satya Sundaram (1999): *Rural Development.* B.R.Publishing Corporation, New Delhi. p. 171.

21. I. Satya Sundaram: ' Government and voluntary Agencies' In I. Satya Sundaram (Ed.1989): Rural Poverty and Area Planning. B.R. Publishing Corporation, New Delhi. p. 354.

20

NGOs and RD:

An Appraisal

Dr. P. Jegadish Gandhi

Introduction

Social sector development and anti-poverty programme have been integral elements of India's development strategy. Several programmes have been in operation since 1951 focusing the poor as the target group. These include programmes for the welfare of backward classes, weaker sections, women and children and a number of special employment programmes for self and wage employment in both rural and urban areas.

The government has relied mainly on three approaches for reduction of poverty and unemployment: the first entails pursuit of higher economic growth which will improve the levels of all groups of people in the society including the poor, the second involves direct anti-poverty and employment programmes; and third has stressed high priority to government expenditure on social sectors. The reforms underway since the economic crisis of 1991 have sought to strengthen these approaches.

The NGO Sector

Voluntary organisations have played an important role in India since Independence. There is a common stereotype held by many observers and policy planners that NGOs are small, convivial, participative and innovative, demonstrate a high leadership quality, are cost-conscious and austere, locally rooted and responsive, and thus a worthwhile instrument for welfare, developmental and mobilisation and organisation of programmes. The contribution of voluntary organisations in promoting micro-level development is universally acclaimed. Voluntarism has taken deep roots in India during the past two centuries. The voluntary organisations have certain advantages over Government agencies. They have greater freedom to adapt themselves to changing needs and ideas and can modify their methods and areas of work. They have better rapport with the people and naturally get better response from them in their activities. Since voluntary organisations are charecterised by greater human touch, and closer personal contact they are potent agents in mobilising community resources for welfare programmes.

Relationship with the Government

The most important relationship for the NGO sector is with the government. Since both the government and the NGOs represent a diverse and confused universe, there is no fixity to their relationship, which is marked by admiration as also suspicion and hostility. Thus conflicting relationship has itself gone through different phases, occasioned both by shifts in the environment and in official policy and perception. It is not just the government but also the NGOs who react to any move that they perceive to be detrimental to their own interest. Though the government often complains that NGOs neither meet their targets nor submit accounts, the current trend is changing. The Seventh Plan (1985-90) recognised the importance of voluntary effort, and financial provisions were made to give grants to voluntary oraganisations to take up developmental works in rural areas. The NGOs, while obviously relishing their newly instituted status and importance including the increased availability of funding, are still very critical of the operationalisation of this relationship.

Institutional Support

Under the Ministry of Rural Areas and Employment, the Council for Advancement of People's Action and Rural Technology (CAPART) was set up in 1986 to promote voluntary action and propagate appropriate rural technologies for the benefit of the rural masses. It provides assistance to NGOs under different programmes such as the Indira Awas Yojana, watershed management, social forestry, link roads in hilly areas, promotion of voluntary action in rural development and the development of women and children in rural areas. Assistance is also provided to NGOs involved in the organisation of beneficiaries of anti-poverty programme, Central rural sanitation programme, drinking water under the technology mission on accelerated rural water supply programme and advancement of rural technology. Since its inception, CAPART has assisted 6401 voluntary organisations and sanctioned 17877 projects. While the amount sanctioned works out to Rs. 475.04 crores, the total amount released was to the tune of Rs. 349.75 crores. All this is, however, not having the desired impact on the development activities in the rural regions.

During the period of three years 1995-96, 1996-97 and 1997-98, as many as 1980 NGOs were helped by CAPART. As far the state-wise list is concerned, West Bengal leads with 314 NGO, followed by Uttar Pradesh (303), Andhra Pradesh (276) and Tamil Nadu (172). An amount of Rs.

171.75 crores has so far been forwarded by CAPART in these three years to NGOs. The maximum assistance was cornered by voluntary organisations in Andhra Pradesh (Rs. 33.63 crores) followed by West Bengal (Rs. 23.72 crores), Tamil Nadu (Rs.17.42 crores) and Karnataka (Rs. 15.29 crores).

Scheme-wise, the Indira Awas Yojana tops the list with Rs. 36.11 crores. It is followed by advancement of rural technology (Rs. 25 crores), accelerated rural water supply programme (Rs.20 crores), Jawahar Rozgar Yojana (Rs. 15.50 crores), Central rural sanitation programme (Rs. 14.70 crores), the promotion of voluntary action in rural development (Rs. 13.90 crores) and Rs. 4.88 crores for the organisation of beneficiaries. The remaining schemes include IRDP,DWCRA, training to Panchayatraj functionaries, million wells scheme and watershed development.

"Seepage" Effect

As many as 248 NGOs are on the black list of CAPART. This follows reports of widespread corruption, misuse/diversion of funds and false claims by the affected NGOs. Of these, 61 cases had been referred to the CBI for investigation and 58 has been investigated by CAPART evaluators. Apart from these, 23 representations had been further received by CAPART and action had been initiated on 106 NGOs on the basis of records available. The Council, had taken serious note of the misuse of resources meant for rural development and was determined to streamline its functioning.

To voluntary organisers, the proliferation of NGOs and massive misuse and appropriation of funds and diversion of funds into self-channels by some agencies are all NGOs unfairly with the same brush. According to Dipankar Dasgupta in a theoretical plane, it is well-known of course that the contribution by any individual (or a group of individuals) towards a public good (Such as preservation of environment) gives rise to unavoidable externalities and hence an incentive for others to free-ride. As a consequence, the market mechanism fails to achieve a proper allocation of resources. It is also acknowledged that voluntary organisations have no mandate from the people and their strength emanates from their commitment to those served. It is therefore necessary that they are accountable not only to their donors and government, but also to those whom they serve.

Efforts have been made to form a commission that can act as a watchdog as well as develop into a bridge linking the Non-government sector with government agencies for the benefit for the people. This could be on the lines of the University Grants Commission which has authority to withdraw funds from grant-receiving colleges that do not follow rules laid down by the Commission. Unfortunately, these recommendations have not been followed up. Tamil Nadu is often referred to as an NGO factory but this is also a state where development work has been fairly successful. The total number of NGOs in India is believed to be around 1,00,000 but when people talk of accountability it is not clear to whom they are to be accountable in the country, the donor, the beneficiaries or themselves. There have been instances of malpractice and funds being siphoned-off to individuals/office bearers, even of some agencies using the organization for anti-national or criminal purposes. There are certain rules to be adhered to in the running of voluntary agencies.

Inherent Deficiencies

We have to acknowledge the catalyst role of voluntary agencies in rural transforming process in the post-Independence era. But every voluntary agency devotes only to micro-aspects of rural life due to its limited funds and short span of its life in the rural scene. Once the agency's funds are exhausted, they quit the area without taking care of its reconstructive ripple effect. Then another agency enters and starts work, not from the former agency's end-point but from their own first point. This duplication process has become common due to agency's ego to keep aloft its own banner. This causes distortions in rural structure undermining the very roots of development despite varied expertise and high expectations. In their bid to reorient the rural life, the voluntary agencies are involuntarily creating a new rural class society-agents of the agency and anti-agents of the agency. Instead of creating proper rural atmosphere this kind of self-anchored rural re-constructive programmes sows the seeds of disruption not only on the rural economic front, but also in rural social life.

Redifined Role in the 21st Century

It is recognised that voluntary effort will grow, and then it is necessary to create an environment conductive to their functioning on a much larger scale than at present. While actually participating in the development process, voluntary organisations can play a dynamic role in empowering the poor by fostering greater mobilisation and awareness-generation among them. They must train social animators and rural organisers. These, in turn, would help the poor to form groups and would organize them to take advantage of the system, programmes and opportunities that exist for their betterment but which normally elude them. In other words, NGOs can help to motivate, organise and conscientise the 'poor' and provide them with an interface with the bureaucracy and elected bodies. Also, they can partake in developmental projects, with the active participation of the beneficiaries. Success stories abound. In the long-run, however, it is important for NGOs to build up the confidence of the people at the grassroots level and ensure their active participation in the decision-making process. The NGOs should then withdraw from active involvement into a more passive role.

If the voluntary agencies are genuinely interested in the uplift of rural masses, they should pool all their men and materials along with available rural potential and chalk out a common comprehensive rural development programmes to be implemented wholeheartedly and fully till the point of self-reliance of the particular rural area. This makes the particular area to gain the levers of self-developmental forces on their own way. Rural development is not only a process, a method, a programme, but also a movement in our country.

REFERENCES

1. Dasgupta, Dipankar, (1997), "Voluntary contributions to the Public Goods: A Parable of Bad Samaritans", Issues in Economic Theory and Public Policy, Eds. Amitava Bose et al. Oxford University Press, New Delhi.
2. Gandhi, Jegadish, (1982) "Role of Voluntary Agencies", *The Hindu,* August 21.
3. Gandhi, Jegadish, (1996), "The Concept of Development: Its Dialects and Dynamics", *Indian Journal of Applied Economics,* October-December.
4. Gandhi, Jegadish, (1997) "Development – The 21st Century Perspectives", *Business Line*, May 24.
5. Gandhi, Jegadish, (1998), "Issues in Social Development in present Context: An Economist's Perspective", Seminar paper at Social Workers' Association (SWAN),Vellore, October 2.
6. Gandhi, Jegadish, (2000), "Rural development and the role of NGOs in India: An Appraisal" NGOs and Socio-Economic Development Opportunities, Ed. Kamta Prasad, Deep and Deep publications, New Delhi.

7. Mathivaanan, S.C., (1991), Voluntary Agencies and Social Change, Manas Publications, New Delhi.

8. Shakuntala, B. and Visa Ravindra (1998), "Changing Face of Voluntarism", *The Hindu,* November 29.

9. Sheth, D.L. and Harish Sethi (1996), "The NGO Sector in India: Historical Context and Current Discourse", Government Policy and Administration, Ed. Kuldeep Mathur, Sage Publication, New Delhi .

21

Empowerment of Rural Women Through Local Self-Government in Afro-Asian Countries*

S.P. Jain

1. Introduction—Rural Women and Development

A very large majority of rural women in most of the countries of Africa and Asia belongs to the poor or low income families. Their lot tends to be harder and the satisfaction of their basic needs are more inadequate as compared with menfolk or else with women from more prosperous and enlightened families of rural and urban areas. Keeping this in view, specific strategies to integrate rural women and agricultural development have been designed in a number of countries in South Asia.[1]

In recent years, there has been an increasing realisation that the age-long discriminations and inhibitions imposed on rural women are unjust and that they need to be brought into the mainstream of

* Originally Published in Journal of Rural Reconstruction, 31(2) 1998, New Delhi.

development, rather than remain at the periphery. Though the perception varies from one country to the other but the general trend for improving their quality of life and productive skills is beginning to gain headway to a great extent. This is mostly due to proper articulation of their cause at the international forums (especially the ones belonging to UN and its agencies), at regional and national forums (especially the ones belonging to UN and its agencies), at regional and national forums (especially the ones sponsored by voluntary agencies and women's movements) as well as in the legislatures and other political/social institutions in which leaders are beginning to be awakened to the legitimacy of women's rights in the desired egalitarian society.

New legislations have been enacted by several governments to remove discrimination and exploitation in regard to women. Many development programmes such as education, health, nutrition and family planning are beginning to take into account the needs of women which had remained largely invisible to planners earlier. Women's cooperatives have been set-up in several places to improve the income and also the levels of living among women through collective and well organised action. Statutory provisions have also been made by several governments to ensure women's representation in local government bodies, though the quantum and mode differ from place to place. Several voluntary organisations have also set up projects aimed at encouraging 'group' and 'self-help' efforts among women to improve their lot. Moreover, newly created women's associations and groups as organised under various projects, serve as a receiving mechanism for governmental delivery of services and inputs.

Despite these efforts, there is a long way to go to bring the rural women on par with men and bring the two sexes as equal partners in the great but highly challenging adventure of national development in different countries. It is agreed that various measures to integrate women with development can hardly succeed unless these are backed by appropriate strategies for the empowerment of women, particularly in the sphere of political participation. The phenomenon of empowerment represents the fourth phase of policy approach in respect of women's participation in development process.

2. Empowerment of Women

The phenomenon of empowerment of women in the Afro-Asian context has been considered as an important variable for integration of women in development process. Though the term 'empowerment' has been defined by different scholars differently, there appears to be a consensus that the term broadly indicates the process of 'giving power to', developing conditions for "generating power within", facilitating acquisition of power" and lastly "building capacities for utilisation of power." Conceptually, therefore, the term empowerment has multi-dimensional focus and can be described as a process wherein a group or individuals are enabled to enhance their status in the society, on the one hand, and overall participation in growth and development, on the other. The process thus covers elements such as availability of opportunities in different spheres of life, improvement in knowledge base, development of skills and elevation of ones status in society. Broadly, therefore, the process envisages greater access to knowledge and resources, greater autonomy in the decision making process for home as well as matters concerning society. The process of empowerment has been considered as time consuming and gradual. As the success of empowerment process depends on environmental factors in a given society, it's outcome cannot always be predicted.[2]

Empowerment has been considered as a result of participation in decision-making. An empowered person is one who can take initiative, exerts leadership, display confidence, solves new problems, mobilise resources, and undertakes new initiatives. Empowerment is an important outcome of high levels of participation involving control over decision-making for a range of activities. Hence empowerment is a leading outcome of successful capacity building at the individual and institutional levels.

In recognition to the fact that for empowerment of women is essentially a need of development, the subject is gaining increasing attention all over the world. As a result, specific measures to empower women have already been initiated or are underway in most of the countries. Most of the democracies and developing countries are already working on this theme and have a public agenda for the process of empowerment of women. It is more or less a kind of 'national commitment' which is prevalent in different Afro-Asian countries in different forms.

In recent years, there has been considerable work on the question of empowerment, and on developing a clearer conceptual framework for this rather vague notion. The most notable contributions came from Sen and Grown, Sharma, Kabeer and others who have attempted definitions keeping in view their own experiences and data base. All these analyses seem to concur with the view that empowerment aims to increase women's access to and control over social, economic and intellectual resources. Furthermore, it is also agreed that the central objective of women's empowerment is the transformation of traditional gender relations both in the private and public sphere. This is manifest, among others, in changes in the gender based division of labour, women's equal access to private and public resources (including food, health care, education, credit and employment) changes in legislation, public policies and programmes, and women's increased participation in private and public decision making.[3]

The South Asian framework is perhaps most relevant to the subject of empowerment. Here, women's empowerment has been defined as 'the process and the result of the process' of (i) challenging the ideology of male domination and women's subordination; (ii) enabling women to gain equal access to and control over resources (material, human, intellectual); and (iii) transforming the institutions (family, education, religion, media, and so on) and structures (legal, political, economic and social) through which the ideology and practice of subordination is reinforced and reproduced.[4]

The debate on empowerment strategies have not, however, sufficiently explored or analysed the role of the state. The construction and reinforcement of gender roles and the mediation of women's access to resources and decision making power, are both largely located within the family, household and community. Therefore, whether state intervention is effective or even desirable becomes a critical question. Field experiences from different countries have made it increasingly clear that women's empowerment processes must take the form of social movements located within communities. They are best initiated through raising the consciousness of oppressed women themselves to initiate and lead struggles for change within their own contexts and according to their own priorities.[5]

The process of women's empowerment clearly requires two synergistic processes: social change agents and women working at the grassroots level in their constituencies to renegotiate the gender contract, and the state with its many arms working to facilitate and legitimise women's entry into new spaces. The role of the former is to raise consciousness, mobilise and organise women, and engage in struggles for change at various levels. The role of a state genuinely committed to gender equality, on the other hand, lies in transforming its own institutions and structures, scrutinising its policies and schemes for ideological biases against women, and ensuring them equal access to resources. In other words, the state must create a kind of suction effect, which both accelerates the momentum of and absorbs the thrust for change emerging from the base.[6]

3. Political Empowerment of Women

The word 'empowerment' has come to be widely used to denote the need to fill up the gap between the rights granted by the Constitution, legislations and policy measures and the actual exercise of the same by the women. In a way, these provisions, by themselves, are meant to strengthen the hands of women and increase their capacity to utilise what belong to them as natural rights and justice. However, in practice, each law/policy provision seem to need another follow up step by way of law/administrative measure to make the previous one effective. It is then that, in what looks like a contradiction, the need has been felt for strengthening the capacities of women, so as to enable them to utilise the political and other powers granted by the Constitution and other statutory provisions, towards realisation of their rights for justice, equality and development.[7]

'Political Empowerment' thus is a phrase referring to the acquisition of the capacity as well as the adoption of the needed strategies by women in order to exercise their powers more effective, and profitably for their own development as well as the development of the society they live in, and for participating meaningful in decision-making process in the governmental operations at the local and higher levels.

4. Women Empowerment in Retrospect

Development of societies requires a balanced contribution of all human beings, men and women, according to their capabilities and capacities. Until recently, in most of the Afro-Asian countries, women's contribution was marginal because of a number of socio-cultural factors, though there has always been a thinking that society must have equality in all spheres of human activity. The Greek Philosopher Plato had advocated for a complete equality between the sexes, pleaded for active involvement of women in all spheres of life. Eminent thinkers and social reformers in later centuries also lent a powerful support to this plea. It was only during the last century that women all over the world started demanding equal rights including the right to vote. The civilization of China, India and Rome and some of countries in Western Europe did have small groups of highly cultivated women. Ever since the middle of the 19th century, there has been substantial progress towards equality in spheres such as education, suffrage, property rights, equality in industrial sphere and freedom to choose professions and position in public life.[8]

The movement for granting political equality to women dates back to 1848 when Susan Anthony gave a call to women in the United States of America to fight for their rights. As a result, the end of the nineteenth century saw a small fraction of women participating in the political life of their country. New Zealand was the first country to enfranchise its women in 1893. Then followed Australia in 1899, Finland in 1906, the Scandinavian countries in 1915, all the provinces of Canada (except Quebec) in 1916, the dominion followed in 1917, England, Soviet Union., Netherlands and the Ukraines in 1918, USA in 1920 and Switzerland as late as 1971.[9]

Historically, English Common Law had low regard for women. Commonwealth accommodated this assumption, thereby tending to include discriminatory provisions. As a result, women in most of the Commonwealth countries have by and large identical legal constraints as far as women's participation in political bodies is concerned.

The Charter of the United Nations included "promoting and encouraging respect for human rights and for fundamental freedoms for all without distinction as to race, sex, language or religion", while the preamble to the Charter stated of "the equal rights of men and women". Originally, the UN Commission on the status of women was established as a subsidiary of the Commission on Human Rights but became a permanent body of the Economic and Social Council in 1946. When the UN was founded in 1945, about half of the 51 members had extended franchise to women. The Commission therefore first concentrated on political rights which were regarded as fundamental. The convention on the Political Rights of Women adopted by the General Assembly in 1952 stated: "Women shall be entitled to hold public offices and to exercise all public functions, established by national law, on equal terms with men, without any discrimination". This was the first instrument of International Law aimed at granting and protecting of women's rights on a world wide basis.

The United Nations declared 1975 as the 'International Women Year' and 1980 as the 'Year for Development of Women'. The decade 1975-85 was hailed by the member nations as the Women's Development Decade'. During this period, many countries across the globe focused their attention and resources on the problem of women with the objective of integrating women with the social, economic and political activity. In most of the countries, legal steps were initiated to encourage women's participation in decision making bodies working at various levels. It was felt that the greater participation of women in these bodies will not only enable them to articulate their problems at different levels but will also be helpful in making decisions which are favourable to them.

Despite all these efforts, the number of women, in high positions of political power and influence, is still small.

Only five have to date been Prime Ministers. Although there have been women ministers, some of cabinet rank, in many countries, very few have held office outside the spheres that are usefully considered women's interests such as social welfare, public health and family affairs.[10]

5. Participation of Women in Local Government

Women's participation in the political process of development has been rightly considered as crucial from the point of view of both equity and production. Although women have been a partner and a substantial contributor to societal economy since time immemorial, they are still subject to neglect and enjoy marginal status in a number of societies. These conditions depress the overall capacity of a society for a balanced development. Since local government is a sub-system of national government, women's involvement and representation is not only desirable but essential from the point of view of their empowerment. And consequential enhancement of status. Since local government generally provides for services and facilities to the people of a specified area, women, being nearly half of human resources, have to be the contributors and recipients of various services.[11]

The extent to which participation of women was restricted in local government system in a number of countries is evident from the fact that they were not eligible even to exercise their role in the elections the right to vote depended on possession of property, tax payment and educational qualification for a long time. The situation is, however, changing gradually in different countries and more and more women are not only having the right to vote but are also contesting elections in conformity with democratic principles and practices. In some of the countries where they are not eligible to contest the elections for one reason or the other, provisions have been made to co-opt them in local bodies through the procedure of nomination.

6. Empowerment of Women through Local Government Institutions in Afro-Asian Countries

An assessment of the policies, strategies and trends in respect of women empowerment through local government institutions in countries of Asia and Africa is beset with the non-availability of micro level data. In the absence of specific data, it becomes difficult to arrive at generalisation based on empirical evidence. Some of the factors responsible for this situation are as follows: first, women are mostly engaged in most of these countries as housewives which prevent their direct participation in societal institutions. Secondly, there is a perceptable absence of policy framework favourable to women's participation in local institutions. Thirdly, socio-cultural factors inhibit free access to women in these institutions in terms of holding elective management positions.

Notwithstanding these limitations a definite change in most of the Afro-Asian countries towards empowerment of women is visible, though in a limited way. For, an exercise involving comparisons across the countries is constrained by differences in the (a) political set up, (b) socio-cultural practices, (c) strategies for empowerment of women, and (d) availability of data. Although information on comparable basis is not available for different countries in the Afro-Asian region on relevant aspects and there are differences in definitions and coverage in respect of data that are available an attempt has been made to discern broad trends in the aspect of women empowerment and highlight basic common as well as country-specific situations relating to their participation in local government. An attempt has therefore been made in the present paper by providing case illustrations of some selected countries in Afro-Asian region. Though such an exercise may not indicate the trends in respect of individual countries, this will certainly facilitate understanding about the possible direction in respect of political empowerment of women.

Although information about the representation in central parliaments and state assemblies in most of the countries is available, very little is known as far as their representation in local bodies is concerned, as may be seen from Table 1 to 2. It is evident from the available data that the percentage of women's representation is alarmingly low in different countries, with some exceptions where representation is as high as 28 per cent. On the basis of available information, it can safely be presumed that the position in respect of local government institutions is no better even in countries which are developed and are generally characterised by progressive and modern attitude.

7. Country Cases

In view of the non-availability of data in respect of women's participation across the countries in Afro-Asian region, it is not possible to have situational analysis of individual countries. However, a search of literature on the subject does provide information in respect of some selected countries in the region. It is, therefore, proposed to use information of these countries for purposes of analysis. These are Bangladesh, Pakistan, India, the Philippines. Sri Lanka and Taiwan. From African subcontinent, the case of Zambia has been included.

These cases do indicate the trends which are likely to shape in respect of empowerment of women in the years to come.

7.1 Bangladesh

A three-tier system of rural local government i.e., Union Parishad, Up-Zila Parishad and Zila Parishad is functioning in 61 districts all over the country. However, no Palli Parishad, which was supposed to comprise one elected Pradhan and eight elected members and two women members, has yet been created in the country. The

Table–1. Percentage of Women in Parliament and Local Assemblies in Selected Countries since 1960

	National Parliament (% women)	*Local Assemblies (%women)*
Developing Countries		
Egypt	0.0 (1970)	
Philippines	2.4 (1970)	
W. Pakistan	3.8* (1970)	
Mexico	4.8 (1968)	
Bangladesh	5.0* (1970)	
India	7.0 (1963)	
Ghana	13.6* (1966)	
Developed countries		
Canada	1.6** (1968)	
France	1.6 (1969)	2.4 (1971)
United States	2.3 (1974)	6.0 (1971)
Japan	2.9 (1970)	
United Kingdom	4.1 (1970)	12.0 (1971)
Australia	8.2 (1970)	8.0 (1970)
West Germany	8.8 (1963)	
Scandinavian countries		
Norway	9.3 (1968)	9.5 (1972)
Sweden	10.4 (1968)	
Denmark	11.2 (1970)	10.5 (1970)
Finland	21.5 (1970)	
Eastern European		
Socialist countries		
Poland	12.4 (1968)	15.1 (1968)
USSR	28.0 (1968)	42.8 (1968)
Czechoslovakia	17.6 (1967)	19.9 (1967)

Source: Women Roles and Status in Eight Countries (ed) by Janet Zollinger Giela and Andry Chapman Smock

*Seats reserved for women **Five of six women were appointed

Table–2. Gender Empowerment Measures (Asia)*

	Gender Empowerment Measure (GEM) rank	*Seats Held in Parliament (%women)*
East and South-East Asian Countries		
Indonesia	61	12.2
Philippines	39	9.5
S. Korea	78	2.0
Thailand	53	4.8
China	29	21.0
Japan	37	6.7
South Asia countries		
India	93	8.0
Pakistan	101	1.6
Bangladesh	77	10.6

***Source:** Human Development Report, 1996.

composition of Up-Zila Parishad includes three women members nominated by the government from amongst the women residing in the Up-Zila. Likewise, there is a provision for nomination of women members by the Government in the Zila Parishad. It is, thus seen that representation of women in the local government bodies is essentially through nomination.

During the last three local government elections held in Bangladesh (1973, 1977 and 1984) only nine women were elected as chairpersons of Union Parishads.

In accordance with the provision for three nominated women members in each Union parishad the number of nominated members for the 4460 Union Parishads works out to be 13380 women. There are to be 1380 nominated women members for the 460 Upazila Parishads. The total number of nominated women members in rural local bodies in Bangladesh works out to be 14,760. Although the total number of nominated women members appears to be quite significant but given the fact that women constitute half of the nation's population, their representation compared to men is still grossly inadequate.

Although the nominated women members in the Union Parishads are required to specialise in the area of family planning, social welfare and cottage crafts and to be the members of concerned committees, their actual participation has been found to be peripheral.[12]

7.2 India

Ever since the introduction of the system of rural self-government (Panchayati Raj) in India in the early sixties, women were included in these bodies through the procedure of co-option. This procedure enabled a few women from the area to get nominated to serve as members in these bodies provided no women had been elected in the normal course. It was however, found that the co-option procedure did not help the women much except that some of them, particularly those belonging to the elite class, could get themselves nominated to these bodies. It, nevertheless provided avenues to rural women to take up leadership role in a traditional society.[13]

In order to promote participation of women in real measure, a revolutionary measure was introduced through 73rd Constitutional Amendment in 1992. India amended its Constitution to bring in local self-government widely endowed in terms of functions, elected through multi-party competitive politics and universal franchise. In a sense, the 73rd Amendment is a reaffirmation of India's long tradition of decentralised governance. For a vast and diverse country like India, decentralised governance has been considered not just desirable but essential. If India truly believes in democracy as conceptualised by Lincoln's immortal words 'for the people, of the people, and by the people then grassroots democracy is a must, and the Constitutional Amendment could not have come any sooner.

The Indian experiment with local self-government is one of many in the world. What makes India unique is the introduction of affirmative action or positive discrimination by 'reserving' 33.3 per cent of local government seats for women only, including those belonging to weaker sections of the society. India has already held elections for these local bodies at rural level in almost all the states.[14]

The 73rd Constitutional Amendment act has thus increased the representation of women in local bodies to not less than one third of the total members. These women, in turn, are to be elected by direct elections. The Act further provides that not less than one third of the total number of offices of chairpersons in the local bodies at each level shall be reserved for women. Significantly, with this provision, nearly 7.95 lakhs women are holding elective positions in local bodies all over the country. Of these there would be about 80,000 women as chairpersons of these bodies.

7.3 Pakistan

The existing rural local government system owe its existence to the uniform system of local government which was introduced in 1979. It consisted of a two tier structure, namely, Zila Councils (84) at the district level and union councils (4100) at the union level. The union council is the basic and lowest tier in the rural local government system. The next higher tier is the district council. The representatives of these councils are directly elected on the basis of adult franchise for a period of four years. The local council is composed of three categories of members i.e., Muslim members, non-Muslim members and members representing special interest groups including women. Their representation is as follows: union Council-two and District Council-minimum one and maximum two. They are elected by the respective Councils.

To what extent the special interest groups are elected directly or indirectly in local bodies is evident from Table 3.

Table–3. Representation of Special Interest Groups in Rural Local Bodies

(Per cent)

Body	*Peasants*	*Workers*	*Women*	*Minorities*
Union Council	0.6	–	10.25	4.65
District Council	0.16	0.9	0.36	0.14

It is apparent that representation of women is only to the extent of about 10 per cent in the Union Councils where as it is only 0.36 per cent in the district councils indicating thereby that very few women are able to reach upto to the higher tier of local government.[15]

7.4 The Philippines

Philippines introduced democratic decentralisation only after a long period of centralised rule. Although President Marcos had initiated a Local Government Code in 1983, its success was limited as authoritarian rule proved to be a constraint to achieving full autonomy. In 1991, the democratically elected President Aquino was successful in passing a remarkable piece of democratic legislation, the Local Government Code to usher in local governments across the Philippines. The Code is a new strategy for pursuing development goals through people's participation, and is perceived as the means to attain sustainable development.

As some of provisions show, the Code has teeth. For instance, it devolves significant powers, authority and personnel to local government. It has develoved responsibility for provision of basic services such as health, infrastructure, social welfare etc., to the local councils. To enable them to carry out these functions they have also been empowered with wide ranging taxing powers and have been allowed to national internal revenue taxes. Between 1991 and 1994 their share had increased from 11 per cent to as much as 40 per cent.

A space has also been provided for women with mandatory sectoral representation (at least one seat) for women in municipal councils. Women's associations have also applied to be accredited as POs in some places, hence ensuring that women's voices are heard even from the NGO sector. It has certainly provided power to women to articulate their needs in the local government system.

7.5 SRI LANKA

The country has had, unlike India, a long tradition of political devolution which came to an abrupt end with the advent of British rule. A new phase of devolution began from the last quarter of the 19th Century. This took some time to develop into a structure consisting of provincial councils, Pradeshya Sabhas and the gramodya mandalyas. There has been a universal commitment to the values of local governance based on the concept of peoples participation. As adopted in the 13th Amendment the different tiers function in a coordinated manner and provide various services to the people. Participation by women was found to be very poor, on account of ignorance, lack of awareness and their inability to spare time for community activities.

7.6 TAIWAN

In the Taiwanese democratic government system, man and woman have been accorded equal status. As a result, women have the same rights to participate in political affairs such as election, recall, initiative and referendum as well as to take public examinations and hold public offices. Earlier in the traditional Chinese society, man's status was higher than woman's, women's opportunity to receive education was rare, women's economy was not independent, even they acquire the status of legal equality, they hardly can rival with man under same standards, so women's protective quota for women include national assemblymen, legislators, provincial and metropolitan councilwomen, country/city council women and town councilwomen. The protective status in the city councils is as follows:

7.6.1 County/city and town/city councilmen

One protective women's quota at least corresponds to each 10 councilmen or below 10 but above 5 councilmen. So far as various elections are concerned, the elected quota in a majority of electorates is between 4 and 5 which is below the stands of women's protective quota. As a matter of fact, now a days, women are entitled to an approximate 10% average protective quota, wherein the rate for central people's representatives is lower but that for local people's representative is higher.

7.6.2 Present status of women's participation in political affairs

The present of women's participation in political affairs in Taiwan region is through the female public functionary personnel elected at various levels including the female representatives to the parliamentary organisations. It has been concluded that for the people's representatives at various levels, except the councilmen of Kaohisiung city, the elected women are more than the protective women's quota, and most of them are elected without relying on the said quota. Further, the women's quota and proportion of people's representatives at various levels remain less than those of men's.

7. Zambia

The role of women in local government is very minimal as there are very few women councillors. Most of the councils in Zambia do not have women councillors and those who have either one, two or three women councillors only against 17 or 22 men councillors. Since a majority of councillors in most cases are men, most of the decisions, if not all, are made by men.

There are also very few women in management positions in councils. However, the trend is now changing as more and more women are being appointed to higher positions but the pace at which this is being done is too slow.

8. Conclusions

As already stated the non-availability of information about most of the Afro-Asian countries makes the task difficult to arrive at conclusions on the specific subjects which have been initiated to promote women's empowerment through local self-government. The main reason is that the issue of women empowerment has yet to receive a prime concern in the national development strategies of the respective governments. Secondly, there appears to be lack of clear policy direction in most of the countries as far as the extent to which women's participation in political institutions such as local government is to be achieved. Thirdly, in most of the countries local government institutions have not yet been established or integrated fully with the administrative system of the country. Lastly, the need to empower women through the local self-government institutions has not yet been recognised. Efforts in this direction in most of the countries are feeble and are overshadowed by issues such as alleviation of poverty and development of infrastructure. The case illustrations of some selected countries do indicated that issue of empowerment of rural women through local self-government institutions still remain a far cry as far as the Afro-Asian region is concerned. Since the rural local government system is the gateway for political participation of people in the larger politico-administrative system in any country, it is only necessary that specific steps are called for towards bringing in more and more women members into the folds of these institutions. The Indian case is a good example wherein one-third of the women members has been brought into elective positions through constitutional mandate. It is only because of the constitutional protection that the representation of rural women in local government bodies has gone up to as much as about 9 lakh as against about one lakh prior to the Amendment.

Another obvious general implication that can be drawn from the foregoing analysis is that, in the long run, steps which ensure empowerment of women will have to be taken in order to ensure their meaningful participation in decision making process. If women are not provided assured entry into local institutions, their role in the higher level political institutions will continue to be marginal. No doubt, any such steps will have to be based on the socio-cultural pattern of a given country besides the structure of local government. Above all, it will also require a high degree of 'political will' and commitment' on the part of national leadership towards empowerment of rural women. It is also necessary to recognise the issue of empowerment of women as a need of development and an essential input for the progress of society and development of human resources.

REFERENCES

1. Jain, S.P. 1995. "Integration of Women with Agriculture and Rural Development in South Asia" *DEVINSA*. Colombo.

2. See, Hall, C M. 1992. *Women and Empowerment: Strategies for Increasing Autonomy,* Hemisphere Publishing Corporation, Washington.
3. Batliwala, Srilatha. 1997. "Empowerment of Women" in *Seminar*, No. 449, January, New Delhi, p. 89.
4. *Ibid.*
5. *Ibid.*
6. *Ibid.*
7. Kaushik, Susheela 1993. "Strategies for Political Empowerment of Women", paper presented in the Seminar on *Women and panchayati Raj* held at NCERT, New Delhi.
8. Suba, K. 1994. *Women in Local Governance,* RBSA Publishers, Jaipur, pp. 1-2.
9. Mehta, Usha. 1978. "Indian Women and their Participation in Politics" *in Social Change"* 8(3).
10. Suba, K. *Op. cit* pp. 3-4.
11. AARRO, 1996. *Role of Local Self-Government in Rural Development* (Report of International Workshop), New Delhi, p.85.
12. *Ibid.*
13. Jain, S.P. 1983 "Leadership Pattern among Rural Women and the Impact of Women's Groups in Social Change *"in Social Change,* 13(3); 8-12,
14. See, Jain, Devki. 1997. *For women to lead... Ideas and Experiences from Asia* (A Study and Political Impediments to Gender Equality in Governance) National Commission for Women. New Delhi.
15. Siddiqui, K (ed.) 1992. *Local Government in South Asia,* University Press, Dhaka, pp. 98-140.
16. Alex B. Brillantes Jr. 1996. "Local Government and Decentralisation: The Philippines Experiences", in Abdul

Aziz and Davi D. Arnold (eds.) *Decentralised Governance in Asian Countries*. Sage Publications, New Delhi, pp. 97-214.

17. Miao-Chuan Lin, Republic of China, *Op.cit.* pp. 92-94.

18. Elizabeth Pezo Kanoka, Zambia, *Op.cit.* pp. 134-35.

Index